Plumbing Contractor
Start and run
a money-making business

R. Dodge Woodson

TAB Books
Division of McGraw-Hill, Inc.
Blue Ridge Summit, PA 17294-0850

FIRST EDITION
FIRST PRINTING

© 1994 by **R. Dodge Woodson**.
Published by **TAB Books.**
TAB Books is a division of McGraw-Hill, Inc.

Library of Congress Cataloging-in-Publication Data

Woodson, R. Dodge (Roger Dodge), 1955-
    Plumbing contractor : start and run a money-making business / by
R. Dodge Woodson
       p.   cm.
    ISBN 0-8306-4323-0 (p)
    1. Plumbing industry—Management. 2. Contractors. I. Title
TH6238.W66 1993
    696'.1'068-––dc20   93-11833
                                                               CIP

Editorial Team: Kimberly Tabor, Acquisitions Editor
                Joanne Slike, Executive Editor
                Barbara M. Minich, Book Editor
                Joann Woy, Indexer
Production team: Katherine G. Brown, Director
                Wanda S. Ditch, Layout
                Susan E. Hansford, Typesetting
                Nancy K. Mickley, Proofreading
                Ruth Gunnett, Computer artist
Design team: Jaclyn J. Boone, Designer
                Brian Allison, Associate Designer
Cover design: Carol Stickles, Allentown, Pa.   TAB1
Cover photograph: Brent Blair, Harrisburg, Pa.   4344

Contents

Dedication

This book is dedicated to my daughter, Afton Amber Woodson, and my wife, Kimberley. Kimberley has been my best friend for 12 years, and Afton is my inspiration. These ladies of my life are my life.

Acknowledgments

I would like to acknowledge and thank my parents, Maralou and Woody, for all the help they have given me over the years. They have been more than parents; they have been close friends.

Thanks is extended to the Department of Treasury, the Internal Revenue Service, and the U.S. Government for the use of selected forms as illustrations.

Introduction

If you are considering opening your own plumbing business, this book was written just for you. Between these pages you will find a wealth of information that has been compiled over the 20-year career of R. Dodge Woodson. Dodge is a licensed master plumber and a licensed business consultant. He has worked with plumbing and plumbing companies for two decades.

Dodge has owned and operated many types of businesses, beginning with a one-man plumbing company. His plumbing work has included commercial and residential work, as well as many forms of specialty plumbing. A survivor, Dodge has weathered many economic slumps and emerged a successful business owner. His experience is invaluable to anyone wishing to open their own contracting business.

What will you learn from this book? Chapter 1 asks you to define your goals and plans for your business, then helps you tie them all together into achievable steps. Chapter 2 tells you about the various plumbing specialties and encourages you to find your niche.

Chapter 3 clears up the mystery surrounding corporations and partnerships. With this information, you can determine the best structure for your business.

Chapter 4 examines legal and tax considerations that will directly affect your business. Learn how to survive an IRS audit, how to document your business activities, and see examples of contracts and change orders.

Chapter 5 encourages good organizational skills. Learn the right and wrong way to conduct business. Chapter 6 shows you how to budget your time, recognize wasted time, and even find time for working out.

Chapter 7 looks at your financial start-up requirements and then helps you build a spreadsheet so you have an accurate accounting of the money you will need to get your business off and running.

Chapter 8 helps you build a viable business plan that will enable you to meet your business goals and establish business credit. If you don't have credit or have bad credit, this chapter will show you how to overcome these obstacles.

Chapter 9 tells you step by step how to collect money owed you. Chapter 10 goes even further by looking at ways to manage your money for maximum efficiency.

Chapter 11 looks at schedules, budgets, and job costing. These three activities will help you stay organized and aware of your profit margins.

Chapter 12 considers factors that influence the price of your labor and materials. Equipment and inventory needs are discussed in Chapter 13. Learn how to separate your needs from your desires.

How to decide what products you will carry is discussed in Chapter 14. You will see that it takes more than choosing products, you must stay on top of orders and deal efficiently with suppliers.

Chapter 15 helps you answer the question of where you should locate your office. Check out your self discipline and decide if you can really work from your home. The computer you need in your office is described in Chapter 16.

Customer relations is the topic discussed in Chapter 17—specifically how to maintain relations that result in jobs. Learn the techniques and tactics that have worked for other contractors.

Chapter 18 looks into sources for plumbing work. From word-of-mouth referrals to government jobs, this chapter will tell you what you need to know.

Chapter 19 helps you create a successful public image. Learn how your image affects your fee schedule and the public's perception of your business' success.

Where to advertise for maximum efficiency and how to track the responses to your advertisements are just two of the pointers you will receive in Chapter 20.

Chapter 21 delves into the world of employees. Find out why most business owners want employees until they have individuals on their payrolls. Discover the true costs of employees and explore the benefits of subcontractors versus employees.

Chapter 22 discusses the various insurance and retirement options open to you and your employees. Liability and worker's compensation insurance is also explored.

Chapter 23 shows you how to avoid some common business traps. These final words will give you the confidence and insight you will need to operate a successful business.

The reader-friendly text is complemented by many illustrations that show you what forms should be used in your business. The index at the end will acquaint you with the words and terms you are likely to encounter. IRS forms used by businesses are found in the appendix.

All in all, you couldn't ask for more information from a more knowledgeable source. Unlike other business books that are written to apply to any type of business, this book is written for the working plumber by a working plumber. The words come from experience, not from theory. Dodge has had his ups and downs, and now, for the first time, you can learn from his mistakes and experience.

1

From worker to owner

Opening your own business is no small undertaking. The time and financial requirements of starting a business can be overpowering. Before you jump into the deep, and sometimes turbid, water of being self employed, you should give careful consideration to your goals and desires. Strong business goals pave the way to higher income and a more enjoyable life. Without goals, you have no direction. A business without direction is almost certain to go down.

Many people start a business without goals, and then, after spending considerable sums of start-up money, realize the business is not what they want. These people have two options. They can shut down the business, or they can go on with a business that does not make them happy. If they close the business, they lose money. If they continue with the business, they are no happier than they were before they started it. Neither option is desirable.

It is not uncommon for people to put themselves into business situations that they regret. For some, the stress of owning and operating a business is too much. For others, the financial ups and downs are more than they can handle. Being in business for yourself is not all leisure time and big bank accounts. Being self employed requires discipline, long hours, dedication, and persistence. Owning your own business is not the glorified cake walk some people fantasize it to be, but it can be the best job you will ever have.

While being self employed is rarely easy, it can be financially and mentally rewarding. This chapter is going to show you how to use your goals to obtain the results you want. If you are thinking you don't need to set goals, think again.

WHEN YOU ARE THE BOSS

When you are the boss, life changes. Owning and running your own business is not the same as going to your old job. You don't have a company supervisor to answer to, but you still have a boss: your customers. If you don't do your job to the satisfaction of your customers, you won't have your new, self-employed job for long.

The truth is, being in business for yourself can be much more demanding than having a job. When you work for someone else, all you have to worry about is the quality of your plumbing work and the basic responsibilities of an employee: showing up for work on time, giving a fair day's production, and so on. You go to work, do your plumbing, and go home. Once you're home, the rest of the day, evening, and night is yours, unless you are on call for emergency service repairs. This is not usually the case when you are in business for yourself.

As a self-employed plumber, you have to perform all the normal plumbing duties, but your job does not stop there. Paperwork must be done. Phone calls must be returned. Estimates must be made. Complaints must be answered and solved. Marketing strategies must be developed. Accounts receivable and payable are a routine chore. The list of additional duties goes on and on.

When your job becomes your business, you have many more job-related responsibilities. Time with your family will be at a premium. Time once spent on week-end outings may be used to catch up on business matters that were not completed during the week.

WHAT DO YOU WANT FROM YOUR BUSINESS?

This would seem to be a simple question, yet many people can't answer it. As a business consultant, I talk with a wide variety of people. When I go in to troubleshoot a business, the first question I ask the owner is, "What do you want from the business?" More often than not, the owner doesn't know what he wants. Generally, the answer is broad and unfocused.

When I opened my first business, a plumbing business, I wanted to be my own boss. I wanted to work my own hours and not be worried about putting in 18 years, only to be let go before retirement. My dream called for building a powerful business that would take care of me in my old age. Well, I started the business, and I was relatively successful. Looking back I can see countless mistakes that I made.

Since my first business, I have gone on to open many new businesses. Each time I start a new venture I seem to find new faults with my procedures. It is not that my methods don't work, but I always seem to find ways to improve them. I wouldn't begin to tell you that I know all the answers or can tell you exactly what you need to know to make your business work. But I can give you hundreds of examples of what not to do. I can tell you what has worked in my business endeavors and those of my clients.

I don't believe you ever finish refining your business techniques. Even if the business climate is stable, you can always find ways to enhance your business. If you are going to start and maintain a healthy business, you must be willing to change.

Take some time to think about what you want from your business. Write down your desires and goals on a sheet of paper. You must write down your goals and desires. For years I refused to believe that writing my goals and desires on paper would make a difference, but it does.

After you have compiled your list, check it over. Break broad categories into more manageable ones. For example, if you wrote that you want to make a lot of money, define how much is a lot. Is it $30,000, $50,000, or $100,000 a year? If you jotted down a desire to work your own hours, create your potential work schedule. Will you work 8-hour days or 10-hour days? Will you work weekends? Are your scheduled hours going to comply with the needs of your customers?

Your work schedule might show you will work from 7:30 A.M. to 4:30 P.M., with an hour off for lunch. How realistic is this? The answer depends a great deal on the type of plumbing work you will be doing. If you are working all new-construction jobs, your schedule might work. If you are running a service and repair business, your schedule will never work. If a person's toilet is overflowing just after supper, the customer is not likely to wait until the next morning to have it fixed. If you are going to be competitive in this type of service business, you must be available for emergency calls on a 24-hour basis.

The point is this: look over your list and rate each goal and desire. You want to make a lot of money. That can be done by working over-time calls, but are you willing to sacrifice the time with your family? Go through your list with this type of question-and-answer procedure. Evaluate your goals and your willingness to achieve them. This is the first step toward starting or improving your business.

Make your goals realistic. Realistic goals can mean the difference between the success and failure of your business. If you set your goals too high, you will struggle to achieve them. If you continually struggle, you might decide the fight for your business is not worth the effort. A series of simple goals will keep you motivated and feeling good about your accomplishments.

DEVISE A BUSINESS PLAN

A business plan is simply a blueprint of your business. It diagrams where you are, where you want to go, and how you are going to get there. A business plan should include as much about your business as possible. The more you put into your business plan, the better you will be able to track your success.

How can you learn to devise a business plan? You could go to specialized classes and have an instructor teach you. But this would take significant time and money. You could attend seminars, and this is not a bad idea, but it can get expensive. Reading is another way to gain the knowledge you will need to build a successful business plan. Books may not be cheap, but they are generally a good value.

Hiring a professional consultant is a quick way to have your questions answered. Consultants, accountants, and attorneys might seem expensive, but if they are good, they are well worth the expense. A combination of reading, seminars, and consultations is probably the quickest way to hit the fast track.

In my early years, I never had a viable business plan. My plan was to work as hard as necessary and to make as much money as possible doing what I wanted to do. As time and money passed, I learned the value of a solid business plan. I can tell you, from my expensive experience, a good business plan is instrumental to your success. A business plan does not have to be complicated, only complete.

WHERE DO YOU WANT TO BE IN FIVE YEARS?

A key step toward securing a good future for your business is the development of goals and plans. Let's take a moment to look closer at some thoughts for your business future.

How big do you want to become?

Do you want a fleet of trucks and an army of employees? If you answer yes to these questions, you must ask yourself more questions. Are you willing to pay the high overhead expenses that go hand in hand with a large group of employees? Will you need to take classes in human resources to manage your employees? Will you have the knowledge to oversee accounting procedures, safety requirements, and insurance needs?

In business, almost every answer raises new questions. As a business owner, you must be prepared to answer all the questions. It is all but impossible for an individual to have the experience and knowledge to answer correctly so many diversified questions.

For example, let's say you are about to hire your first employee. Do you know what questions you may ask without violating the employee's rights? Are you aware of the laws pertaining to discrimination and labor relations? The chances are good that you don't and aren't, so what do you do? You could play it by ear and hope for the best, but that type of action might result in a lawsuit and the loss of your assets. You should consult with professionals in the field of expertise pertaining to your questions.

Are you willing to diversify?

Plumbers hit dry spells when work is hard to find. Should you consider expanding your business parameters to include heating, air conditioning, or electrical work? The first consideration should be how much you know about other trades. If you are capable of doing any of them yourself, and are licensed to do so, adding the service to your business should increase your income. If you don't know much about air conditioning work, should you hire a cooling mechanic to run this side of your business? The good side of adding a cooling mechanic will be the increased revenue to your business. But just because your gross sales go up doesn't mean your net profits will escalate. What will you do with the cooling mechanic during the cold months? How will you know if your employee is doing a good job? Suppose your cooling mechanic quits on short notice, what will you tell your customers? Your life will not be pleasurable if angry customers are calling you in July, wanting to know when their air-conditioning job will be finished.

I think it is healthy for businesses to diversify, but I believe the conditions must be right. In my opinion, you should not hire people to do a job of which you have no knowledge. For example, as a plumbing contractor, I could hire a master electrician and expand my business base. It would appeal to general contractors to be able to deal with one subcontractor for all their plumbing and electrical needs. So, why don't I do it? I haven't hired an electrician because I have limited knowledge of electrical wiring.

If my plumbers make a mistake or leave me out on a limb, I have the ability to work myself out of the jam. But if the same happened with an electrician, I would be helpless. Without a master electrician, I would not be able to complete work that was started or repair work already installed. I see the potential dangers of expanding with electrical service as being too great for the rate of return. However, I am capable as a builder, so I have no reservations about expanding as a remodeling contractor or home builder. You can apply this type of logic to any business venture. You can even use it to evaluate if going into business is the right move for you.

How big is big enough?

When you plan the destiny of your business, you must know what measuring sticks to use. Do you think in terms of gross sales, number of employees, net profits, tangible assets, or some other means of comparison?

Gross income is one of the most common measurements of a business. However, gross income can be deceiving. Theoretically, a higher gross income should translate into a higher net income, but it doesn't always work that way. Having a fleet of new trucks and several employees might produce a high gross income, but the associated expenses might cause your business to fail.

The best measurement of your business is the net profit. It has been my experience, and the experience of my clients, that you must base your growth plans on net income, not gross income. Determine how much money you want to make, and then create a business plan that allows you to reach your goal.

WHAT TYPES OF CUSTOMERS DO YOU WANT?

It is important for you to determine the type of clientele with which you wish to work. During the initial start up of a business or during poor economic times, it is easy to justify taking any job that comes along. While this type of approach may be necessary for the short term, never lose sight of your business goal. For example, if you choose to specialize in new construction, make every effort to concentrate on this type of work. When you are forced into remodeling or repair work, do it to pay the bills, but continue to pursue new construction. If you bounce back and forth between different types of work, it will be more difficult to build a strong customer base and to streamline your business. Let me give you an example from my past.

When I opened my first plumbing business it was my only source of income. I wanted to be known as a remodeling plumber. After extensive research, I determined I could make more money doing high-scale remodeling than I could in any other field of plumbing in which I was interested. I reasoned that remodeling was more stable than new construction and required less running around and lost time than service work. So, I had a plan. I would become known as the best remodeling plumber in town.

During the development of my business, it was tough finding enough remodeling work to make ends meet. I took on some new-construction plumbing, cleaned drains, and repaired existing plumbing. I was tempted to get greedy and try to do it all, but I knew that wouldn't work, at least not while I was the only plumber in the company. Why wouldn't it work? It wouldn't work because of the nature of the different types of work.

With new-construction, bid prices were very competitive. To win the job and make money, I had to work fast and eliminate lost time. If I was plumbing a new house and my beeper went off, I had to pick up my tools and stock and leave the job to call the answering service. Then I would have to call the customer. I would have to either respond to the call or try to put the customer off until I left the new-construction work. The time I spent picking up and responding to service calls ate into my narrow profit margin on the house.

Service customers were annoyed if I didn't respond within an hour. I was losing money and running the risk of making customers angry. The same was true if I left a remodeling job to answer a service call. The remodeling customer became distressed because I left his job to take a service call. It didn't take long for me to see the potential for problems.

I set my sights on remodeling and put all my effort into getting remodeling jobs. In a matter of months I was busy, and my customers were happy. My net income rose because I eliminated wasted time. In time, I added more plumbers and built a solid service and repair division. Then I added more plumbers and took on more new-construction work. But you see, you must carefully structure your business plan, or it will get away from you and cause you to work harder while making less money.

When you define your desired customer base and work type, do it judiciously. If you live in a small town you might not be able to specialize in just one type of plumbing. You might have to do a little of everything to stay busy. But if you want to specialize in a certain field, never stop pursuing your desired type of work and customers.

WHAT POSITION WILL YOU PLAY?

Just like setting a goal for the type of work your business will do, you should establish a goal for the type of work you want to do. Do you want to work in the field or in the office? Will you trust important elements of your business to employees or will you want to do it all yourself?

The delegation of duties and proper management are difficult for many first-time business owners. Most people fall into one of two traps. The first group believes that they must do everything themselves. This group hesitates to delegate duties. Even after assigning the task to competent employees, they must keep their fingers in the work. The second group believes everything can be delegated and passes on responsibilities to people that are not in a position to make the call. Somewhere between these two extremes you will find most successful business owners.

It is counterproductive to hire employees if you are not going to allow them to do their jobs. Supervise and inspect the employees' work, but don't look over their shoulders every five minutes. If you did a good job screening and hiring your employees, they should be capable of working with limited supervision. When you spend time hovering over employees, you neglect many of your management and ownership duties.

If you decide to do everything yourself, you must recognize that a time will come when you have to turn away business. One person can only do so much. It is better to politely refuse work than it is to take on too much work and not get it done.

Will you be content to stay in an office? If your nature tends to keep you outside and doing physical work, being office based can be a struggle. It has its advantages, but office work can be a real drag to the person accustomed to being out and about.

If you don't want to work in the office, make arrangements to allow you freedom of movement. Answering services and machines afford some relief. A receptionist is another way to keep the office staffed while you are out, but this is an expensive option. If you will be in the field, a pager and cellular telephone might be your best choice for keeping in touch with your customers. It will be up to you to devise the most efficient way to stay on the job and out of the office. Don't overlook this question when you plan your business.

Now for the reverse situation, suppose you want to be in the office. Who will be in the field? The solution to this problem is not easy for the new business owner. If you hire employees to do the field work, you will need enough work to keep them busy. Getting steady work is rarely simple, and for a new business it can be nearly impossible.

Most new businesses are run by the owners. For plumbers, it is common to do field work during the day and office work at night. While this is usually mandatory, it doesn't have to stay that way forever. Decide where you want to be, in the field or in the office, and work up a plan to meet your goal.

MENTAL REQUIREMENTS

You can buy tools and inventory, but you cannot buy the mental capacity to make your business work. You can, however, buy products and services that will help prepare you mentally for owning your own business. These products and services might be books, college courses, seminars, cassette tape sets, professional consultations, and similar goods and services.

Few potential business owners consider the mental aspects of starting a business. Because they want to own their own business, they assume they will have the skills and determination to make the business a success.

Before you open a business, make sure you are prepared for the task and truly want to own and operate your own business. If you find that what you really want is an endless supply of money produced by others, opening your own business might be a mistake. Having your own business doesn't guarantee you will make plenty of money with very little effort. In fact, the opposite is more likely to be true.

When you start your business, you must perform many functions and devote a major portion of your time to it. If you like having afternoons off and your nights and weekends free, owning a business might be more pain than pleasure for you. There will be plenty of times when you will have to work nights and weekends to keep your business afloat.

2

Find
your niche

When you first start your plumbing business, you will probably be happy to get any work you can. As your business grows, it will be important for you to find your niche in the industry. Most plumbers are better at one type of work than others. If you recognize this fact and act on it, you can make more money. It stands to reason that if you are more efficient doing repair work than you are doing installation work, you should make more money doing repairs. Not only will you make more money, you will be happier when you do the work you do best.

Finding an area of specialization shouldn't require much effort. Look at the type of work you enjoy and the type of work you do best. That should be your specialty.

It is not always possible to specialize in a narrow field of plumbing. Plumbers working in rural locations have a harder time specializing than plumbers working in major metropolitan areas. Big cities provide opportunities for plumbers to specialize in such narrow fields as drain cleaning or water heater replacements.

It is not unusual for rural plumbers to work in all fields of plumbing and to diversify into other areas. For example, I diversified my plumbing company to include residential remodeling services as a general contractor. From there, my business expanded into home building. In later years, a real estate sales and management division was added. What started as a one-plumber business grew into a major corporation with many employees, subcontractors, and investors.

I chose to diversify to increase my profits and to hedge my business against economic slowdowns. I felt that all of the businesses I grouped with my plumbing business were natural additions and enhancements to my existing business. This is not to say that you must expand the way I did. Some people will be much happier keeping their business small and targeted toward one area of specialization.

I have known plumbers that did nothing but drain cleaning, and they made good money. Some of my business clients have specialized in the installation of back-flow preventers. While back-flow preventers are not big business in many small towns, they can produce a good income for plumbers in large cities. Many plumbers, myself included, choose to do only residential work. Others prefer commercial work. Your specialization could be as broad as residential plumbing or as narrow as drain cleaning. How will you decide where you fit? Let's spend some time looking at the pros and cons of various specialties.

RESIDENTIAL vs. COMMERCIAL

I have always preferred residential work, but many people enjoy commercial work. You know the type of work you prefer. However, it might be worthwhile to note some of the differences between the two types of work.

Residential work

Residential work is often done on a relatively small scale. By that I mean residential work can involve only one house, and often does. You could, however, take on a residential project with 100 townhouses or condos. Even on large residential jobs, the procedures vary greatly from commercial work. Normally, work restrictions and safety requirements are more lax on residential jobs. Residential blueprints are commonly less extensive than those used on commercial jobs. Penalties for completing the work after the proposed completion date often don't exist or are minimal on residential jobs. Equipment needs are different for residential work and are usually not as expansive as the requirements of a commercial job.

Residential work offers many advantages. It is usually a more relaxed atmosphere than commercial work. The size of the jobs are generally small and can be completed in a short time. This helps with cash-flow needs. The amount of credit needed to finance a residential job is less than that needed for a commercial project. Work crews tend to be smaller on residential jobs, often involving only one person. This makes residential work ideal for the plumber just opening a new business.

Commercial work

Commercial work is usually more structured than residential work. Blueprints for commercial jobs are extensive and contain many details and diagrams that generally are not found on residential jobs. On the right jobs, safety can be better than it might be on a residential job. Because commercial jobs are larger than most residential jobs, the potential profit from each job is much higher. This means you can win less bids and make more money. However, big jobs often require bonding, which can be difficult for new companies to obtain. License requirements might also be stiffer for commercial jobs. The best advice I can give you is to choose the field with which you are the most comfortable.

REPAIR WORK

Repair work can be very profitable. Since the work is usually done on a time-and-material basis, it is hard to lose money with repair work unless you have uncollectable accounts receivable. The percentage of mark up on service and repair items is also quite good, usually at least 10 percent better than what you could charge for competitive-bid jobs.

Repair work can usually be done by a single plumber. Unlike commercial jobs and large residential work, where a helper or additional plumbers are often needed, a one-plumber company can do repair work with great efficiency.

Repair job costs are rarely more than $500, and many of them for less than $150. This limits your loss to a deadbeat customer. Unlike a commercial job, where you might be waiting for a $20,000 check, repair jobs don't carry the same risks. Most service and repair plumbers get paid right on the spot. This reduces billing time and keeps up your cash flow.

One drawback to repair work is the need for a good supply of rolling stock. If you don't keep parts on your truck, you can't sell them. A well-stocked service truck might carry $10,000 in mobile inventory. You can start out with a smaller inventory, but you should expect to tie up several thousands of dollars in truck stock for a successful service and repair business.

An advantage to repair work is its consistency. New-construction work runs in cycles and falls off when the real estate market slumps. Repair work is often unaffected by such slumps. While people may put off some replacements and repairs, they won't try to live long with a stopped up toilet or a shower valve that will not cut off. In the long run, there is usually more security in repair work than there is in construction work.

DRAIN CLEANING

Drain cleaning can produce phenomenal profits, especially in urban areas. If your area has a large enough population, you could specialize in drain cleaning and roll money over faster and in larger amounts than you ever dreamed possible.

Why is drain cleaning so profitable? Many people will try to do minor plumbing repairs on their own, but a lot of people have strong aversions to cleaning their own drains. Even those that are willing to clear their own blockages often find that homeowner-type tools and liquid cleaners just won't cut it, forcing them to call professionals.

Homeowners and businesses might put up with a dripping faucet for months, but let their toilet facilities stop up and somebody is going to get a call to clear the blockage. If you have a large ad in the phone directory or have used direct-mail or name-recognition advertising effectively, you are going to get that call.

When you respond to the call, you are going to collect your normal hourly rate and you are going to charge a rental fee for your equipment. Drain cleaners are not cheap, but you can get good equipment, capable of clearing all common drains, for less than $1,500. When you consider you can charge a rental fee of $45 to $75 each time you use your drain cleaner, you can see it won't take long to recover your $1,500. After running 20 stoppage calls you can pay for your equipment. From then on out, you pocket the extra profits made from your equipment rental fees.

Let's say you are a service and repair plumber. Your hourly labor rate is $40. You bill out 32 hours a week and gross $1,280 a week. You also make money on the parts you sell. Let's say you average a 30 percent mark up on them. If your average service call nets a mark-up profit of $5, and you make 32 calls a week, you make an extra $160, for a weekly total of $1,440. Most people would agree that this is not a bad income. Now let's compare it to an income from drain cleaning.

For the sake of simplicity, we will assume you make no material sales or mark-up profits. Of course, in the real world, drain-cleaning companies do make retail sales and do pocket handsome mark-up profits. You bill 32 hours of drain cleaning time at $40 per hour and charge an average machine rental fee of $50 for each of your 32 calls. If your equipment is paid for, you make $2,880 for your time. Not bad, huh?

The equipment rental fee for drain cleaning doubles your income! You work the same number of hours, generally do less strenuous work, and make twice as much money. This is what I call a spectacular specialty.

There is another significant advantage to specializing in drain cleaning. Let's assume you are ready to hire some help for your business. If you send your employee to a job without your direct supervision, for most specialties the person must be a licensed journeyman plumber. Let's assume that the going hourly pay rate for journeyman plumbers is $12 per hour. Wouldn't it be great if you could hire unlicensed people at hourly rates around $7.

You can as a drain-cleaning company. Most jurisdictions don't require drain-cleaning mechanics to be licensed plumbers. You can hire help at lower rates and charge the same amount for their time. This is an excellent way to pick up an extra $5 per hour. Based on a 32-hour week of billable time, the savings add at least $160 to your income. Few plumbing contractors think of this option, but it is a good one.

One disadvantage to drain cleaning is the need to be available on a 24-hour basis, but this is no different from the requirements of most service and repair plumbers. And, if you run the calls after normal business hours, you can charge considerably more for your time.

Health risks are another consideration that some plumbers feel outweigh the advantages of drain cleaning. However, if you have good equipment, wear the proper clothing, and professionally perform your job, there should be very little risk associated with drain cleaning.

NEW-CONSTRUCTION WORK

New work is what many plumbers prefer. The work is clean, and it is done during normal business hours. Inventory needs for new work are low, and it is possible to schedule work out for months in advance. There are, to be sure, many advantages to new work.

On the downside, new plumbing work often requires the efforts of more than one person. Another disadvantage to new work is its dependence on good economic times. When recessions hang over an area, new work withers. However, some types of commercial work, like schools, tend to keep going, even in bad times.

New work can be found through bid sheets, and new companies don't need a long work history to get involved with the jobs. The amount of money on these jobs can be great, but the percentage of mark up on material is usually lower than what it would be in other types of work. The fact that much new work is issued through a bid process limits the excess profit a plumber can make.

Since new work can provide jobs for many months, you will be competing against a number of large companies. Some large companies receive volume discounts that you can't get. This can kill your chances for winning the jobs.

New work involves high risk. Unless you are getting advance deposits for labor and material, you might get stiffed and lose thousands of dollars on a single job.

New work is a great specialty for plumbers that can work fast, but if you are a perfectionist, forget new-construction work.

REMODELING WORK

Remodeling work has always been one of my favorite specialties. Remodeling is a lucrative specialty for plumbers, regardless of whether you limit your work to plumbing or expand it to include general contracting.

Since most plumbers limit their work to plumbing, we will keep our look at remodeling to those circumstances. If you are a good remodeling plumber, you can charge more for your services than most other plumbers. To do this, you must also possess and use sales skills to convince homeowners and contractors to deal with you. If you simply put in bids at high prices, you won't get the jobs. But if you sell yourself as a specialist and play on the fear factors most homeowners harbor, you can command attractive rates for your services.

Remodeling work is not as clean as new work, nor is it as predictable. If you are not an experienced remodeling plumber, you can lose a bundle of money if you make mistakes in your estimates. This is especially true for plumbers that remodel or restore properties damaged by fire. You might look at these jobs and think sections of piping are fine, when in reality they must be repaired or replaced.

When you do remodeling work, your career is likely to be more stable than it might be with new work. While recessions can reduce the number of homeowners looking to remodel their houses, it can also increase your business. Homeowners that can't sell their homes, due to market conditions, often turn to remodeling as an alternative.

General contractors that specialize in remodeling know that it takes a special kind of plumber to make them look good. Plumbers with heavy remodeling experience and good reputations can ask for, and often get, top dollar for their time. Seasoned general contractors know what a mess an inexperienced remodeler can make of a job, so they are willing to pay extra for plumbers with well-honed remodeling skills.

New-construction work can get boring, especially if you are plumbing a housing project where every fourth house is the same. This is not the case with remodeling. Every remodeling job will be different and present its own unique challenges.

Remodeling plumbers can work all year. Many new-construction plumbers have times of the year when weather conditions affect their work. Often they can't work at all. At other times, the work is uncomfortable due to weather. Remodelers do most of their work within functional buildings. There is heat in the winter, a roof over their head, and usually air conditioning in the summer. The climate-controlled work conditions make remodeling a good option for plumbers looking to specialize.

If you have the experience to be a good remodeling plumber, you can make good money and usually work under comfortable conditions. When you build a reputation as a remodeling specialist, there shouldn't be any shortage of work.

CLINICAL WORK

Clinical work is a specialty many plumbers never consider, but it is an area of plumbing that can be very lucrative. Clinical work involves special equipment that is normally installed in medical and dental facilities. The devices used in these clinical jobs are often complex and difficult for the average plumber to install. Many plumbers are not fluent in the code requirements for clinical equipment, and don't know how to install a sterilizer or fluid-suction system. If you do, you have the opportunity to make major money.

Hospitals, doctor's offices, dentist's offices, and similar buildings are built during good times and bad. Some of these jobs, like hospitals, can keep a few plumbers busy for many months. If you like knowing where you will be working for the next six months or the next year, hospital plumbing is worth considering.

Not only are new buildings available to plumbers experienced with clinical equipment, there is plenty of service and repair work associated with these fixtures. Convalescent homes, hospitals, and even laboratories are equipped with plumbing that an average plumber might never have seen. This is a prime market for a person with the skills needed to repair and replace clinical equipment.

Money is always a motivator in business, and the money that can be made with clinical work is extremely good. One drawback to clinical work is that much of it usually requires at least two people, but one of the people may be an apprentice.

SPECIALIZED WORK

In the specialties that we have already covered, we talked mostly about broad categories of work. Now we are going to concentrate on highly specialized work.

Well pumps

For rural plumbers, well pumps can be something of a specialty. Few people will be able to put off having their well pumps repaired. This leaves an open market for pump specialists, both as installers and repairers.

If you want to work with pumps, it helps to have some special equipment. A pump puller will allow you to work alone and to work quickly. By being faster than the plumbers that don't have this equipment, you can price your work lower, get more work, and still make good money.

Water treatment equipment

Water treatment equipment is a growing industry that offers many opportunities to plumbers looking for an area of specialization. Both rural and urban areas can offer strong demand for water treatment systems. A lot of plumbers don't install water conditioning equipment, but there is a big market for it.

Learning to install, service, and repair water conditioning equipment doesn't take long. Attend a few seminars and read some product literature. You can become proficient in installing and troubleshooting water systems.

Water heaters

In big cities, some plumbers make good livings doing nothing but replacing water heaters. These plumbing companies advertise heavily and become known as water-heater specialists. They respond to calls quickly and often charge competitive prices. Customers pay a fixed price that includes a good mark up on the water heater and a flat-rate fee for labor. These plumbers make a better than average profit on the job.

Back-flow prevention

Back-flow prevention is an area of specialization that many plumbing companies overlook. With all the new laws pertaining to back-flow prevention, there are thousands of buildings in every major city that are required to be equipped with them. Many of these buildings were not equipped with back-flow preventers when they were built. This opens the door for retrofitting the systems with new back-flow prevention devices.

When the local code authorities require existing buildings to install back-flow preventers, and they do so frequently, the building owners must find someone to do the work. If you have done a targeted mailing to the owners of buildings that are not equipped with back-flow protection, you are likely to be flooded with work. An ad in the phone directory will also bring in the work.

Back-flow preventers for commercial buildings are very expensive. This allows for a good profit on the sale of the device. Not only will you earn a good hourly rate doing this type of work, the mark-up profits are very high.

Rounding out the list

Several specialties round out the list of potential fields, including gas piping. If you work in an area with enough new construction, gas piping can pay your bills.

If you are licensed to install fire sprinkler systems, the pay can be quite good.

Installing roof-drainage systems is another possible specialty if you are working in an area with plenty of commercial work. Even if you are not installing the plumbing inside the building, there is a good chance the roof work can be bid separately.

Government contracts might become your specialty. The work you do under government contracts can be diverse. Learn the system for getting government work and you can keep busy all year long.

It might be feasible to specialize in the installation of water services and sewers, but unless new housing is going up rapidly, this is not a booming business.

JUGGLING YOUR WORK

It is very likely that when you first open your business you will have to learn to juggle your work. You might have to be on service calls in the morning, new-construction work in the afternoon, and back on service calls in the evening. You might find yourself switching back and forth from commercial jobs to residential work. The struggle to stay busy can force you to take work you don't like. To get established as a specialist, you will probably have to juggle your work load for several months.

One of the best ways to juggle your work involves good communication channels with your customers. Customers seeking emergency repair service are not likely to leave a message on an answering machine or with a known answering service. If they call and know they are talking to an answering machine or service, they will hang up and call another plumber. You can, however, avoid losing these calls.

Hire a human answering service and have them answer with your company name. Ask them not to identify themselves as an answering service, unless the customer asks directly about their identity. Most customers will assume they have reached someone in your company that can dispatch a plumber, and in a way, they have. After the answering service has the customer's name, address, and phone number, the service can contact you immediately.

If you have a pager and a cellular phone, you can respond to the customer in a matter of minutes. Call back customers quickly, and you will keep them from moving down the list of plumbers in the phone directory.

You have some options when you return a customer's call. You might be able to schedule the service call for later in the day. If you can, leave the job you are working on a little early and take the service call. Some calls will be emergencies. With those you will either have to leave immediately or refer the customer to another plumber. Never tell a customer you will be there at a certain time when you don't intend to arrive until well past the scheduled appointment. Some plumbers do this to monopolize the customers, but the practice will brand you as an unreliable company.

Time management is the key to successfully juggling work. First you must have good, open communication, and then you must schedule your time carefully. When you perfect these skills, you can juggle your work effectively and fairly.

3

Determine your business structure

The first step toward setting up your business is deciding on a business structure: corporation, sole proprietorship, or partnership. Each of these structures has its own advantages and disadvantages.

WHAT STRUCTURE IS BEST FOR YOU?

Before we get started, let me say that I am not an expert on tax and legal matters. The information in this chapter is based on my personal experience and research. As with all the information in this book, you should verify the validity of the information before you use it. Laws change and different jurisdictions have different rules. I am not attempting to give you tax or legal advice. I am only trying to make you aware of questions to ask the proper experts. Now, with that out of the way, let's dig into the various types of business structures.

What is a corporation?

A corporation is a legal entity. To be legal, the corporation must be registered with and approved by the secretary of state. A corporation can live on in perpetuity and may operate under general management. It may provide limited liability to its shareholders. Stock may be transferred when you work with a corporation.

What is a Subchapter-S corporation?

A Subchapter-S corporation differs from a standard corporation. Commonly called an S-Corporation, these corporate structures must meet certain requirements. For example, an S-Corporation may not have more than 35 stockholders; stockholders must provide personal tax returns; and stockholders must show their share of capital gains and ordinary income on their individual tax returns. The corporation files a tax return, but does not pay income tax. This type of corporation allows stockholders to avoid double taxation. Another restriction is that Subchapter-S corporations may not receive more than 20 percent of their income from passive sources. Passive income could be rent from an apartment building, book royalties, and so on.

What is a partnership?

A partnership is an agreement between two or more people to do business together. In a general partnership, each partner is responsible for all of the partnership's debt. This is an important factor. If you have a bad partner, you could be held liable for partnership debts the partner incurs. Most partnerships don't pay income taxes, but they must file a tax return. The income from the partnership is taxed through the personal tax returns of the partners.

Partnerships can be comprised of general partners or one general partner and any number of limited partners. General partners do not have limited liability. Each general partner can be held accountable for all actions of the partnership. Limited partners might have limited risk. For example, a limited partner may invest $10,000 in a partnership and limit personal liability to that $10,000. If the partnership loses money, goes bankrupt, or has other problems, the most that the limited partner stands to lose is his investment of $10,000. The general partner, however, will be held responsible personally for all actions of the partnership.

What is a sole proprietorship?

A sole proprietorship is a business owned by an individual. The business must file a tax return, but any income tax is assessed against the individual's tax return. Sole proprietors are exposed to full liability for their business actions.

SHOULD YOU INCORPORATE?

The primary advantage of a corporation is the possibility of limited liability, but the protection might not be as good as you think. There are several misconceptions about corporations. Let's explore some of them.

WILL A CORPORATION PROTECT YOU FROM LIABILITY?

The answer depends on what type of liability you are seeking protection from and how your business operates. Let me get specific on these issues.

Protection from lawsuits

If your business is a corporation, your liability might be limited to the corporate assets, but don't count on it. Let's consider an example where the corporate structure might not protect you.

You go to a home to thaw some frozen water pipes. Being a one-employee corporation, you do all the work yourself. Your torch sets the house on fire and burns it to the ground. The customer decides to sue for damages. Can the customer sue the corporation and go after its assets? Yes. Can the customer sue you as the primary stockholder of the corporation? Not really, though anyone can sue anyone else for any reason. But don't relax, you're not safe. Since you did the work yourself, the customer can sue you as an individual for the mishap. This is a fact that most business owners don't understand.

Again, let me stress the importance of seeking professional legal and tax advice. This example is for illustrative purposes only.

If you had sent an employee or a subcontractor out to do the work, your risk of being sued for personal assets, in addition to corporate assets, would be minimal. If you don't do your own field work, a corporation can help protect your personal assets.

Personal financial protection

Personal financial protection is another goal of people who incorporate their business. If a corporation gets into financial trouble, it can file for bankruptcy without affecting the personal assets of the stockholders. However, most lenders and businesses that extend credit to corporations require someone to sign personally for the debt. If you personally endorse a corporate loan, you will be responsible for the loan, even if the corporation goes belly up. Before you spend needed money on false protection, talk to experts for details on how incorporating will affect you and your business.

PARTNERS AND PARTNERSHIPS

My worst business experiences have involved partners. It would be easy to think that my bad track record with partners has been my fault. However, the clients that I consult with have shared similar bad experiences with partners. I can think of very few successful partnerships. If you are considering going into business with a partner, go into the arrangement with your eyes wide open.

Partnerships should be treated seriously. If you are a general partner you can be held accountable for the business actions of your partner or partners. This fact alone is enough to make partnerships a questionable option. There are very few advantages to partnerships, but the potential problems are numerous.

If you decide you want to set up a partnership, consult an attorney. It is much better to invest in a lawyer to form the partnership than it is to pay legal fees to resolve partnership problems. Now, let's look at the pros and cons of each type of business structure.

THE PROS AND CONS OF EACH STRUCTURE

Before you can make a final decision on what type of business structure to assume, you need to know the pros and cons of each form of business. Let's take each type and examine the advantages and disadvantages.

Corporate advantages

Corporate advantages are abundant for large businesses, but a standard corporation might not be a wise decision for a small business. Depending on the size and operational aspects of your business, a corporation might protect you from personal lawsuits and financial problems.

Since corporations can issue stock, there is the possible advantage of generating cash from stockholders. Large sums of money can be generated when a corporation goes public, but this is not usually a feasible option for a very small business.

By incorporating your business, some expenses that are not deductible as a noncorporate entity become deductible. Insurance benefits might be an example of this type of deductible advantage.

Corporate disadvantages

The first disadvantage is the cost of incorporating. There are filing fees that must be paid. Most people use lawyers to set up corporations, which adds legal fees. The cost of establishing a corporate entity can range from less than $200 to upwards of $1,000. This can be a lot of money for a fledgling business.

To keep the advantages of a corporation effective, you must maintain certain criteria. You will have to have a registered agent. Many people use their attorney as the registered agent. If you use an attorney in this position, you will spend extra money. There are board meetings to be held, corporate officers to be appointed, and the corporate book must be maintained. A board of directors must be established, and written minutes must be recorded at meetings. Annual reports are another responsibility of corporations. Again, many people have an attorney tend to much of this work.

If the corporate rules are broken, the corporation loses much of its protection potential. If an aggressor can pierce the veil of your corporation, you could be exposed to personal liability.

Small business owners that incorporate their business with a standard corporation face double taxation. These owners will pay personal income tax and will also pay corporate taxes. This extra taxation is a serious burden for most small businesses.

The advantages of a Subchapter-S corporation

One of the biggest advantages of a Subchapter-S corporation over a standard corporation is the elimination of the double taxation. Stockholders of Subchapter-S corporations pay personal taxes on the money they and the corporation earn, but they only pay taxes on the money once. S-Corporations offer the other advantages you would receive with a standard corporation.

Disadvantages of S-Corporations

The cost of setting up and maintaining the corporation are still there. Once you have more than 35 stockholders, you will not be able to use an S-Corporation. If more than 20 percent of your corporate income will be passive, you cannot use a Subchapter-S corporation.

The advantages of a partnership

About the only advantage to a partnership is that it will cost less to set up than a corporation.

Disadvantages of partnerships

In my opinion, the disadvantages of partnerships are abundant. Partnerships have a place in business ventures, but I don't like them for most types of business. If you are a real estate investor partnerships can work, but why gamble with a partnership for a service business. Hooking up with a bad partner might ruin your business and your future. If you decide to set up a partnership, get legal counsel to understand what you are getting into.

The advantages of a sole proprietorship

A sole proprietorship is simple and inexpensive to establish. You are your business, so there are no complicated corporate records to keep. You can get tax advantages as a sole proprietor, as you can with other forms of business structure. You are the boss. There is no partner to argue with over business decisions. There are no stockholders to report to. Tax filing is relatively simple, and you don't have to share your profits with others.

Disadvantages of a sole proprietorship

As a sole proprietor you will have to sign for all your business credit personally. If your business gets sued, you get sued. There also might be some tax angles that you will miss out on as a sole proprietor.

Give a lot of consideration to the type of business structure you want before you make a decision. It would be a shame to spend a lot of money setting up a standard corporation only to discover you would have been better off with an S-Corporation or a sole proprietorship.

4

Legal and tax considerations

Using and maintaining the proper paperwork can make all aspects of your business better, especially when it comes to taxes and legal issues. If you ever have to go to court, you will learn the value of well-documented notes and agreements. An Internal Revenue Service (IRS) audit will prove the importance of keeping good records.

Professional help is not inexpensive, but it is better to pay an attorney to draft good legal documents than it is to pay to have improper documents defended in court. The same can be said about accountants. A good certified public account (CPA) can save you money, even after the professional fees you are charged.

THE LEGAL SIDE OF BUSINESS

It is your responsibility as a business owner to comply with all laws. Ignorance of the law is not a suitable defense. Penalties for breaching some of these laws are extensive and might involve imprisonment and cash fines.

There are so many laws to abide by that the average person has trouble keeping up with them (FIG. 4-1 through FIG. 4-6). There are laws that require certain posters to be displayed for employees. Contract law is an issue for any contractor. Laws pertaining to legal collection procedures for past-due accounts can affect your business. Discrimination laws come into play when you deal with employees and customers. The list of laws that might affect your business could fill a small library.

If you are not well versed in business law, spend some time studying the topic. You might find it necessary to go to seminars or college classes to gain the knowledge you need. Books that specialize in business law can be a big help. If you have specific questions, confer with an attorney that concentrates on business law.

Employers Holding Federal Contracts or Subcontracts

Applicants to and employees of companies with a Federal government contract or subcontract are protected under the following Federal authorities:

RACE, COLOR, RELIGION, SEX, NATIONAL ORIGIN

Executive Order 11246, as amended, prohibits job discrimination on the basis of race, color, religion, sex or national origin, and requires affirmative action to ensure equality of opportunity in all aspects of employment.

INDIVIDUALS WITH HANDICAPS

Section 503 of the Rehabilitation Act of 1973, as amended, prohibits job discrimination because of handicap and requires affirmative action to employ and advance in employment qualified individuals with handicaps who, with reasonable accommoda- · tion, can perform the essential functions of a job.

4-1 Labor laws U.S. Dept. of Labor

LICENSES

Licenses are required for most businesses. Some businesses only require a general business license, but as you probably know, a plumbing business also requires a master plumber's license.

Having or obtaining the proper licenses is the responsibility of the business owner. If you operate a business without the required licenses, you can get into trouble from all angles. Consumers will have grounds to be upset, and local authorities will have something to say about your failure to be licensed. The penalties for operating a business without a license can be

4-2 Labor laws U.S. Dept. of Labor

steep. Check your local regulations to see what licenses you must obtain. Don't do business without them.

CHOOSING AN ATTORNEY AND ACCOUNTANT

These two professional fields incorporate an enormous amount of facts and requirements under two simple names. An individual attorney cannot possibly be fluent in all areas of law. Accountants cannot be expected to know every aspect of finance. For these reasons, you must look for professionals who specialize in the type of service you require.

Most professionals list their specialties in their advertising. For example, an attorney that specializes in criminal law will often make this point clear in advertising. CPAs that concentrate on corporate accounts will direct their advertising to this form of service.

Once you narrow the field to professionals working within the realms of your needs, you must further separate the crowd. Begin your process of elimination with technical considerations. Make a list of your known and expected needs. Ask the selected professionals how they can help you meet

AGE

The Age Discrimination in Employment Act of 1967, as amended, protects applicants and employees 40 years of age or older from discrimination on the basis of age in hiring, promotion, discharge, compensation, terms, conditions or privileges of employment.

SEX (WAGES)

In addition to sex discrimination prohibited by Title VII of the Civil Rights Act (see above), the Equal Pay Act of 1963, as amended, prohibits sex discrimination in payment of wages to women and men performing substantially equal work in the same establishment.

Retaliation against a person who files a charge of discrimination, participates in an investigation, or opposes an unlawful employment practice is prohibited by all of these Federal laws.

If you believe that you have been discriminated against under any of the above laws, you immediately should contact:

The U.S. Equal Employment Opportunity Commission (EEOC), 1801 L Street, N.W., Washington, D.C. 20507 or an EEOC field office by calling toll free (800) 669-4000. For individuals with hearing impairments, EEOC's toll free TDD number is (800) 800-3302.

4-3 Labor laws U.S. Dept. of Labor

Private Employment, State and Local Governments, Educational Institutions

Applicants to and employees of most private employers, state and local governments, educational institutions, employment agencies and labor organizations are protected under the following Federal laws:

RACE, COLOR, RELIGION, SEX, NATIONAL ORIGIN

Title VII of the Civil Rights Act of 1964, as amended, prohibits discrimination in hiring, promotion, discharge, pay, fringe benefits, job training, classification, referral, and other aspects of employment, on the basis of race, color, religion, sex or national origin.

DISABILITY

The Americans with Disabilities Act of 1990, as amended, protects qualified applicants and employees with disabilities from discrimination in hiring, promotion, discharge, pay, job training, fringe benefits, classification, referral, and other aspects of employment on the basis of disability. The law also requires that covered entities provide qualified applicants and employees with disabilities with reasonable accommodations that do not impose undue hardship.

4-4 Labor laws U.S. Dept. of Labor

4-5 Labor laws U.S. Dept. of Labor

INDIVIDUALS WITH HANDICAPS

Section 504 of the Rehabilitation Act of 1973, as amended, prohibits employment discrimination on the basis of handicap in any program or activity which receives Federal financial assistance. Discrimination is prohibited in all aspects of employment against handicapped persons who, with reasonable accommodation, can perform the essential functions of a job.

If you believe you have been discriminated against in a program of any institution which receives Federal assistance, you should contact immediately the Federal agency providing such assistance.

4-6 Labor laws U.S. Dept. of Labor

Programs or Activities Receiving Federal Financial Assistance

RACE, COLOR, NATIONAL ORIGIN, SEX

In addition to the protection of Title VII of the Civil Rights Act of 1964, Title VI of the Civil Rights Act prohibits discrimination on the basis of race, color or national origin in programs or activities receiving Federal financial assistance. Employment discrimination is covered by Title VI if the primary objective of the financial assistance is provision of employment, or where employment discrimination causes or may cause discrimination in providing services under such programs. Title IX of the Education Amendments of 1972 prohibits employment discrimination on the basis of sex in educational programs or activities which receive Federal assistance.

these needs. Inquire about the past performances and clients of the professionals.

After you have covered all the technical questions, ask yourself some questions. How do you feel about the individual professional? Would you be comfortable going into a tax audit with this CPA? Are you willing to bet your business on the knowledge and courtroom prowess of this attorney? Are you comfortable talking with the individual?

How you feel towards the professional as a person is important. You will very likely expose your deepest business secrets to your accountant and your attorney. If you are not comfortable with the professional, you will not get the most out of your business relationship.

Another key factor to assess when choosing professionals is the ease with which you understand them. The subject matter you will discuss is complex and possibly foreign to you. You need professionals who can decipher the cryptic information that confuses you and present it in an easy-to-understand manner.

TAXES ARE PART OF ANY BUSINESS

Unless you are a tax expert, consult someone who is. If you prepare your own taxes, you might be giving the government more money than necessary.

If you wait until a month before tax time to meet with a tax specialist, there might not be much the expert can do for you, short of filing your return. If you consult with a tax expert early in the year, you can manage your business to minimize the tax bite. Early consultations can result in significant savings for you and your business.

Tax manipulation is an art, and CPAs are the artists. When you meet with these professionals you might find numerous ways to save on your taxes. You might be told to lease vehicles, instead of buying them. You might be shown how to keep a mileage log for your vehicle to maximize your tax deductions. A CPA might recommend a different type of structure for your business. For example, if you are operating as a standard corporation, the accountant might suggest that you switch to a Subchapter-S corporation to avoid double taxation.

If you work from home, your tax expert can show you how to deduct the area of your home that is used solely for business. A tax specialist can show you how to defer your tax payments to a time when your tax rate might be lower. Investment strategies can be planned to make the most of your investment dollars.

Perhaps one of the most important aspects on which a tax specialist can educate you is what is a legitimate deduction. I see numerous businesses where the business owners are required to pay back taxes. Most of these business owners had no idea they owed taxes, until they got a notice to pay them. These people found deductions that they thought were legitimate were not allowable. It can be a major burden to catch up on taxes that were due last year or years before. This type of expenditure is never planned for and can drive a business to financial hardship.

The best way to avoid unexpected tax bills is to make sure your taxes are filed and paid properly. The most effective way to ensure that your taxes are done properly is to hire a professional to do them for you. If you resent paying someone to do a job you think you can do, you are not alone, but you might find that by paying a little now, you will save a lot later.

YOU CAN SURVIVE AN IRS AUDIT

If you are concerned about surviving an IRS audit, don't worry. I did it, and you can do it. For years an audit was one of my greatest fears. Even though I knew, or at least thought, that my tax filings were in order, I worried about the day I would be audited. It was a lot like dreading the semi-annual trip to the dentist. Then one day it happened. I was notified that my tax records were going to be audited. My worst nightmare became a reality.

Before the audit I scrambled to gather old records and went over my tax returns for anything that might have been in error. I couldn't find any obvious problems. I went to my CPA and had him go over the information I would present in the audit. There were no blazing red flags to call attention to my tax return.

When I called the individual that was to perform my IRS audit, I was told that my return had been chosen at random. The person went on to say that probably nothing was wrong with my return, that a percentage of returns are picked each year for audit. Gaining this information made me feel a little better, but not a lot.

My CPA represented me on the day of the audit. I was not required to attend the meeting. Even though I wasn't at the meeting, my mental state was miserable that day. When my CPA called, he told me the meeting had gone well, but that I had to provide further documentation for some of my deductions. These deductions primarily were travel expenses and books.

After digging through my records, I found most of the needed documentation. However, there were some receipts that I couldn't document. For example, I had written on receipts that they were for book purchases, but I hadn't listed the title of the book. The IRS wanted to know what books I had purchased. I couldn't remember what the titles were, so I put notes on the receipts to explain that I could not document the book titles.

The travel expenses were easier to document, most of them had been paid for with credit cards. After finding the old receipts, I was able to remember where I had gone and why. After finding as much documentation as I could, the package was given back to my CPA.

Another meeting between the auditor and my accountant took place. I was expecting the worst, and thought I would have to pay back taxes on items I couldn't identify properly. But to my surprise, I was given a clean bill of health. The auditor accepted my I-can't-remember receipts. Since most of my receipts were documented and I hadn't written fictitious names on the receipts, my honesty prevailed.

I always thought an audit would be horrible. However, I didn't have to attend the audit personally, my CPA did a great job, and I didn't have to pay any serious tax penalties. My audit was over, without much pain. I can't say that all audits are this easy, but mine was.

Going through that audit convinced me of what I had believed for years. Accurate records are the key to staying out of tax trouble. If my records had been misplaced or substantially incomplete, I could have been in a serious bind. However, my good business principles enabled me to survive the audit, with relative ease.

If you are afraid of being audited, begin keeping detailed records. Before you take a questionable deduction, check with a tax expert to confirm the legality of the deduction. Don't cheat on your taxes. Not only is it wrong, you never know when you will be caught. Honesty is the best policy.

DOCUMENT YOUR BUSINESS ACTIVITY

Documenting your business activity is an absolute must. The documentation may be used to track sales, keep up with changes in the market, forecast the future, defend yourself in court, or substantiate your tax filing, just to name a few.

There are many good reasons for and ways to document your business activity. A carbon-copy phone-message book is a simple, effective way to log all of your phone activity (FIG. 4-7). Written contracts document your job duties and payment arrangements. Change orders and addendums are the best way to document actions that cause you to deviate from the original agreement. Letters can be used to confirm phone conversations, creating a paper record and avoiding confusion. Tape recorders can help you remember your daily duties.

Service Call

Date_____ Time_____

Customer name_____

Address_____

Type of service requested_____

Call taken by_____

Call assigned to_____

Service promised by_____

4-7 Service call (message)

CONTRACTS, CHANGE ORDERS, AND ESSENTIAL PAPERWORK

While most people abhor paperwork, it is recognized as a necessary part of doing business. The use of computers has helped reduce the amount of paper and made the task of doing paperwork easier, but even computers cannot eliminate the need for accurate paperwork. To understand the need for so much clerical work, let's take a closer look at the various needs of business owners.

Contracts

Contracts are the lifeblood of your business. There are two types of contracts—verbal and written. Verbal contracts are legal, but they are essentially unenforceable. Written contracts are the other choice. These agreements are enforceable (FIG. 4-8 and FIG. 4-9).

A written contract should be used for every job, except small repairs. Even with repairs, it is best to use a written service order or some type of agreement. Contracts help protect you. They provide physical evidence of the understanding between you and the customer.

Contracts give a full description of the work you are being engaged to perform. When written properly, contracts leave little room for misunderstandings (FIG. 4-10 through FIG. 4-13). Good contracts include the date work will start and the hours that may be worked. If you have a customer that doesn't want anyone on the job until 10:00 A.M., you will have trouble scheduling your workers for maximum efficiency. If you know this in advance, you can adjust your price to reflect the inconvenience on your company. If you take the job and don't find out about the allowable work hours until a raging customer chases your workers off the property at 8:00 A.M., you will have problems on the job.

By inserting a starting date in the contract, both you and the customer know when to expect the work to begin. This eliminates the customer calling and hounding you about when the job will start. A written start date also will help you organize your schedule and prepare for the job. Some contractors need this committed discipline to run their businesses effectively.

Contracts address how much you will be paid and in what increments you will receive your money. If you are to get a deposit before starting the job, the date the deposit is due, and the amount of the deposit will be stipulated in the agreement. Money is a major cause of job-related problems. The more documentation you have on the financial aspects of the job, the better off you will be.

Most contracts go on to cover a wide variety of other variables. These variables might include who is responsible for cleaning up after the job, what will happen with the debris from the job, the length of the job guarantee, and so on. Generally speaking, a written contract is the foundation for your business.

Your Company Name
Your Company Address
Your Company Phone Number

PROPOSAL

Date: _____

Customer name: _____

Address: _____

Phone number: _____

Job location: _____

Description of Work

<u>Your Company Name</u> will supply, and or coordinate, all labor and material for the above referenced job as follows:

_____

_____

_____

Payment Schedule

Price: _____ ($_____),

Payments to be made as follows:

_____

_____

_____

All payments shall be made in full, upon presentation of each completed invoice. If payment is not made according to the terms above, <u>Your Company Name</u> will have the following rights and remedies. <u>Your Company Name</u> may charge a monthly service charge of <u>one-and-one-half percent (1.5%), eighteen percent (18%)</u> per year, from the first day default is made. <u>Your Company Name</u> may lien the property where the work has been done. <u>Your Company Name</u> may use all legal methods in the collection of monies owed to it. <u>Your Company Name</u> may seek compensation, at the rate of $_____ per hour, for attempts made to collect unpaid monies.

Page 1 of 2 initials _____

4-8 Proposal

Your Company Name may seek payment for legal fees and other costs of collection, to the full extent the law allows.

If the job is not ready for the service or materials requested, as scheduled, and the delay is not due to Your Company Name's actions, Your Company Name may charge the customer for lost time. This charge will be at a rate of $_____ per hour, per man, including travel time.

If you have any questions or don't understand this proposal, seek professional advice. Upon acceptance, this proposal becomes a binding contract between both parties.

Respectfully submitted,

Your name and title
Owner

Acceptance

We the undersigned do hereby agree to, and accept, all the terms and conditions of this proposal. We fully understand the terms and conditions, and hereby consent to enter into this contract.

Your Company Name   Customer

By _____   _____

Title_____   Date_____

Date_____

Proposal expires in 30 days, if not accepted by all parties.

4-8 Continued

Addendums

Addendums (FIG. 4-14) are extensions of a contract. Addendums are used to add language to contracts after the contracts are written. In some cases, where fill-in-the-blank contracts are used, addendums provide a means for making the contract more explicit.

Change orders

Change orders (FIG. 4-15) are written agreements that are used when a change is made to an existing contract. It might seem unlikely that a customer would ask you to alter the plans of an original agreement and then sue you for doing what you were told, but it is possible. Without a written change order you would be at the mercy of the court.

Renaissance Remodeling
357 Paris Lane
Wilton, Ohio 55555
(102) 555-5555

REMODELING CONTRACT

This agreement, made this _____th day of _____, 19____, shall set forth the whole agreement, in its entirety, between Contractor and Customer.

Contractor: Renaissance Remodeling, referred to herein as Contractor.

Customer: _____, referred to herein as Customer.

Job name: _____

Job location: _____

The Customer and Contractor agree to the following:

Scope of Work

Contractor shall perform all work as described below and provide all material to complete the work described below: All work is to be completed by Contractor in accordance with the attached plans and specifications. All material is to be supplied by Contractor in accordance with attached plans and specifications. Said attached plans and specifications have been acknowledged and signed by Contractor and Customer.

A brief outline of the work is as follows, and all work referenced in the attached plans and specifications will be completed to the Customer's reasonable satisfaction. The following is only a basic outline of the overall work to be performed:

_____

_____

_____

_____

_____

_____

_____

_____

_____

(Page 1 of 3 initials_____)

4-9 Remodeling contract

Commencement and Completion Schedule

The work described above shall be started within three days of verbal notice from Customer; the projected start date is _____. The Contractor shall complete the above work in a professional and expedient manner, by no later than _____ days from the start date. Time is of the essence regarding this contract. No extension of time will be valid, without the Customer's written consent. If Contractor does not complete the work in the time allowed, and if the lack of completion is not caused by the Customer, the Contractor will be charged _____, per day, for every day work is not finished beyond the completion date. This charge will be deducted from any payments due to the Contractor for work performed.

Contract Sum

The Customer shall pay the Contractor for the performance of completed work, subject to additions and deductions, as authorized by this agreement or attached addendum. The contract sum is _____, ($_____).

Progress Payments

The Customer shall pay the Contractor installments as detailed below, once an acceptable insurance certificate has been filed by the Contractor, with the Customer:

Customer will pay Contractor a deposit of _____,
($_____), when work is started.
Customer will pay _____,
($_____), when all rough-in work is complete.
Customer will pay _____,
($_____) when work is _____ percent complete.
Customer will pay _____,
($_____) when all work is complete and accepted.

All payments are subject to a site inspection and approval of work by the Customer. Before final payment, the Contractor, if required, shall submit satisfactory evidence to the Customer, that all expenses related to this work have been paid and no lien risk exists on the subject property.

Working Conditions

Working hours will be ___ A.M. through ___ P.M., Monday through Friday. Contractor is required to clean work debris from the job site on a daily basis and to leave the site in a clean and neat condition. Contractor shall be responsible for removal and disposal of all debris related to their job description.

(Page 2 of 3 initials_____)

4-9 Continued

Contract Assignment

Contractor shall not assign this contract or further subcontract the whole of this subcontract without the written consent of the Customer.

Laws, Permits, Fees, and Notices

Contractor is responsible for all required laws, permits, fees, or notices required to perform the work stated herein.

Work of Others

Contractor shall be responsible for any damage caused to existing conditions. This shall include work performed on the project by other contractors. If the Contractor damages existing conditions or work performed by other contractors, said Contractor shall be responsible for the repair of said damages. These repairs may be made by the Contractor responsible for the damages or another contractor, at the sole discretion of Customer.

The damaging Contractor shall have the opportunity to quote a price for the repairs. The Customer is under no obligation to engage the damaging Contractor to make the repairs. If a different contractor repairs the damage, the Contractor causing the damage may be back-charged for the cost of the repairs. These charges may be deducted from any monies owed to the damaging Contractor.

If no money is owed to the damaging Contractor, said Contractor shall pay the invoiced amount within _____ business days. If prompt payment is not made, the Customer may exercise all legal means to collect the requested monies. The damaging Contractor shall have no rights to lien the Customer's property for money retained to cover the repair of damages caused by the Contractor. The Customer may have the repairs made to his satisfaction.

Warranty

Contractor warrants to the Customer all work and materials, for one year from the final day of work performed.

Indemnification

To the fullest extent allowed by law, the Contractor shall indemnify and hold harmless the Customer and all of their agents and employees from and against all claims, damages, losses and expenses.

This Agreement entered into on _____, 19_____ shall constitute the whole agreement between Customer and Contractor.

_____   _____
Customer   Date   Contractor   Date

_____
Customer   Date

4-9 Continued.

Commencement and Completion Schedule

The work described above shall be started within <u>three (3)</u> days of verbal notice from the customer, the projected start date is _____. The subcontractor shall complete the above work in a professional and expedient manner by no later than <u>twenty (20)</u> days from the start date.

Time is of the essence in this subcontract. No extension of time will be valid without the general contractor's written consent. If subcontractor does not complete the work in the time allowed and if the lack of completion is not caused by the general contractor, the subcontractor will be charged <u>one-hundred dollars ($100.00)</u> for every day work is not finished after the completion date. This charge will be deducted from any payments due to the subcontractor for work performed.

4-10   Sample completion clause

Subcontractor Liability for Damages

Subcontractor shall be responsible for any damage caused to existing conditions. This shall include new work performed on the project by other contractors. If the subcontractor damages existing conditions or work performed by other contractors, said subcontractor shall be responsible for the repair of said damages. These repairs may be made by the subcontractor responsible for the damages or another contractor, at the discretion of the general contractor.

If a different contractor repairs the damage, the subcontractor causing the damage may be back-charged for the cost of the repairs. These charges may be deducted from any monies owed to the damaging subcontractor, by the general contractor. The choice for a contractor to repair the damages shall be at the sole discretion of the general contractor.

If no money is owed to the damaging subcontractor, said contractor shall pay the invoiced amount, to the general contractor, within <u>seven (7)</u> business days. If prompt payment is not made, the general contractor may exercise all legal means to collect the requested monies.

The damaging subcontractor shall have no rights to lien the property where work is done for money retained to cover the repair of damages caused by the subcontractor. The general contractor may have the repairs made to his satisfaction.

The damaging subcontractor shall have the opportunity to quote a price for the repairs. The general contractor is under no obligation to engage the damaging subcontractor to make the repairs.

4-11   Sample damage clause for contract

Certificate of Completion and Acceptance

Contractor: _____

Customer: _____

Job name: _____

Job location: _____

Job Description: _____

_____

_____

_____

Date of completion: _____

Date of final inspection by customer: _____

Date of code compliance inspection & approval: _____

Defects found in material or workmanship: _____

_____

Acknowledgment

Customer acknowledges the completion of all contracted work and accepts all workmanship and materials as being satisfactory. Upon signing this certificate, the customer releases the contractor from any responsibility for additional work, except warranty work. Warranty work will be performed for a period of one year from the date of completion. Warranty work will include the repair of any material or workmanship defects occurring between now and the end of the warranty period. All existing workmanship and materials are acceptable to the customer and payment will be made, in full, according to the payment schedule in the contract, between the two parties.

_____   _____
Customer   Date   Contractor   Date

4-12 Certificate of completion & acceptance

Change orders should include basic information: the name and address of the customer, the location of the job, and the date and reference number of the original contract. A specific description of the work being altered should be included in the body of the change order. For example, don't

Certificate of Subcontractor Completion Acceptance

Contractor: _____

Subcontractor: _____

Job name: _____

Job location: _____

Job description: _____

_____

_____

_____

_____

_____

Date of completion: _____

Date of final inspection by contractor: _____

Date of code compliance inspection & approval: _____

Defects found in material or workmanship: _____

_____

_____

_____

_____

Acknowledgment

Contractor acknowledges the completion of all contracted work and accepts all workmanship and materials as being satisfactory. Upon signing this certificate, the contractor releases the subcontractor from any responsibility for additional work, except warranty work. Warranty work will be performed for a period of one year from the date of completion. Warranty work will include the repair of any material or workmanship defects occurring between now and the end of the warranty period. All existing workmanship and materials are acceptable to the contractor and payment will be made, in full, according to the payment schedule in the contract, between the two parties.

_____   _____
Contractor   Date   Subcontractor   Date

4-13 Certificate of subcontractor completion acceptance

Addendum

This addendum is an integral part of the contract dated _____, between the Contractor, _____, and the Customer(s), _____, for the work being done on real estate commonly known as _____. The undersigned parties hereby agree to the following:

_____

_____

_____

_____

_____

_____

_____

_____

_____

_____

_____

_____

_____

_____

The above constitutes the only additions to the above-mentioned contract, no verbal agreements or other changes shall be valid unless made in writing and signed by all parties.

_____   _____
Contractor   Date   Customer   Date

                                            _____
                                            Customer   Date

4-14 Addendum

Change Order

This change order is an integral part of the contract dated_____, between the
customer, _____ , and the contractor,_____, for
the work to be performed. The job location is _____.
The following changes are the only changes to be made. These changes shall now become a part
of the original contract and may not be altered again without written authorization from all parties.

Changes to be as follows:

_____

_____

_____

_____

_____

_____

These changes will increase/decrease the original contract amount. Payment for theses changes
will be made as follows:_____. The amount of change in the
contract price will be _____ ($). The new total contract price
shall be _____ ($).

The undersigned parties hereby agree that these are the only changes to be made to the original
contract. No verbal agreements will be valid. No further alterations will be allowed without
additional written authorization, signed by all parties. This change order constitutes the entire
agreement between the parties to alter the original contract.

_____   _____
Customer   Contractor

_____   _____
Date   Date

_____
Customer

_____
Date

4-15 Change order

write a change order that says the kitchen sink will be changed from a single-bowl sink to a double-bowl sink. For this type of a change, include all pertinent data on the new sink: the make, model number, color, style, and whatever else is applicable.

Always provide documentation on how the change order will affect the cost of the job. If the change will result in a credit to the customer, put the amount of the credit in the paperwork. If the change will be reason for you to charge more money for the job, detail the extra charges in writing. Dictate how the credits or extra charges will be accounted for and when they will be paid.

Require all parties who signed the original contract to sign the change order. I have seen contractors write up a change order and give it to the customer, without receiving a signed copy for their files. I have also seen change orders signed by only one of the parties of the original contract. Both of these practices are bad business. Treat change orders with the same respect you would a contract and keep signed copies on file.

Service orders

Service orders are the small tickets that customers are asked to sign, generally after the work is done, to acknowledge that the work was satisfactory. This is fine, except for the fact that most customers are not asked to sign the service order until the work is complete. This practice puts the business owner at risk. The customer should be asked to sign the service order before the work is started and again when the work is completed.

The wording in your service contracts should include payment terms, guarantees, liability restrictions, and much more. An attorney can help you design a service order that will best suit your needs.

Service orders also should document the time your employees arrive on a job and the time they leave the job. This helps to keep your employees productive and gives you an edge in management.

Inventory control is another feature service orders can give you. Have your service technicians list all materials used on the service ticket, and you can maintain an accurate inventory of your rolling stock. When designed and used properly, service orders will make your business better.

Liability waivers

These forms protect contractors from being accused of acts that were nearly unavoidable. Use liability waivers any time you believe your actions might cause a confrontation.

For example, assume a customer asks you to replace the flush valve in a very old toilet. Being an experienced plumber you know that when you try to loosen the nut on an old flush valve there is a risk of breaking the toilet. Because of the possibility of damaging the toilet, you have the customer sign a liability waiver. This way, if the toilet is broken accidentally, you are not held responsible for the damage.

You probably won't find many preprinted liability waivers. I suspect that in time, companies will make generic waivers, much like the fill-in-the-blank contract forms. For now, you will need to consult an attorney.

When you talk with your attorney, explain all aspects of your business. The attorney will not be able to give you a comprehensive liability waiver, unless you are specific about your work requirements. While you are talking with your lawyer, ask for some boiler-plate language that you can use in on-the-spot cases. Even a customized waiver form will not fulfill all of the potential needs. There will come a time when special circumstances will require you to draft a liability waiver on the job.

Check to make sure you can draft your own waiver legally. Some states are very stringent on what individuals, other than attorneys, can do to prepare legal documents. If you can create your own liability waiver, obtain suitable language for the waiver from your attorney. If you are prohibited from drawing up your own document, let your attorney make a fill-in-the-blank waiver. Then you can add specific details to the waiver as required.

Written estimates

Written estimates (FIG. 4-16 and FIG. 4-17) reduce the risk of confusion when you give prices to customers. They also advise the customer of your terms and conditions, and provide a written description of the work to be performed. This helps protect you and creates a professional image.

Specifications

Written specifications are another way to avoid confrontations with customers. With small jobs, the specifications can be included in the contract. When you are embarking on a large job, the specifications will generally be too expansive to put in the contract. In these instances, make reference to the specifications in the contract and attach the specification sheets to the contract, to make them part of the contract.

When you are developing specifications for a job, be as detailed as possible. Include model numbers, makes, colors, sizes, brand names, and any other descriptions of the labor and materials you will provide. Once you have a good spec list, have the customer review and sign it. Unsigned, specification sheets carry little weight in a legal battle.

Credit applications

Credit applications should be filled out by all credit customers. These forms allow you to check into an individual's past credit history. Just because a person has good references now doesn't guarantee you will be paid, but your odds for collecting the money owed you are better.

As a business owner, you can subscribe to the services of a credit reporting bureau. For a small monthly fee and an inexpensive per-inquiry fee, you can get a detailed credit history on your customers. You will, of course,

Green Tree Lawn Care
987 Willow Road
Wilson, Maine 55555
(101) 555-5555

WORK ESTIMATE

Date: _____

Customer name: _____

Address: _____

Phone number: _____

Description of Work

Green Tree Lawn Care will supply all labor and material for the following work:

_____

_____

_____

_____

_____

_____

_____

_____

Payment for Work as Follows

Estimated price: _____, payable as follows

_____

_____

If you have any questions, please don't hesitate to call. Upon acceptance, a formal contract will be issued.

Respectfully submitted,

J. B. Williams
Owner

4-16 Work estimate

Your Company Name
Your Company Address
Your Company Phone Number

Quote

This agreement, made this _____ day of _____ , 19_____, shall set forth the whole agreement, in its entirety, by and between Your Company Name, herein called Contractor and_____, herein called Owners.

Job name: _____

Job location: _____

The Contractor and Owners agree to the following:

Contractor shall perform all work as described below and provide all material to complete the work described below. Contractor shall supply all labor and material to complete the work according to the attached plans and specifications. The work shall include the following:

_____

_____

_____

Schedule

The work described above shall begin within three days of notice from Owner, with an estimated start date of _____. The Contractor shall complete the above work in a professional and expedient manner within ___ days from the start date.

Payment Schedule

Payments shall be made as follows:

_____

_____

This agreement, entered into on _____, shall constitute the whole between Contractor and Owner.

_____   _____
Contractor   Date   Owner   Date

                                              _____
                                              Owner   Date

4-17 Quote

need the permission of your customers to check into their credit back-ground. Credit applications provide documentation of this permission.

Even if you don't belong to a credit bureau, you can call references given by the customer on the credit application. This type of investigation is not as good as the reports you receive from credit agencies, but it is better than nothing.

Cash receipts

If you keep records of all your cash purchases, you can take advantage of all your tax deductions. Receipts serve as documentation for your deductions. If the receipt does not state clearly what the purchase was, write what the item was and its use. If the item was for a particular job, write the job name on the receipt. In a tax audit your documented receipts may mean the difference between an easy audit and having to pay back taxes.

Inventory logs

Inventory logs can be used to maintain current information on your inventory needs and supply. If you take materials out of your inventory, write in the log what the items were and where they were used. At the end of the week go over your log and adjust your inventory figures. If you need to replace the inventory, you will know exactly what was used. If questions arise at tax time, you can identify where your inventory went. Something as simple as an inventory log can save you from lost money and time.

Repair vouchers

If your customers bring items in for repair, use repair vouchers (FIG. 4-18). Repair vouchers are similar to service orders. They detail the work to be done, for whom the work is being done, the item that is being worked on, and other necessary information.

Repair vouchers should include a complete description of the item being left by the customer. Always include the item's serial number on the voucher. Ideally, your repair voucher should have a questionnaire on it for the customer to fill out. The questions should inquire about the present condition of the item being left for repair. These vouchers can save you from being accused of breaking this or scratching that. If you see a visible defect on the item, note it on the voucher. Have the customer sign to accept the known defect. Repair vouchers offer good protection from disputes and accusations.

CONCISE CONTRACTS MAKE FOR HAPPY CUSTOMERS

When you prepare contracts, put as much information in them as possible. Once the contract is written, go over it with the customer. Allow the customer plenty of time to read and absorb the contents of the contract. Answer any questions the customer might have. If necessary, reword the

Repair Voucher

Date_____

Time_____

Received of_____

Address_____

Phone number_____

Item to be repaired_____

Serial number_____

Make_____

Model_____

Nature of problem_____

Item accepted by_____

4-18 Repair voucher

contract to eliminate confusion. Once the contract is agreeable to all parties, execute it, preferably in front of a witness.

After the contract is signed, don't deviate from its contents. If changes are to be made, use addendums or change orders, and make sure they are signed by all of the signatories on the contract. If you follow this type of procedure in all of your jobs, you should have more happy customers and fewer problems.

DEALING WITH CONTRACTORS AS A SUBCONTRACTOR

Dealing with general contractors as a subcontractor can be an unpleasant experience. Most general contractors have good intentions, but it is not uncommon for generals to be slow to pay their subcontractors. Your best line of defense with subcontracting work is a good contract (FIG. 4-19). The contract should state clearly the terms and conditions of all your work and fees.

Most general contractors are reluctant to give contract deposits. Part of their reasoning is cash-flow. If a contractor gives each subcontractor front money, the contractor will have less cash with which to work. Another reason general contractors refuse to give deposits is the potential for losses. The general who gives a generous deposit might never see it again, or the

Subcontract Agreement

This agreement, made this ____th day of _____, 19___, shall set forth the whole agreement, in its entirety, between Contractor and Subcontractor.

Contractor: _____, referred to herein as Contractor.

Job location: _____

Subcontractor: _____, referred to herein as Subcontractor.

    The Contractor and Subcontractor agree to the following:

Scope of Work

Subcontractor shall perform all work as described below and provide all material to complete the work described below.

Subcontractor shall supply all labor and material to complete the work according to the attached plans and specifications. These attached plans and specifications have been initialed and signed by all parties. The work shall include, but is not limited to, the following:

_____

_____

_____

_____

_____

_____

_____

_____

Commencement and Completion Schedule

The work described above shall be started within three days of verbal notice from Contractor, the projected start date is _____. The Subcontractor shall complete the above work in a professional and expedient manner by no later than _____ days from the start date. Time is of the essence in this contract. No extension of time will be valid without the Contractor's written consent. If Subcontractor does not complete the work in the time allowed, and if the lack of completion is not caused by the Contractor, the Subcontractor will be charged <u>fifty dollars</u> <u>($50.00)</u> per day, for every day work extends beyond the completion date. This charge will be deducted from any payments due to the Subcontractor for work performed.

Page 1 of 3 initials___

4-19 Subcontract agreement

Contract Sum

The Contractor shall pay the Subcontractor for the performance of completed work subject to additions and deductions as authorized by this agreement or attached addendum. The contract sum is _____($_____).

Progress Payments

The Contractor shall pay the Subcontractor installments as detailed below, once an acceptable insurance certificate has been filed by the Subcontractor with the Contractor.
Contractor shall pay the Subcontractor as described:

_____

_____

_____

_____

_____

_____

_____

_____

_____

_____

_____

_____

_____

_____

_____

_____

All payments are subject to a site inspection and approval of work by the Contractor. Before final payment, the Subcontractor shall submit satisfactory evidence to the Contractor that no lien risk exists on the subject property.

Page 2 of 3 initials____

4-19 Continued

Working Conditions

Working hours will be 8:00 A.M. through 4:30 P.M., Monday through Friday. Subcontractor is required to clean his work debris from the job site on a daily basis and leave the site in a clean and neat condition. Subcontractor shall be responsible for removal and disposal of all debris related to his job description.

Contract Assignment

Subcontractor shall not assign this contract or further subcontract the whole of this subcontract, without the written consent of the Contractor.

Laws, Permits, Fees, and Notices

Subcontractor shall be responsible for all required laws, permits, fees, or notices, required to perform the work stated herein.

Work of Others

Subcontractor shall be responsible for any damage caused to existing conditions or other contractor's work. This damage will be repaired, and the Subcontractor charged for the expense and supervision of this work. The Subcontractor shall have the opportunity to quote a price for said repairs, but the Contractor is under no obligation to engage the Subcontractor to make said repairs. If a different subcontractor repairs the damage, the Subcontractor may be back-charged for the cost of the repairs. Any repair costs will be deducted from any payments due to the Subcontractor. If no payments are due the Subcontractor, the Subcontractor shall pay the invoiced amount within 10 days.

Warranty

Subcontractor warrants to the Contractor, all work and materials for one year from the final day of work performed.

Indemnification

To the fullest extent allowed by law, the Subcontractor shall indemnify and hold harmless the Owner, the Contractor, and all of their agents and employees from and against all claims, damages, losses and expenses.

This agreement, entered into on _____, 19_____, shall constitute the whole agreement between Contractor and Subcontractor.

_____		_____	
Contractor	Date	Subcontractor	Date

4-19 Continued

work that was supposed to be done. Control is another factor. Giving people money for work that hasn't been done is a sure way to lose control. Money is an excellent lever to keep subcontractors in line. If a deposit is given, the general has less control.

So here's the problem: generals won't give deposits and you won't work without a deposit. Most subcontractors give in and do the work, hoping to get paid later. The fact is, if you want to work for general contractors, you will generally have to work without deposits. Don't do so blindly. Just as a general might lose a deposit, you could lose your labor and materials.

Before you work for a new contractor, check him out. Get the names of other subs who work for the general. Call the subcontractors and see how the contractor is to work for. If you are a member of a credit reporting bureau, get permission to pull a credit report on the contractor. Check with local agencies for any complaints that might have been filed against the contractor. Get a physical address for where the general contractor can be found. If you must serve legal papers on a general contractor, it is hard to serve them to a post office box.

Once you have done your homework, proceed with caution. Your contract should stipulate when you will be paid and what your remedies are if the contractor doesn't pay. Check with your attorney on lien rights and legal actions that might help you recover your money. Know in advance how to deal with deadbeats, and you will save valuable time and make the right moves when it counts.

Don't become too dependent on one or two general contractors. It is nice to get steady business from the same source, but if something happens to the general you will be out of work. It is wise to spread out your work so you can survive, even if your best accounts dry up.

Never get too comfortable with a general contractor. It is easy to slack off on paperwork and rules once you get to know someone, but it is a mistake. Keep your relationship on a business level. If you mix too much business with pleasure, you might wind up in a mess.

BUILD GOOD RELATIONS WITH CODE OFFICERS

If your business depends on the approval of code officers, you will do well to get to know the inspectors. Code officers are often scorned. Contractors that have problems with inspectors cuss them and buck against the system. If these contractors would direct the same amount of energy in a more productive direction, they could solve their problems.

Like it or not, code officers are a fact of life for most plumbers. The relationship between code officers and contractors can go one of two ways—good or bad. As a contractor, you can influence which way the pendulum swings.

If you want to make your life easier, get to know your code officers. I'm not saying you have to become best buddies, but at least be civil. Your attitude will have a great deal of influence on the posture assumed by the code officer. Don't be afraid to smile and talk with your inspectors. If you get to know each other, problems will be easier to resolve.

Code Violation Notification

Contractor: _____

Contractor's address: _____

City/state/zip: _____

Phone number: _____

Job location: _____

Date: _____

Type of work: _____

Subcontractor: _____

Address: _____

Official Notification of Code Violations

On March 22, 1993, I was notified by the local code enforcement officer of code violations in the work performed by your company. The violations must be corrected within two business days, as per our contract dated March 1, 1993. Please contact the codes officer for a detailed explanation of the violations and required corrections. If the violations are not corrected within the allotted time, you may be penalized, as per our contract, for your actions in delaying the completion of this project. Thank you for your prompt attention to this matter.

_____

General Contractor   Date

4-20 Code violation notification

AVOID REJECTED CODE-ENFORCEMENT INSPECTIONS

One of your goals must be to avoid rejected code-enforcement inspections (FIG. 4-20). This goal is not difficult to achieve. Work gets rejected because it is not in compliance with the local code requirements. If you know and understand the code requirements, you shouldn't get many rejection slips. If you don't understand a portion of the code, consult with a code officer. It is part of an inspector's job to explain the code to you.

Again, attitude can have a bearing on the number of rejections you get. If you walk around with a chip on your shoulder, inspectors might look more closely for minute code infractions. If you play by the rules, you won't have much trouble with the officials. But don't ever try to put one over on a code officer. If you get caught, your life on the job will be miserable for a long time to come. Inspectors can be a close-knit group. When you con one, others will get the word, and your work will be put under a microscope.

5

Plan for success

Very few people stumble onto wealth and success. To reach the pinnacle of your profession, you must learn how to plot a path to success. If you fail to recognize the need for solid plans, your business will not make it. This chapter is going to take you on a tour down the path of business ownership.

ACHIEVE YOUR GOALS

We talked about setting goals in the first chapter, here we are going to see how to achieve those goals. Setting goals is important, but achieving them is the key to success.

Bite-size goals

When you first start your business, think of yourself as an infant. Set small goals and practice accomplishing them, like a baby learns to eat. As you develop to the toddler stage, begin to make the goals a little more difficult. By the time you get your adult business teeth, you will be ready to chew any size goal you bite off.

Reading goals

Set aside time to read a certain amount of material on a daily basis. Whether it is 15 minutes or an hour, schedule reading time and use it to broaden your knowledge. There are a multitude of good books available to help new business owners in every facet of the business world. By setting and meeting reading goals, you practice self discipline and learn how to build a better business.

Fight frustration

Goals can cause frustration, and fighting this frustration can be stressful. The best way to avoid goal frustration is to set achievable goals. Don't set your goals too high or move your goal sticks too quickly. If you want to run your own show, you must find effective ways to deal with frustration and stress.

SOLID ORGANIZATION IS KEY TO SUCCESS

The need for proper organization ranges from being able to find a pen to take down a phone message to starting a job on schedule. If you don't take the time to stay organized, your business will suffer. Let's look at some specific examples of how organizational skills and techniques affect your business and your profits.

Telephone organization

Most service businesses make their first impression on customers with their telephone organization. Whether you make a favorable or foul impression will influence the success of your business.

When your phone is answered, what is said? If you simply answer with a quick "hello," callers will get the impression of a small business, probably one run from home. This isn't always a bad impression, but it may not be the image you wish to present. On the other hand, if the phone is answered, "Good morning, Pioneer Plumbing, how may I help you?," people will feel they are talking to a business with good business manners and a professional approach.

Your phone should be answered in a consistent manner. Switching back and forth between answering messages will imply that the business is unorganized and unprofessional. Pick a greeting and stick with it.

If I call your business and ask to leave a message for you, what will happen? Am I going to be put on hold indefinitely? Will the person I'm talking to have to scurry around to find a pen and paper to take down the message? If either of these events occur, I'm not going to be favorably impressed with your business. Before you ever have the opportunity to return my call and talk with me, I've already formed an opinion that will make me less receptive to what you have to say.

When I leave a message, will I be advised when I can expect to hear back from you? If you don't want to interrupt your field work to return calls during the day, have your answering service or receptionist tell me that I won't hear from you until after you are off the job. With the easy and affordable availability of pagers and cellular phones, there is little reason why you shouldn't be able to return my call during business hours. Perhaps you will need to set aside specific times to return calls. Then you know your day will be disturbed at given times, and callers will know when to expect you to return their calls.

What system will you employ to assure you get all your phone messages? If you use an answering machine you can be reasonably certain you will get all your calls. But what if your secretary or spouse takes messages for you? Can you be sure you will get all the messages? Writing messages and phone numbers on scraps of paper is a poor way to run your business. Buy a phone log with duplicate pages or make one (FIG. 5-1) and use it. Not only will using this type of message book reduce the chances of missed messages, it might come in very handy for other reasons.

For example, if Ms. Smith called two weeks ago and you need to follow up on the estimate you gave her, you can use the message book to retrieve her phone number. If you are forced into court over a customer dispute, the message book can serve as evidence. The usefulness of a message book far outweighs its cost.

If you have a professional answering service take your calls, how will you track your messages? It is tough to maintain control on answering services. Most services maintain copies of all messages left and delivered, but you will have no way of knowing if you have gotten all of your messages. More importantly, it is difficult to determine how the service is treating your customers.

When you use a human answering service, check up on the service from time to time. You can monitor the skills of the people answering your phones by having your friends leave messages and by asking your customers how they were treated on the phone. By asking your customers, you not only get valuable information on the performance of your answering service, you make a great impression on your customers by being concerned about how they were handled on the phone.

Scheduling

Scheduling cannot be effective if you are not organized. It will not do any good to devise a perfect schedule if you can't find the schedule. Whether you are scheduling appointments for estimates or starting dates for jobs, you must be organized enough not to establish conflicting times. Once you have a good working schedule, you must be able to access it quickly and maintain it.

Many plumbing contractors use a scheduling board (FIG. 5-2) to keep track of their jobs. Many of these same contractors fail to precisely schedule estimates and meetings. If your business is doing well and you're busy, scheduling can be difficult. If you agree to meet a customer at a specific time and don't make the meeting, you may lose a sale. At the least, you have made a bad impression on the customer.

My schedule is full of appointments, deadlines, and events. I use a bulletin board, a wipe-off wall calendar, a desk-top day book, and a briefcase appointment book to maintain my schedule. This may sound like overkill, but it works for me. If I'm in the field, I refer to my briefcase appointment book to make on-the-spot decisions about my availability and requirements. If I'm at the phone in my office, I flip through the desk-top day book to schedule my work. When I walk into the office, I look up at the wall calendar and bulletin board for a quick assessment of my time needs. With this system, very little slips between the cracks.

Phone Log

Date/Time	Company Name	Contact Person	Remarks

5-1 Phone log

Service	Vendor	Phone	Date
Trench	K & B Diggers	555-5555	5-5-93
Welding	Blue-Tip Welder	555-5555	6-10-93
Trash	Rubbish, Inc.	555-5555	7-25-93

5-2 Production schedule

I'm not suggesting that you go to the extremes that I do. Find a system that works for you, and use it.

Office organization

Office organization is one of the most common organizational failures of my business clients. Usually I can tell when I walk into a client's office if the business runs smoothly. If I look at a desk and see papers neatly stacked and placed in descending order along the desk, I'm impressed. This shows me that the client has his work organized and prioritized. On the other hand, if I see a desk covered in scattered papers, folders, and coffee cups, I jump to the conclusion that the client needs help getting organized. My visual impressions are not always correct, but they usually are. Even if the cluttered desk is more productive than the neat desk, the visual impact of the well-organized workspace on customers is more favorable.

Filing cabinets and in-out baskets are tools you can use to stay on top of your office organization. It is embarrassing to have a customer sitting at your desk while you rummage through boxes, stacks of papers, or your briefcase, looking for the estimate you presented last week. If you show customers a lack of organizational skills in your office, how much confidence will they have in you to perform satisfactorily on their job? Would you want someone who couldn't find a recent estimate to plan the complete remodeling of your bathroom plumbing? My point is this: be organized and professional at all times. Every contact you or your representatives have with customers will affect your business.

In-field organization

Most contractors practically live out of their trucks. It's easy to stick a phone number over the sun visor and forget where you put it. It is also entirely possible that the paper under the visor will blow out of the truck and be lost forever. To cut down on in-field losses, you need a mobile filing system.

A mobile filing system might consist of a portable filing box, the type sold in most department stores and office supply stores. A briefcase can serve as your rolling file cabinet. Once you determine what type of container will best hold your field records, set it up in your truck and use it.

In addition to needing an in-truck filing system, stock the vehicle with various office supplies. Paper clips, rubber bands, business forms, file folders, and related office supplies should be close at hand. I have found that a two-briefcase system works well for me. I stock one large briefcase with all the office supplies and small office equipment I may need. Then I use a smaller, less intimidating briefcase for my in-home appointments.

I am always prepared with the two-briefcase system. If my small briefcase is running low on estimate forms, I can restock it with forms from the larger in-truck briefcase. Once I've met with my customers, I set up a file for them in my truck. When I return to the office, I make copies of the truck file and file them in the office. This way, if I'm caught on the road with the need to contact a recent customer, I have a copy of the customer's file with me. This dual filing system also reduces the odds of losing a file. I admit this takes up some space in the vehicle, but I'm always ready to do business.

DEVELOP GOOD HABITS

Customers enjoy doing business with people who are organized and professional. You can eliminate much of the competition by acting like a professional. Let's look at two examples of how your organizational skills can help you get and keep more customers.

In our first example, the plumbing contractor is going to be unorganized. He is going to talk with Mr. Williams about a remodeling job. Mr. Williams wants to install a bathroom in his basement and finish off part of the basement into a family room. Our unorganized contractor, Ray, knows this is a job that will offer good work and great profit. Ray knows in advance about the job and has plenty of time to prepare for it. Now, let's see how Ray handles the estimate.

On the day of the big estimate, Ray has been crawling around under an old house replacing drainage pipes. His estimate with Mr. Williams is scheduled for 6:00 P.M. Ray leaves the drainage job at 5:00 P.M. He goes to a fast-food place for supper and washes up in the men's room. Ray eats his meal and heads over to see Mr. Williams.

On his way to the Williams' residence, Ray realizes he left the address of the property in his office. Ray thinks he remembers the house number, so he continues on his way. By the time Ray figures out that he is lost, it is getting close to 6:00 P.M. Ray gives up and searches for a public phone to call his office. He finds a phone and calls the office. His wife answers the phone and, after digging around, finds Mr. Williams' address. Ray writes down the address and rushes to the estimate. He arrives about 30 minutes late.

Mr. Williams meets Ray at the front door. There is Ray, standing at the front door of a well-appointed home, dressed in torn jeans that are covered in dirt and unidentified stains. Ray's shirt is dirty and his boots look like they have been through a war.

After seeing Ray's clothing, Mr. Williams asks Ray to meet him behind the house at the basement entrance. Ray comes into the basement and looks over the job. As Mr. Williams talks, Ray nods his head and looks around. When Mr. Williams finishes describing the work he wants done, Ray tells him that he will get back to him in a few days.

Ray leaves and Mr. Williams shakes his head. After going upstairs, Mr. Williams tells his wife about his meeting with the plumber. The Williams decide not to even consider Ray's bid. After looking at what they presently know about Ray, they wouldn't consider having him work in their home. What did Ray do wrong? Let's look at some of his key mistakes.

Ray made many mistakes. He was late for the appointment. His tardiness could have been avoided with proper organization. Even after losing the address, Ray could have asked his wife to call the Williams and explain that he was running a little late. Instead, Ray just showed up late, didn't apologize, and started off on the wrong foot.

Ray's personal appearance was a big mistake. Even though the stains on his clothes were old and the soles of his boots were clean, he looked as if he would be a major threat to the floor coverings, walls, and furniture in the house. His lack of proper dress eliminated any chance to sit down and talk with Mr. and Mrs. Williams. Further, his appearance gave the impression of someone who has little respect for his customers or himself. This was not the image of a contractor that the Williams wanted.

Ray made another mistake while listening to Mr. Williams. He did not take notes. Remember, this estimate was for extensive work. How could Ray remember all the details? Ray's lack of response to Mr. Williams and his choice not to take notes made a bad impression. Ray didn't offer any suggestions or advice to Mr. Williams. By saying nothing, he appeared uninterested in the job and possibly incompetent.

Ray left saying he would get back to Mr. Williams in a few days. This left Mr. Williams not knowing when he would hear from Ray. If Mr. Williams had still been interested in dealing with Ray, he would have appreciated a specific date for the delivery of his estimate. Obviously, Ray blew this deal. Now, let's see how Craig handled the same estimate.

Craig is given the same circumstances as Ray, but he does business in a different manner. Prior to the day of the estimate, Craig rides by the home of Mr. Williams to locate the house and assess the neighborhood. Craig can see that the home is well-appointed and that Mr. Williams is a man who appreciates neatness.

On the day of the estimate, Craig leaves his drainage job at 4:00 P.M. He goes home and showers, shaves, and dresses in clean clothes. He wears jeans, a flannel shirt, and boots, but they are clean and neat. Craig collects his photo album of similar jobs he has done and gathers his notes and briefcase. He leaves early for the appointment and is in the neighborhood with time to spare.

When Craig pulls into the driveway, Mr. Williams comes to the door. Craig is right on time. The two men shake hands and Mr. Williams invites Craig into the living room. Craig speaks with Mrs. Williams and then they all go down into the basement.

As Mr. and Mrs. Williams describe the work they want done, Craig takes notes and makes comments and suggestions. He makes measurements with his tape measure and asks questions about particulars of the job. After going over the plans for the basement, Craig and the Williams go back up to the living room.

Sitting down, Craig shows the Williams the photo album of his previous jobs. As conversation ensues, Craig gets to know more about the Williams. By the end of their talk, Craig is no longer a number from the phone book; he is a person, with the possibility of becoming a friend.

As Craig leaves, he tells the Williams that he will mail them letters of reference from his office the next morning. He explains that due to the size of the job, he will need a day to work up the estimate. Then Craig asks to meet with the Williams on Saturday morning to go over the estimate with them, in case they might have questions about the job. The meeting is set and Craig leaves. On Saturday Craig meets with the Williams and goes over the cost of doing the job. In less than two hours Craig has a signed contract and a deposit check.

What did Craig do differently? It should be obvious: he was organized, neatly dressed, and professional in his business manners. By wearing jeans and boots, Craig gave the appearance of someone who was not afraid to get involved in the physical work of the job, yet he didn't look like he spent all of his time in the trenches. By talking to the Williams, Craig developed a rapport and gained the confidence of his customers. Talking allowed Craig to show his knowledge of the work required and his interest in the customer.

By taking measurements and making notes, Craig demonstrated his thoroughness in job planning and pricing. The photos Craig showed built a level of credibility. By offering to mail the Williams reference letters, Craig took the first step toward overcoming an objection to closing the deal. By setting an appointment to go over the estimate, Craig created a setting for signing the contract. All in all, Craig did everything right. Much of what he did had to do with good organizational skills.

LEARN STRONG ORGANIZATIONAL SKILLS

Some people seem to have a natural ability to get and stay organized. Others seem never to be able to remember where they left their truck keys. Fortunately, good organizational skills can be learned. As a business owner, you owe it to yourself to learn as much as you can about effective organizational skills.

There are many ways to learn good organizational skills. You can read books, go to seminars, listen to cassette tapes, and meet with business consultants. Any of these methods can prove effective. The way that you choose to learn is not as important as the fact that you choose to learn.

Begin your learning experience by making a list of all the areas on which you need to concentrate. There are many ways to do this, but keeping a diary may be the best.

Keep a diary for a week, and then review what your week was like. You answered the phone, returned phone calls, went out on estimates, dealt with customer complaints, and so on. From the contents of your diary you will be able to see the areas of business on which you should concentrate.

Once you have an outline of your daily duties, choose methods of study that will enhance your day-to-day organization. Maybe you need to take a seminar that teaches effective time management. You might benefit from reading a book on professional secretarial duties. Whatever your weakness, work to improve it. The time and money you invest in getting organized will be returned to you many times over as you build your business.

6

Fine-tuning your fledgling business

True success will come as you learn the art of fine-tuning your fledgling business. All businesses need to be monitored and altered as they grow. This process starts the day you open for business, and it doesn't stop until the business is closed permanently.

How well your business prospers will depend largely on how proficient you become at keeping up with market trends. Running a business is a time-consuming responsibility, but if you don't make time to improve your business as you go along, the business might not last five years. Let's take some time now to see how you can fine-tune your plumbing profits.

TIME IS MONEY

It is a cliché, but time is money. Whether you bill your time on an hourly basis or a contract basis, lost time translates into lost money. To get the most out of your business, you have to get the most out of your time. How many times have you said you don't have time for this or that? Do you find yourself rushing around to get everything done, only to be frustrated that you didn't accomplish your goals? Poor time management is usually a factor in these circumstances.

There is a difference between not having time to accomplish a task and not taking the time to complete the job. Let's look at a quick example. Consider yourself a busy business owner. Your morning starts early, and you work until the phone stops ringing at night. If you have ever done this, you know your day can include 12 to 14 hours of work. Obviously, time is a coveted commodity in this situation.

Your business is a success, and you have become a desk jockey. Since getting out of the field, you have started putting on weight. You want to work out, but when can you possibly find the time?

This scenario is not unusual. Business owners are often obsessed with the advancement of their business. This obsession can ruin marriages, damage relationships with children, and drive the business owner to extreme behavioral swings. If you are going to survive in the fast lane, you have to learn how to make pit stops or you are going to burn out. I'm not a great one to preach slowing down, since I always seem to be in high gear, but it is true that you need to allow some time for yourself.

Over the last 12 years I have changed my work habits considerably. I no longer go from 6:00 A.M. to 11:00 P.M. I spend time with my wife and daughter. I pursue some hobbies, and I'm going to start working out real soon, really I am. Okay, so some nights I write until 3:00 A.M., but I'm not missing time with my family; they are asleep. I wouldn't consider myself a workaholic, but I am very aggressive. If you want to win the business battle, you have to be aggressive. If you move too slowly in the rat race, the faster rats will run over you.

When you have something you want to do, or something you should do, you can probably make time to do it. In the case of making time to work out, you can work out before work, at lunch, or after work. When you consider that most authorities say you only need 20 minutes of exercise every other day, that's not much time. You probably spend that much time reading the paper, drinking coffee, or thinking about what you are going to do on your day off, if you ever take one. Time management is an individual act. Every individual will adjust to changes in their schedule differently. Let's see how you can budget your time better.

BUDGET YOUR TIME

Most people don't budget their time. They react rather than act. This is a major mistake for a business owner. If you compare it to a football game or boxing, it is easy to see. The team that gets off the ball first or the man who throws the first punch has the advantage. The other side has to react to this aggressive action. The opponent of the aggressive team or fighter doesn't have the luxury of planning the attack. They are too busy trying to thwart the offensive action. The same is true in business. Let me show you what I mean.

Consider this example. You are a remodeling plumber and you do much of your own work. Your strongest competitor is also a remodeling plumber, but she has an outside sales staff and uses subcontractors for her jobs. This leaves your competitor with more time to spend on business projections and evaluations. Both of you make about the same amount of money.

You try to be on the job by 7:30 A.M., and you rarely leave before 4:00 P.M. When you leave the field, you take care of estimates and paperwork. By 6:30 P.M. you're home and having supper with your family. Then from 8:00 P.M. to 10:00 P.M., you return phone calls and pay bills, among other things. By midnight you're in bed. This is a tough schedule to keep, but is not an uncommon one for owners of small plumbing companies.

While you are thrashing around and working yourself into exhaustion, your competitor seems to be gliding through life. She is in her office by 9:00

A.M., a full hour and a half after you are on the job. She handles her office work during the day, while you sweat it out in the field. She tends to customer service and supervision, while subcontractors do the heavy work. Her commissioned salespeople make the estimate calls and sales.

At 5:00 P.M., your competitor goes home. An answering service picks up her business calls and transfers them to the appropriate salesperson or worker. From 5:00 P.M. on, your competitor has a personal life. What are you doing wrong?

If you're happy, you're not doing anything wrong. If you resent your competitor, you need to work smarter, not harder. Both of you are operating profitable businesses, but you are working much harder. Your competitor has outmaneuvered you in the business arena. There are pros and cons to the life each of you live, but she seems to have the better life.

Doing business your way, you probably have less on-the-job problems because you are on the job. You are not paying out money to commissioned salespeople. You are in total control of your business, as much as anyone ever is. You are basically married to your business. You have chosen to create a working life, your competitor has created a business. Which would you prefer to have? Your competitor has her business running smoothly because she has made good management decisions. Part of this management is time management.

KNOW WHEN YOU WASTE TIME

To effectively manage time, you must know when you are wasting it. It is easy to get caught up in the heat of the battle and lose your objectivity. If this happens, you will not realize you are working harder and losing ground. To run a good business, you must be able to step back and look at the business operation from an objective point of view.

Taking an unbiased look at your operational procedures can be troublesome. Many of my clients engage me to troubleshoot their businesses for just this reason. They are too close to the fire to see the individual flames. However, you don't have to hire an outside consultant to evaluate your business. You can do it yourself.

To determine how much time you are wasting, you may have to waste a little time. I realize this may seem redundant, but it's true. One of the best ways to pinpoint your wasted time is to spend time making a time log. This log will expose how and where you are losing time.

Your log can be written or taped on a tape recorder, whichever makes you most comfortable. As soon as you wake up, start your log. Keep track of everything you do from the time you wake up until you retire for the evening. The log should include your business and personal activities.

I know it might be inconvenient, but discipline yourself to make entries in your log for every activity you undertake. Whether it is brushing your teeth, walking the dog, going to the mailbox, or making business calls, enter your actions in the log. If you don't take the log seriously, this experiment will not work.

Keep your log for at least two weeks. Review the log at the end of that time. Scrutinize your entries for possible wasted time. For instance, if you find you talk for more than 5 minutes on your business calls, take a close look at what you are talking about. There are times when business calls deserve 30 minutes or more, but most calls can be accomplished in 5 minutes or less.

Look for little aspects of your daily life that could be changed. Do you sit at the breakfast table and read the paper? How long do you spend reading the paper? Does this reading help you in your business? If your reading doesn't pertain to your business, maybe you should consider curtailing the time you spend at the table. If you derive pleasure from reading the paper, it's not a bad thing to do. If you are caught up in a habit of reading the paper for half an hour, and wouldn't feel deprived without this time, you have just found time for your workout.

You will probably find many red flags as you go down your time log. Almost everyone has little habits that rob them of time. Most of these routine activities will have little impact on your daily life, but they go on because they are habits. Before you can change your bad habits, you must identify them. A time log will help you expose your wasted time.

CONTROL LONG-WINDED CONVERSATIONS

Part of your time management routine should include controlling long-winded gab sessions with employees. If you spend too much time talking with employees, you lose money in two ways. You are not free to do your job, and when your employees are talking to you, they're not working.

SET YOUR APPOINTMENTS FOR EFFICIENCY

Arrange your meetings in a logical order. It is also beneficial to schedule meetings in your office, instead of a customer's home or office. By meeting in your office, you save time. However, if you are having a sales meeting, you might be better off to sacrifice some time and meet with the potential customers on their home turf. People are more comfortable in their own home or office. When you are in a sales posture, you want the customer to be as comfortable as possible. For now we are dealing with time management, so let's concentrate on why you want the meetings to convene in your office.

Set appointments in your office

Schedule appointments for your office whenever possible. If your client is late, you will be able to continue working. If the appointment is broken, you won't lose any time from work. You also will be more at ease, and the people you are meeting will feel at a disadvantage. This can be detrimental in a sales meeting, but typically it will work to your advantage. Under these circumstances, you have the control. How much you use or abuse it is up to you.

Did you know that most people will feel more intimidated when there is a desk between you and them? Are you aware of the signals you send when you put your hands behind your head and rear back in your chair? Body language says a lot. If you investigate sales techniques, you will discover how your body language influences your meetings.

For example, you will often be in a more advantageous position if you move out in front of your desk. People will be more receptive and less intimidated. Rearing back in your chair, with your hands behind your head, signals that you are in control of the conversation. Body language is a powerful sales tool, and good sales people know how to read the signals people send with their physical movements.

REDUCE LOST OFFICE TIME

It is common to think that if you are in the office, you're working. This isn't always true. A lot of people sit in the office, thinking they are working, without being productive. The people that have these feelings often lose more than time; they lose money.

Where do you lose time in the office? Do you sit in the office for hours at a time, waiting for the phone to ring? If you do, get a cellular phone or an answering service, and go out and look for business. If your phone isn't bringing you business, go out after it.

Do you take an hour to type a single proposal? If you do, it might be worth your while to find a typist that is an independent contractor. Hire the typist to transcribe your voice tapes into neatly typed pages. This eliminates work you are not good at and allows you to do what you do best.

Assess your office skills and rate them. If filing is not your strong suit, find someone to do your filing. If you have an aversion to talking on the telephone, hire someone with an excellent phone presence to tend to your calls. Use a checklist to rate your in-office performance. After referring to your checklist, concentrate on the skills with which you need help.

REDUCE LOST FIELD TIME

There are many ways to reduce the time you lose in the field. A mobile phone can make a huge difference in your in-field production. Working with a tape recorder will give you some advantages. Setting up a filing system in your work vehicle will help you stay organized and save time. Let's take a look at how the wonders of technology can work for you.

USE A TAPE RECORDER

Tape recorders can boost your productivity into a whole new category. Many contractors spend an enormous amount of time driving. Tape recorders can turn this previously wasted driving time into productive time. Letters can be dictated, notes can be made, marketing ideas can be recorded, and scores of other opportunities await the users of tape recorders.

SHOULD YOU HAVE A MOBILE PHONE?

Cellular phones can be a boon to your business. While it is true cellular phones are expensive on a cost-per-minute basis, they can be a bargain. If a $5 call results in a $5,000 job, you've made a wise decision.

With a mobile phone you can call ahead to make sure the next individual on your schedule is home and ready for service. If the homeowner has forgotten the appointment, you can move up the schedule to the next service call. This can save at least an hour's labor charge. When you add up this type of savings over a year's time, the amount can be substantial.

If you have a mobile phone and get stuck in traffic, you can call ahead and let your appointment know you're going to be late. Keep your customers and business associates aware of your schedule, and you will have less broken appointments and disappointed clients.

If you have on-the-road communication, you can always be reached for emergency or highly sensitive issues. When customers know they can reach you at any time, they are more comfortable doing business with you.

Can you afford to operate without a mobile phone? With the progress in modern technology and the competitive nature of service businesses, I think cellular phones are nearly a necessity.

7

Financial start-up requirements

Many new businesses fail within their first year because the owners did not accurately assess their start-up requirements. This type of failure is easy to avoid. While it is nearly impossible to predict how much money you will make in your first year of business, it is not difficult to chart how much money you and your business will spend during that year.

It is not unusual for someone who has always worked as an employee to be unsure of how to build a start-up budget. The fact that at this moment you don't know what is involved with the opening and operational needs of your new business is not a problem because this chapter is going to show you how to predict your start-up needs.

EVALUATE YOUR CASH RESERVES

Every business needs cash reserves to get over the humps in the road to prosperity. A large number of businesses fail each year, many due to limited cash reserves. Without back-up money, what will you do when a scheduled draw payment is held up and your bills are due?

How much money do you need in reserve? The answer to this question relates to the nature of your business and your ability to project and maintain budgets and schedules. Some people say you shouldn't start your own business until you have at least one year's salary in savings. I must admit this would be a comfortable way to get started, but for most people, saving up a year's salary isn't feasible.

When I opened my first plumbing business, many years ago, I borrowed $500 for tools and advertising. I had less than $200 in my savings account. Looking back, I was probably stupid to try such a venture, but I tried it and it worked. I'm not, however, suggesting that you follow in my footsteps. I am a risk-taker. For me, trying a new venture is an adventure. But I have learned never to gamble more money than I can afford to lose. I think this line of thinking is good.

To evaluate how much money is enough, I suggest you play the worst-case game. In this game you draw out scenarios of how your business venture might go. You look for what could be the worst possible outcome of your decision to start a business. Once you have gone "what-if" enough, you will start to develop some insight into what you stand to lose. The next step is to determine how much you are willing or can afford to lose.

Let's look at a quick example. You have $3,000 in your savings account. The tools you must add to your collection will cost $750. You already have a truck and the insurance company is willing to allow you to make monthly installment payments on your liability insurance. The economy is average, and you feel you can get work with minimal advertising. You set an ad budget of $400 per month. You will be doing residential work and will get paid upon completion of your jobs. After making a personal accounting of your budget, you see that you need an income of $2,000 a month to help your spouse meet the bills. Do you have enough money to try jumping into business?

In my opinion, you don't have nearly enough cash to go into a full-time business. At the best, you have enough money to last one month without income. Even if you are lucky enough to get work the first week, how will you pay for materials? What will you do if the customer doesn't pay you? Your odds of survival are very low under these circumstances.

If this is your situation, start your business by working nights and weekends. This type of moonlighting is easy to schedule when you are working small residential jobs. Homeowners like it because they can be home when the work is done. As you do more jobs and your savings and customer base grows, you can consider turning the business into a full-time job.

I don't think there is any clear-cut answer to how much reserve capital is enough. Each individual will have different needs. If I were forced to give an opinion, I would suggest having enough money to last at least four months without income. I would also suggest that when you feel you have established your monthly budget, that you add 20 percent to it. There will always be unforeseen expenses. Even with this reserve, you must monitor your success on a frequent basis. If the business is not going well or your budget spending is running high, look for alternative sources of income.

Let's look at some of the types of start-up money you will need.

START-UP CAPITAL

Start-up capital is the money you will use to get your business off the ground. You will use it for advertising, office supplies, equipment, and other business-related expenses. This start-up money will go faster than you think. How much money do you need? The amount of money required will vary. It will depend upon the type of business you are starting and how experienced you are in business matters.

If you are familiar with marketing procedures, your start-up cash will go further. If you have limited business sense, you will have to do a lot of experimentation. Trial-and-error techniques are excellent teachers, but plan on losing money with your on-the-job learning process.

The amount of money you need could be as little as $1,000. Then again, you might need $5,000 or $10,000. I would say that most small service businesses, if you already have your truck and tools, could be started with less than $2,000 of start-up capital.

RESERVE CAPITAL

Reserve capital is the money you will live off of until your business starts paying its bills and yours. This type of money is also used to cover unexpected expenditures like truck repairs, medical bills, and so on. The amount of reserve capital needed varies from individual to individual. There are some people that live comfortably on an income of $2,000 a month, and others that would feel deprived with less than $4,000 a month. You, like most people, probably fall somewhere in between these two numbers.

If you assume you need $3,000 a month to survive comfortably, your reserve capital should be based on that amount. How long will it take for your business to become profitable? This is a question no one can answer with certainty, but you should expect to live off of your savings for at least a few months.

When you plan the amount you need for reserve capital, make sure you decide if you are working with gross-income needs or net-income needs. Taxes take a big bite out of your gross earnings, so don't forget to allow for them.

BUILD A SPREADSHEET OF YOUR START-UP REQUIREMENTS

Start-up requirements are the items you must have to open and operate your business for the first year. Cash is usually the most important; if you have money, you can buy most of the other items such as tools, equipment, inventory, and advertising.

Arriving at an accurate figure for the amount of money you will need might require some research, but it is not a formidable task. It is, however, one of the first steps toward assuring your business success. To expand on this topic, let's sit down together and project the financial start-up requirements of a new plumbing business. The amounts used in this example are only for illustrating the way the process works, they are not meant to be actual cost projections.

Licenses

Do you have a master plumber's license? How much does it cost to maintain your license? The annual renewal cost of the plumber's license is $125, but a continuing education course is also required each year before the license can be renewed. The cost of the seminar is $35. The total annual cost is $160.

The cost of a general business license is $75 a year. When we total all of the costs associated with licenses, we arrive at a figure of $235.

Property taxes

These taxes might not amount to much in your first year, but it is an expense you are likely to have to pay. You might also to pay local taxes on the personal property owned by the company. Computers, inventory, office furniture, equipment, and similar items might be assessed and taxed. After talking to the tax assessor, you estimate your property taxes will be $195.

Legal fees

You have decided to open your business as a sole proprietor, so no legal fees are involved in structuring the business. A decision to use preprinted forms has eliminated the need for contracts and forms to be prepared by your attorney. Unless you run into unexpected problems, you don't anticipate incurring any legal fees this year. However, since questions about your business are likely to arise, I suggest you factor in $400 for this year's legal fees as a safety buffer.

Certified public accountant

You want to keep your up-front costs to a minimum, so you decide not to meet with a CPA until the end of the year. I advise you to meet with a tax professional now, to plan a tax strategy, but you refuse. Even at the end of the year, you are planning to use a simple tax service to file your tax returns, not a CPA. Your estimated cost for the tax filing at the end of the year is $75. This is the number you want put on your spreadsheet. It's your business, so I don't argue with you, but I reaffirm my opinion that you should meet with a CPA now, and then have the CPA file your taxes. You won't budge on this issue, so we put $75 down as your expected cost for tax services.

Design costs

When we talk about design costs, you tell me you are going to use a generic logo on your paperwork: one offered for free by the company selling you the forms. I explain the advantages of having a custom logo, (FIG. 7-1) but you decline. With your decision, there will be no design costs involved with the opening of your business.

Printing costs

Since you have decided to buy preprinted forms, you will not have any immediate printing costs. The preprinted forms, stationery, envelopes, invoices, and related paperwork you plan to order will cost $175. I raise the point of having flyers and direct-mail pieces printed during the year, and you agree this is a possibility. We build in a figure of $500 for your annual printing budget. The combined cost of your printing needs and preprinted forms is $675.

Pioneer Plumbing
Rt. 2, Box 8999 Buoy Road
Leadbend, Maine 55555
(207) 555-5555

Sold to: Bill to: Job #:
Mr. & Mrs. R. D. Woodson Same   896
72860 Loon Lane
Leadbend, ME 55555

Date: June 10, 1993
Invoice #: 896
Work ordered: June 2, 1993
Work completed: June 3, 1993
Warranty period: One year

Description of Work and Materials	Quantity	Price Per Unit	Unit Total
52 gallon electric water heater	1	$325.	$325.
T & P valve	1	$6.	$6.
3/4" copper tubing	12'	$1.50	$18.
3/4" male adapters	3	$0.85	$2.55
3/4" unions	2	$3.78	$7.56
3/4" copper elbows	4	$0.58	2.32
3/4" gate valve	1	$8.69	$8.69
Removal of old water heater	1	$25.	$25.
Travel expenses	45 min.	$0.75	$33.75
Permit fee	1	$30.	$30.
Labor on the job site	2.5 hrs.	$45.	$112.50
Total amount now due			$571.37

Payment in full is expected within 10 days.
All major credit cards are accepted.

Thank you for your business.

24-Hour Emergency Service Available

7-1 Customized Invoice

Signs

You have decided to buy magnetic signs for your truck. The cost for these signs is $120. When I ask you about buying job-site signs, you feel they are not needed. I disagree, but accept your answer.

Office rent, utilities, and phone service

You will be running your business from home, so you don't have any office rent or utilities to pay. Materials and tools will be stored in your garage. You have, however, decided to have a business phone installed. The installation charge and basic monthly service for your first year will be $580. The phone company has waived the need for a deposit. The phone you will use costs $45. Total phone expenses, excluding long-distance calls, is $625. After talking, we decide on an estimated annual cost of $360 for long-distance calls. The total estimated annual phone expense is $985.

While we were on the subject of phones, we debate answering machines and answering services. You decide to go with a human answering service. After evaluating all aspects of the answering service, we realize call-forwarding must be added to your basic phone service. The cost for this is estimated at $36 a year.

The answering service charges a flat rate of $65 a month. This covers up to 100 calls per month. Additional calls are billed at a rate of 50¢ per call. Since nearly all your phone activity will be routed through the service, we anticipate the total number of monthly calls to be 200. The monthly charge for 200 calls will be $105. This amounts to $1,260 a year.

The discussion on answering services leads us to the issue of pagers and mobile phones. We decide your business will be better if you have both of these items. A decision is made to lease a pager for $23 a month. The mobile phone we decide on will cost $300 installed. The basic monthly service will cost $60. We estimate another $30 a month for additional calls not covered under the basic service. Total associated costs are $3,937 annually.

Office furniture and equipment

When we come to the issue of office furniture and equipment, you say you don't need much of anything. I suggest we look closer at your needs. We decide you need a desk, a chair, and a filing cabinet. We decide these items don't have to be new, so we check out prices on used office furniture and equipment. We estimate the cost for all the items needed to be $375.

Trucks and tools

You already own an adequate truck and most of your tools. It will be necessary to buy a right-angle drill with bits, and a reciprocating saw. These items are expected to cost $425.

Inventory

What are your inventory needs? What type of plumbing are you going to be doing? You are hoping to do mostly residential remodeling work and some service work. We look over your probable needs and arrive at a figure of $2,000 for rolling stock.

Insurance

You will have to have liability insurance, which is going to cost $1,800 a year. Your truck insurance is already in place, but it is going to increase in cost now that the truck will be used for business. The additional truck insurance cost is estimated at $225 a year.

Your health insurance is paid by your spouse's employer, and you already have life insurance. Since you are going to be dependent on your income, you decide disability insurance would be a good idea. The estimated cost for this is $900 a year.

Bid-sheets

Since the work you want to do involves small residential jobs, you will not need bid-sheet subscriptions.

Employees

You are not planning to hire any employees in your first year of business.

Day-to-day living expenses

We estimate your gross needs at $2,500 a month, not counting business expenses. In talking through various scenarios, we decide you should have $10,000 set aside for this part of your start-up requirements.

Operating capital

Since you will set up credit accounts with your suppliers and stay on top of your accounts receivables, we estimate your needs for operating capital to be low. Aside from the hard business expenses in the budget, we allow $1,000 a month for operating capital. We don't expect this money to be out for more than two months at a time, so we set the needed amount at $2,000.

Other expenses

We set an annual budget of $1,500 as a conservative estimate.

Adding it all up

When we begin adding it all up, the numbers are larger than you anticipated. The total for all items is $24,862. You practically fall out of your chair
in shock. When you can breathe again, you tell me there is no way you can
come up with that kind of cash and ask for my advice.

I tell you that the numbers are reality, and that you can't hide from reality. If you want your own business, you must be willing and able to pay
your bills. However, I agree to go over the numbers with you and show you
some options. You roll your head around a few times to relieve the sudden
stress you feel and settle back to see if your dream is still possible.

We start going down the spreadsheet, item by item, looking for alternatives. You want to find out how much cash you must have to open the
doors to your business.

Licenses is the first category on our list of cost projections. There is no
way around this expense, but your plumber's license doesn't have to be renewed until the end of the year. You must buy a business license for $75,
but you don't have to pay renewal fees and continuing education costs in
the beginning. This leaves you with a hard start-up cost of $75.

Your property taxes won't be due right away, so we can drop those for
now. The same is true of your legal expenses and professional fees for tax
advice.

You can't operate without some business forms, but you can eliminate
your projected printing costs for the time being. This gets your estimate for
start-up purposes down to $175 for your preprinted needs.

While signs are advantageous, they are not required in most states, so
you can eliminate that expense.

If you are serious about staying in business, you should have a business
phone installed. This is not only the right thing to do ethically, it also gets
you listed in the phone directory. We will leave the estimated phone expenses alone. However, we don't have to look at the costs on an annual basis for start-up purposes. We can factor in the cost for the first 90 days of
your business. This brings the number down to $364, including call-for-
warding services.

If we also look at the expense of your answering service on a three-
month basis, the cost will be $315. You can get by without the mobile
phone in the beginning, but you will need the pager. The cost of the pager
for three months will be $69.

When we come back to the issue of office furniture and equipment, we
decide you can work from your kitchen table and eliminate the need for a
desk and chair. The used filing cabinet and miscellaneous small items you
need will cost $50.

There is nothing we can do to reduce the cost of your needed tools,
that expense remains at $425. We can, however, get you by with less in-
ventory, so we set a new inventory figure of $700.

You can buy your insurance with monthly installments, so we will look
at premiums for three months. The cost this way is $243.75. You also could

eliminate the disability insurance, but we will leave it in our projections for now.

Your need for money to live on will not change, but you should make some money with your business. If we look at your survival needs for 90 days, the cost is reduced to $7,500. Factoring in some profits, we decide on $5,000.

The need for operating capital could be set at $1,000. This will mean less money for advertising and up-front job expenses, but if your ads work and you promptly collect your money, you can get by on this amount. As for other expenses, we set a three-month figure of $375.

Now, let's see what we are dealing with in hard start-up costs. Our total costs drop from $24,862 to $8,791.75. This is certainly a more manageable figure. While you can take this approach and minimize your start-up costs, you should know what to expect as a total for your first year of operation. You can, of course, make other adjustments and take more risks to reduce the amount of hard money you will need. For example, if you feel you will be earning your keep after your first month in business, you could drop another $2,500 from this projection.

8

Build a viable business plan

A business plan is simply a blueprint of your business. It diagrams where you are, where you want to go, and how you are going to get there. A business plan should include as much about your business as possible. The more you put into a business plan, the better you will be able to track your success.

How can you learn to devise a business plan? You could go to specialized classes and have an instructor teach you, but this would take significant time and money. You could attend seminars, but this can get expensive. Reading is another way to gain the knowledge you need to build a business plan. Books might not be cheap, but they are generally a good value. Hiring a professional consultant is a quick way to have your questions answered. Consultants, accountants, and attorneys might seem expensive, but if they are good, they are well worth the expense. A combination of reading, seminars, and consultations is probably the best, and quickest, way to hit the fast track.

Going it alone is the way most people get into business. Most of them do some reading, but little else. This trial-and-error method might work, but it can be costly. While you save the cost of professional consultations, you pay a price for your experience.

In my early years I never had a viable business plan. My plan was to work as hard as necessary, make as much money as possible, and do what I wanted to do, within reason. As time and money passed, I learned the value of a solid business plan. I can tell you, from my expensive experience, a good business plan is instrumental to your success. A business plan does not have to be complicated, only complete.

A winning plan starts at the beginning. It addresses the design of your logo, your stationery, your company slogan, and much more. The plan details your marketing strategies, your services, your customer-service policies, and your production goals. From there, the plan covers company growth, employee policies, investments, and retirement arrangements.

The first three years are the hardest for which to plan. It is during these early years that you establish business credit, learn the problems and pitfalls of owning your own business, and develop your customer base. If you can get past the first three years you have a good chance of making it over the remaining rough spots.

ESTABLISH CREDIT AND TRADE ACCOUNTS

As you build your new business, you will probably want to establish credit and trade accounts. Very few plumbing businesses run efficiently without credit. Even if you have plenty of cash, credit can make your business run smoother and faster. If you have credit accounts with your suppliers, you can place orders and have them delivered without being present to hand the delivery driver a check. This might not seem like a big deal, but it can be.

Charging material on 30-day accounts will give you time to complete jobs and be paid for them before you must pay for the material. This allows you to maximize the use of your available funds. There is only one drawback to operating this way. If you charge materials to a trade account and customers don't pay their bills promptly, you can get into financial trouble fast! As long as you keep tight reins on customers and don't allow your accounts receivables to become delinquent, trade accounts and lines of credit can get your business booming quickly.

Setting up credit accounts for a new business can be tough for anyone. For people with poor credit histories, the job can seem almost impossible. Vendors don't want to establish credit with you or your company unless you have a good track record. How can you develop a good track record if people won't give you a chance? The dilemma is something of a revolving door. No matter where you enter it, you seem to go around in circles. There are ways to overcome the obstacles of being a new business. There are also ways to beat the odds against you if you have no credit history or a bad credit report. This chapter is going to show you those methods.

GOOD CREDIT IS CRUCIAL

Without good credit, expansion—even survival—can be very difficult. As your business grows, so will your desire for various types of credit. Let's look at some of the types of credit you may need.

Start-up money

The first credit need you have might be to obtain start-up money. It is best to rely on money you have saved for start-up capital. Borrowing money to start your business will put you in a hole right from the start. The burden of repaying a loan used for start-up money will only make establishing your business more difficult. However, many successful businesses are started with borrowed money.

A loan for start-up capital can be one of the most difficult to obtain.

Lenders know that many new businesses don't survive their first year of operation. If you don't have home equity or some other type of acceptable collateral, banks will be reluctant to help you get your business started.

If you wait until you have quit your job to apply for a start-up loan, your chances of having the loan approved drop considerably. Most savvy entrepreneurs arrange personal loans while they have regular jobs and use the funds to start their businesses. This procedure results in more loan approvals.

Some contractors start their businesses on a part-time basis. They are able to obtain the loans they need while they are still employed by someone else, and can build up cash reserves. The work they do on the side produces money with which to repay their loans. They also can accumulate a healthy stockpile of ready cash. The stress and hours of working full-time and running a part-time business can be tiresome, but the results are often worth the struggle.

Operating capital

Once your business is open you will need operating capital to keep the business running. If you don't already have money set aside for this purpose, you might want to apply for an operating-capital loan.

Lenders are a little more willing to make these loans if you have an established track record. However, don't get your hopes up until you can provide two years' tax returns for income verification. Since you will probably need operating capital to survive your first two years, make arrangements for your financing before you jump into business.

Operating-capital loans can come from several types of financing. Some business owners borrow against their home equity to generate operating capital. Lines of credit are often arranged to pull money from as needed. With this type of financing you only pay interest on the money you use. Short-term personal loans are another way of financing your operating capital. These loans are frequently set up with interest-only payments until the note matures, at which time the total amount owed becomes due.

Advertising accounts

Advertising credit accounts are convenient. These accounts allow you to charge your advertising and pay for it at the end of the month. This eliminates the need for cutting a check for every ad you place.

Advertising often pays for itself, but sometimes it doesn't. You cannot afford to charge thousands of dollars worth of advertising that doesn't bring in paying customers. If you do, your business will be crippled before it starts. You will be faced with large payments for advertising that was a dud. Use this credit account prudently.

Supplier accounts

Establish credit with material suppliers and you will not have to take your checkbook with you every time you need to pick up supplies. Since you will probably have to supply and install materials before your customers pay for them, supplier accounts buy you some float time, generally up to 30 days. This gives you time to install the materials and collect from your customers before you pay for the materials. Again, be cautious. If your customers don't pay their bills, you won't be able to pay yours.

Office supplies

Many times you can get better prices on your office supplies by purchasing them from mail-order distributors. Having a credit account with these distributors will make your life easier. You won't have to place COD orders or put business expenses on your personal credit cards. This type of account makes your accounting easier and your business less troublesome to manage.

Fuel

Paying cash for fuel to run your trucks and equipment can be a real pain when you have employees. Keeping up with the cash and the cash receipts is time consuming. Establish a credit account with your fuel provider and your employees will be able to charge fuel for your company vehicles and equipment. At the end of the month, your account statement will be easy to transfer to your bookkeeping system.

Vehicles and equipment

As your business grows, you might need more vehicles and equipment. Most business owners can't afford to pay cash for these large expenses. Financing or leasing vehicles and equipment will require a decent credit rating.

There are a multitude of occasions when you will want to use credit. Sometimes credit will make a difference between the survival and failure of your business. Develop a good credit rating and work hard to maintain it.

LENDING INSTITUTIONS

Not all lenders are alike. Some lenders prefer to make home mortgage loans. Others make car loans or secured loans. Some lenders will make a loan for any good purpose, if they feel the loan is safe. Finding a bank that is willing to make an unsecured signature loan can be perplexing.

Before you set out to find a lender, decide what type of loan you need. If you are not a well-established and financially sound business, be prepared to sign the loan personally. Most lenders will not make a business loan to new businesses without a personal endorsement.

Will you be looking for a secured or unsecured loan? A secured loan is a loan where something of value—collateral—is pledged to the lender for security against nonpayment of the loan. An unsecured loan is a loan that is secured by a signature, but not by a specific piece of collateral. Lenders prefer secured loans.

If you plan to request a secured loan, decide what you have for collateral. The amount of money you wish to borrow will have a bearing on the type and amount of collateral that will be acceptable to the lender. For example, if you want to borrow $50,000 for operating capital, putting up the title to a $10,000 truck will probably not be sufficient.

Real estate is the type of collateral most desired by lenders. If you have equity in your home, and are willing to risk it, you should find getting a loan to be relatively easy. However, home-equity loans can be confusing. Many people don't understand how much they can borrow against their equity. Let me show you two examples of how you might rate the loan value of the equity in your home.

Let's say your home is worth $100,000 and you owe $80,000 on the mortgage. Equity is the difference between the home's appraised value and the amount still owed on it. In this case, the equity amount is $20,000. Does this mean you can go to a bank and borrow $20,000 against the equity in your home? No. Most lenders would consider such a loan a high risk. Some finance companies might lend $10,000 on this deal, but they would be few and far between. In most cases you would not be able to borrow any money against your equity.

Lenders want borrowers to have a strong interest in repaying loans. If a lender loaned you $20,000 on your equity, your house would be 100 percent financed. If you defaulted on the loan you wouldn't lose any money, only your credit rating. To avoid this type of problem, lenders require that you maintain an equity level in your house that is above and beyond the combination of your first mortgage and the home-equity loan. Most banks will want you to have between 20 and 30 percent of the home's value remaining in equity, even after you get a home-equity loan.

Let's say you have the same $100,000 house, but you only owe $50,000 on it. A conservative lender would allow you to borrow $20,000 in a home-equity loan. This brings your combined loan balance up to $70,000, but you still have $30,000 of equity in the home. If you default on this loan, you lose not only your credit rating, but $30,000. A liberal lender might allow you to borrow $30,000, keeping an equity position of $20,000.

If you don't have real estate for collateral, you can use personal property. Personal property might include vehicles, equipment, accounts receivable, or certificates of deposit (CD). Different lenders have different policies, so shop around until you find a lender with whom you like doing business.

Banks are an obvious choice for a loan. Commercial banks often make all types of loans. But banks are not your only option. If you belong to a credit union, check their loan policies and rates. Finance companies are usually aggressive lenders, but their interest rates will probably be high. Private investors are always looking for viable projects to invest in or loan money to. Mortgage brokers are yet another possibility for your loan. A quick look through the phone directory and the advertisements in the local newspaper will reveal many potential loan sources.

ESTABLISHING CREDIT WHEN YOU HAVE NONE

It is better to start with no credit than to start with bad credit. If you have never used credit cards or accounts, you will find it difficult to get even the smallest loans from some lenders. I will give you advice on how to get credit without having a regular job. However, if you have the opportunity to establish your business accounts before you quit your job, do it.

Supplier accounts

Supplier accounts are one of the best places to begin establishing your new credit. When you go into business, suppliers will want to supply you with needed materials. They will be cautious about granting you a credit account, but they will be more liberal than the average bank.

Request a credit application by mail or go to the stores and pick them up from the credit department. Once you have the credit applications, you will need some detailed information to complete them. Most applications will want personal references, credit references, your name, address, phone number, social security number, bank balances and account numbers, business name, and much more.

The application will ask for the amount of credit you want. Don't write in that you are applying for as much as possible. Pick a realistic figure that is a little higher than what you really want. Setting the higher figure will give you some negotiating room.

Most supplier credit applications are similar. Once you fill out the first application, make copies of it for future reference. Not only will the photocopy serve to refresh your memory if the supplier has questions about your application, the copy will act as a template for filling out other credit applications.

Return the applications to the credit departments. You might want to hand deliver the applications. This will give you a chance to make personal impressions on the credit officers. Making good impressions on the credit managers might help get you over the hump.

If you get a notice rejecting your credit request, don't give up. Call the credit manager and arrange a personal interview. Meet with the credit manager and negotiate for an open account. When all else fails, ask for a smaller credit line. Almost any supplier will give you credit for $500. This may not sound like much, but it's a start, and a start is what you need.

Suppliers offer the easiest access to credit accounts. After these accounts are used for a few months, your credit rating will begin to grow. Keep active and current accounts with suppliers and you will build a good background for bank financing.

Other vendor accounts

When you open your business you will need office supplies, the services of a printer, and newspaper advertising. All of these miscellaneous vendors offer you an opportunity to create credit. It can be easy to set up accounts with small businesses. If you are a local resident of the community, small businesses might not even ask you to fill out credit applications. These opportunities are too good to overlook.

Major lenders

Unless you have a strong credit rating, tangible assets, and a solid business plan, many banks will not be interested in loaning you substantial sums of money. But don't despair, there are ways to work with banks.

Banks, like suppliers, should be willing to make a small loan to you. I know $500 will not buy much in today's business environment, but it is a worthwhile start.

Bankers like to have collateral for loans. What better collateral could you give a banker than cash? I know you are thinking that if you had cash for collateral, you wouldn't need a loan, but that is not always true. When you are establishing credit, any good credit is an advantage. Let me tell you how to get a guaranteed loan.

Set up an appointment to talk with an officer at your bank. Tell the banker you want to make a cash deposit in the form of a CD, but that after you have the CD on deposit, you want to borrow against it. Many lenders will allow you to borrow up to 90 percent of the value of your CD. For example, if you put $1,000 in a CD, you should be able to borrow about $900 against it. You are essentially borrowing your own money and paying the bank interest for the privilege. This concept might sound ludicrous, but it will work to build your credit rating.

Banks report the activity on their loans to credit bureaus. Even though you are borrowing your own money, the credit reporting agency will show the loan as an active, secured loan. As long as you make the payments on time you will get a good credit rating. This technique is often used by people repairing damaged credit, but it will work for anyone.

Building a good credit rating can take time. The sooner you start the process, the quicker you will enjoy the benefits of a solid credit history. The road to building a good credit rating can be rocky and tiresome, but it's worthwhile.

OVERCOMING A POOR CREDIT RATING

If you are starting with a bad credit rating, this section will give you options on how to overcome the hurdles that might lie in front of you. There is no question that setting up credit accounts will be harder if you have a poor credit history, but you can do it. If you are battling a bad credit report, plan on spending some time cleaning up the existing report and building new credit. This journey will not be easy, pleasurable, or quick, but the results should make you happy.

Secured credit cards

Secured credit cards are one way for people with damaged credit to begin the rebuilding process. Secured credit cards are similar to the procedure described for CD loans. A person deposits a set sum of money with a bank or credit card company. Then a credit card is issued to the depositor. The card holder can use the credit card with a credit limit equal to the amount of the cash deposit or slightly more. These people are basically borrowing their own money, but they are rebuilding their credit.

CD loans

We have already talked about CD loans, so I won't go into extensive detail on them again. If you need to rebuild your credit, CD loans are a good way to do it. By depositing and borrowing your own money, you build a good credit rating, without risk.

Erroneous reports

Erroneous reports on your credit history are not impossible. If you are turned down for credit, you are entitled to a copy of the credit report information used to make the decision to deny your credit request. If you are denied credit, immediately request a copy of your credit report. Credit reporting bureaus are not perfect; they make mistakes. Let me tell you a quick story about how my credit report was maligned when I applied for my first house loan.

When I applied for a my first house loan, my request for the loan was denied. The reason I was given for the denial was a delinquent credit history. I knew my credit was impeccable, and I challenged the decision. The loan officer talked with me and soon realized something was wrong. My wife's name is Kimberley, and at the time of this credit request I didn't have any children. The credit report showed my wife having a different name and it showed me having several children. Obviously, the report was inaccurate.

Upon further investigation, it was discovered that the credit bureau had issued the wrong credit report to my bank. My first and last name was the same as the person who owned the poor credit history, but my middle initial was different, my wife's name was different, and I didn't have any children. It happened that I lived on the same road as this other fellow. It was certainly a strange coincidence, but if I had not questioned the credit report, I would not have been able to build my first home.

I know from first-hand experience that credit reports can be wrong. I have seen various situations in the past when my clients and customers fell victim to incorrect credit reports. If you are turned down for credit, get a copy of your credit report and investigate any discrepancies you discover.

Explanation letters

If your poor credit rating is due to extenuating circumstances, letters of explanation might help solve your credit problems. A letter that details the circumstances might be all it takes to sway a lender in your direction. Let me give you a true example of how a letter of explanation made a difference to one of my customers.

I had a young couple that wanted me to build a house for them. During the loan application process it came out that the gentleman had allowed his vehicle to be repossessed. On the surface, this appeared to be a deal-stopping problem. I talked with the young man and learned the details behind the repossession. At my suggestion, he wrote a letter to the loan processor. In less than a week, the matter was resolved and the couple was approved for their new home loan. How did this simple letter change their lives?

This man had a new truck with high monthly payments. When he decided to get married, he knew he couldn't afford the payments. My customer went to his banker and explained his situation. The loan officer told the man to return the truck to the bank and the payments would be forgiven. However, the banker never told the man that this act would show up as a repossession on his credit report. My customer returned the truck with the best of intentions and acting on the advice of a bank employee.

When the problem cropped up and the bank employee was contacted, he confirmed my customer's story. The mortgage lender for the house evaluated the circumstances and decided the man was not an irresponsible person. It was decided that he had acted on the advice of a banking professional. Under the circumstances, my customer's loan was approved.

If you have strong reasons for your credit problems, let your loan officer know about them. Once-in-a-lifetime medical problems could force you into bankruptcy, but they might be forgiven in your loan request. If you provide a detailed accounting that describes your reasons for poor credit, you might find that your loan request will be approved.

If you are unable to pay your bills, talk with your creditors. Credit managers are not ogres, they have a job to do. If you are honest and open with your suppliers, most of them will work with you. If you try to ignore the problem, it will only get worse. A healthy business needs a good credit history. If you have good credit, cherish it; if you don't, work to get a good rating.

SEVEN TECHNIQUES TO ASSURE CREDIT SUCCESS

I am about to give you seven techniques to assure your credit success. This is not to say that these seven methods are the only way to establish credit, but they are proven winners. Let's take a closer look at how you can make your credit desires a reality.

Get a copy of your credit report

In most cases, with a written request, you can get a copy of your credit report. This is a wise step to take before you establish new credit. Review your credit report and straighten out any incorrect entries before you apply for credit.

Prepare a credit package

Prepare a credit package before you apply for credit and you will increase your chances of having your credit request approved. What should go into your credit package? If you own an existing business, your package should include financial statements, tax returns, your business plan, a list of current accounts receivable, and all the normal credit information that is typically requested (FIG. 8-1 through FIG. 8-3). If you are a new company, provide a strong business plan and the normal credit information.

Pick the right lender

Do some homework and find lenders that make the type of loans you want. Once you have your target lenders, take aim and close the deal.

Don't be afraid to start small

Any open account you can get will help you. Even a credit line of $250 is better than no credit line at all.

Use it or lose it

Open accounts that are not used will be closed. In addition, an open account that doesn't report activity will not help you build your credit rating.

Checklist of Loan Application Needs

- ☑ Home address for the last five years
- ☑ Divorce agreements
- ☑ Child support agreements
- ☑ Social security numbers
- ☑ Two years, tax returns, if self-employed
- ☑ Paycheck stubs, if available
- ☑ Employee's tax statements (i.e., W-2, W-4)
- ☑ Gross income amount of household
- ☑ All bank account numbers, balances, names, and addresses
- ☑ All credit card numbers, balances, and monthly payments
- ☑ Employment history for last four years
- ☑ Information on all stocks and bonds owned
- ☑ Life insurance face-amount and cash value
- ☑ Details of all real estate owned
- ☑ Rental income and expenses of investment property owned
- ☑ List of credit references with account numbers
- ☑ Financial statement of net worth
- ☑ Checkbook for loan application fees

8-1 Checklist of loan application needs

```
                        Your Company Name
                       Your Company Address
                     Your Company Phone Number


         Date of statement: _____

         Statement prepared by: _____


         ASSETS

         Cash on hand                    $ 8,543.89

         Securities                      $    0.00

         Equipment
         1992 Ford F-250 pick-up truck   $14,523.00
         Pipe rack for truck             $   250.00
         Power tools                     $   375.00
         Hand tools                      $   800.00

         Real estate                     $    0.00

         Accounts receivable             $ 5,349.36


         Total assets                                    $29,841.25

         LIABILITIES

         Equipment
         1993 Ford F-250 truck, note payoff  $11,687.92

         Accounts payable                $ 1,249.56


         Total liabilities                               $12,937.48



         NET WORTH                                       $16,903.77
```

8-2 Financial statement

Pay your bills on time

Having no credit is better than having bad credit. If you have accounts that
fall into the past-due category, your credit history will suffer, and you will
be plagued by phone calls from people trying to collect your overdue
account.

Never stop

Never stop building your credit rating. The more successful you become,
the easier it will be to increase your credit lines. Don't fall into the trap of
getting in over your head. If you abuse your credit privileges it will not be
long before you are in deep financial trouble.

Accounts Receivable

Date	Account Description	Amount Due	Date Due	Date Received
	Total Due			

8-3 Accounts receivable log

9

Collect money owed you

Few people enjoy collecting past-due accounts, and even fewer people are skilled in doing so. Unfortunately, there will be times when people won't pay their bills, and there will be checks that bounce and take you by surprise. This is a natural part of any plumbing business. There is no effective way to eliminate all of the risks.

There are some methods that you can employ to prevent bounced checks and delinquent accounts. Further, there are some ways to collect old money that are more effective than others. This chapter is going to help you avoid bad accounts receivables and show you how to collect money that is overdue.

DEAL WITH THE PAYING PARTY

It might seem like you will always be dealing with a paying party, but that is far from the truth. It doesn't matter whether you are dealing in emergency repairs or new construction, there are times when people that are not the paying party will make requests for work. If you perform the requested work, getting paid can be all but impossible. To expand on this, let's look at two examples.

Our first example involves an emergency service call. Your phone rings and the person on the other end tells you their bathroom is being flooded by an overflowing toilet. It is well into the evening and you will be charging overtime rates. You advise the caller of your hourly rate, and the caller agrees to the rate and asks how soon you can be there.

You drive across town and arrive at the house with the stopped-up toilet. After being greeted by the person that called you, you go into the bathroom and after a few minutes with a closet auger, the toilet's trap is cleared.

At overtime rates, the customer owes you $60. When you present your service ticket for the customer's signature, you are told that the person you are talking to is only a tenant, and that you should send the bill to the landlord. The tenant refuses to sign the work order and gives you the landlord's phone number. Feeling angry, you leave for home to call the landlord.

When you reach the landlord you are told you will not be paid. The landlord insists that you should have sought her authorization before doing work on the property. It turns out the landlord has a handyman on payroll that would have fixed the problem for much less, if the tenant had called the landlord first. You've gotten yourself into a mess.

First of all, you have no proof that you did any work on the home. There is no evidence to support the filing of a mechanic's lien, and a court battle would not be worth the trouble or expense for such a small amount of money. The landlord refuses to pay, the tenant refuses to pay, and you don't have much of a case for collecting your money. Losing $60 will not put you out of business, but you have lost a lot of time trying to earn and collect money that you will never see. This is a prime example of how not to run your business.

Our second example involves the plumbing of a new house. You have been hired by the general contractor to install all the plumbing in the home. A contract has been signed and you have been given blueprints and specifications to follow in the plumbing installation.

You are busy installing the rough-in plumbing when the homeowner comes by to inspect the job. The homeowner walks up to you and tells you he has decided to rough in a future-use bathroom in the basement. He goes on to say that his wife wants the kitchen sink moved to a location for an island sink. You feel frustrated because you were nearly done with the rough-in phase, and now you have a lot of extra work to do.

The next day you have your permit amended to include the extra bathroom in the basement and get on the job. You make the changes with the kitchen sink and install the groundwork for the basement bath. It's been a long day, but you are done. As you pick up your tools, the general contractor arrives. He greets you and asks how the job is going. You explain it was going fine until the homeowner came up with all the changes.

The general contractor's face contorts as he listens to your story. Then you get the bad news. The homeowner is working on a tight budget, and you will probably not get paid for the changes you made. When you throw a fit, the contractor reminds you that you were contracted to do the job with him and to his plans and specs. The contractor doesn't mind that you installed the bathroom in the basement, but he isn't going to pay for it. Further, he demands that you return the kitchen plumbing back to its original condition. The contractor has no plans to install an island sink, and by contract, you were supposed to have plumbed the sink on the outside wall. Now you're really getting mad.

You threaten to lien the house, but the contractor tells you that wouldn't be wise. He explains that you signed a contract, blueprints, and specifications that state clearly what work is supposed to be done and how and where it is supposed to be done. He goes on to remind you of the language in the contract that requires all changes to the agreement to be made in writing and signed by all parties. Your knees begin to feel a little weak.

Not only have you supplied labor and material to install a rough-in basement bath, but you have moved the kitchen sink plumbing and now are going to have to move it again. There is a good probability that you will not be paid for your labor or your materials. This mistake will probably cost you over $500 in time and material. See how easy it is to put yourself in a trap?

QUALIFY YOUR CUSTOMERS

While it is true that the customer is hiring you, you have the right to know a little about the customer. One of the first questions you might ask is what is the customer's ability to pay for the work requested. This might seem like a silly curiosity, but it is not. It is common to have customers who do not pay their bills. The reasons for nonpayment are extensive, but the end result is you do not get paid. No business owner can afford to work for free. Let's look at some of the reasons you may not get paid by your customers.

Loan denial

Loan denial can cause a well-meaning customer to be unable to pay your fees. Repair companies are not the only ones at risk. If you specialize in large jobs, your customers will usually be dependent on borrowed funds to pay you. If their loan isn't approved, there will not be enough money to settle your bill.

To avoid getting stuck on a big job, ask the customer to show evidence of the money required to do the job. This could amount to seeing a loan agreement or a bank statement for the customer's account. You might feel awkward asking to see proof of available funds, but you will feel worse if you don't get paid.

Deadbeats

Avoiding deadbeats can be difficult. They are not always easy to identify. To protect yourself from this undesirable group of customers, get permission and run a credit check on the customer. This is good business for all of your customers. You never know when the sweetest, most trusting person is going to turn out to be a bad debt.

Your fault

Sometimes nonpayment will be your fault. If you have not made the customer happy, you could have trouble collecting your cash. When you qualify your customers, try to read them for trouble signs. If you feel friction in the meeting, perhaps you should pass on the job and look for another customer.

Death

Death is always a good excuse for not paying your bills. Of course, death is no laughing matter, but neither is not getting paid. While you can't avoid a customer's demise with qualifying, you can make arrangements in your contract to cover the death contingency. Ask your attorney for help in drafting a clause that will hold the heirs and estate responsible for your fees if the client passes away.

Bankruptcy

If a customer owes you money and files for bankruptcy protection, your chances of being paid are all but nonexistent. During the qualifying stage, screen the customer's credit rating and financial strength. If the customer is financially healthy when you start the job, there is limited risk of losing your money in the bankruptcy courts.

Insurance

Some customers believe the work they are requesting will be covered by their insurance policy. If your customer tells you that you will be paid by an insurance company, you had better talk to the insurance company before you do any work.

ASK HOW YOU WILL BE PAID

When someone requests you to do work, ask how you will be paid. In the case of our first example, if you had asked the tenant/caller how you would be paid—cash, check, credit card, or established credit account—you might have avoided the lost time, lost money, and frustrations associated with the bad deal.

In reviewing the second example, if you had asked the homeowner who would be paying for the changes and how you would be paid, you might have stopped the problem before it occurred. It never hurts to ask how you will be paid and by whom.

CHECKS

Some contractors don't like taking checks for payment, but most people prefer to pay by check. When you accept a check as payment, you are at risk. The check might not be good for its face amount. There are ways to reduce the risks associated with checks.

As a business owner, there are several things you can do to reduce the number of bad checks you receive. When you accept a check in person, ask to see the customer's driver's license and a major credit card. Write the individual's social security number on the check and confirm that the information on the check matches the information on the driver's license. Retail stores do this all the time. There is no reason why plumbing contractors shouldn't.

A safer alternative is to join a check-protection agency. There are companies that allow you to make a phone call to determine the value of a person's check. You will have to pay to participate in such an agency, but the dues might be much less than the losses incurred from bad checks.

DEPOSITS

If you are doing work that involves a lot of time or material, attempt to get a deposit before you start the job. This is becoming more and more difficult to do, but it is worth a try. Homeowners are afraid, with good reason, to give contractors advance deposits.

When you collect a deposit on a job, at least part of your risk is removed. If you structure your deal to involve advance deposits and progress payments, you can eliminate almost all of your risk.

BEWARE OF EMERGENCY CALLS

Aside from general contractors that don't pay their bills, emergency calls rank near the top of the list for bad debts. People don't plan emergencies, so they often don't budget money to pay for emergency repairs. When you respond to emergency calls you are less likely to take all the proper precautions with signed work orders and contract agreements. This opens you up for a loss.

Treat emergency calls like any other type of call. Insist on knowing who is going to pay you, when you will be paid, and how you will be paid. If you lower your guard, you are likely to lose money.

PROTECT YOURSELF WITH PAPERWORK

Signed documents give you the most leverage in legal litigation. While oral agreements are legal, they are largely unenforceable. Always have customers sign work orders, contracts, and completion certificates. Get a signature authorizing your work on a document that details how and when you will be paid (FIG. 9-1).

Don't deviate from your written agreements. Remember how straying from contract terms cost the plumber money in the new-construction example. The same could happen to you. All of your work and terms should be detailed in writing and signed by all paying parties.

DON'T LET ACCOUNTS RECEIVABLES AGE

The older money is, the harder it is to collect. If you have credit accounts that are not paid promptly, take immediate action. Don't wait several months before you try to collect your accounts. If you wait too long, you will lose your lien rights.

I consulted with a plumbing company that had accounts that had been delinquent for three years, and the owner of the company still had hopes of collecting them. Do you really think someone that didn't pay a $60 bill three years ago is going to pay it today? I was able to help the company collect many of its past-due accounts, even some of the very, very old ones, but there is no excuse for letting your receivables get so old.

Letter of Engagement

Client _____

Street _____

City/State/Zip _____

Work phone _____ Home phone _____

Services requested_____

_____

_____

_____

_____

_____

Fee for services described above $_____

Payment to be made as follows:

_____

_____

_____

By signing this letter of engagement, you indicate your understanding that this engagement letter constitutes a contractual agreement between us for the services set forth. This engagement does not include any services not specifically stated in this letter. Additional services, which you may request, will be subject to separate arrangements, to be set forth in writing.

A representative of _____ has advised us that we should seek legal counsel prior to using information or material received from _____.

We the undersigned hereby release _____, its employees, officers, shareholders, and representatives from any liability. We understand that we shall have no rights, claims, or recourse and waive any claims or rights we may have against _____, its employees, officers, shareholders, and representatives. We further understand that we will pay all costs of collection of any amount due hereunder including reasonable attorney fees.

_____   _____
Client   Date   Client   Date

_____
Company Representative   Date

9-1 Letter of engagement

OFFER DISCOUNTS FOR PROMPT PAYMENT

One way to encourage credit customers to pay on time is to offer discounts for prompt payment. Many businesses follow this guideline, and it can work for you. Before you start giving money away in discounts, make sure you can afford to discount your fee and still maintain your desired profit margin.

REMINDER NOTICES

Reminder notices (FIG. 9-2) are sometimes all it takes to get a delinquent account settled. Some people really do forget to pay their bills. If your money is more than five days late, notify the customer of the delinquency. The first notice should be a friendly reminder, not a legal threat.

9-2 Friendly reminder

> **Friendly Reminder**
>
> Please check your records to see if you neglected to make your scheduled payment on _____. We have not received your payment as of this date: _____. If you have mailed your payment, please call our business office at _____ and notify _____ of the date your payment was mailed. Thank you for your prompt attention to this matter.
>
> Your Company Name
> Your Company Address
> Your Company Phone Number

Phone calls are more effective reminder notices than the type mailed out with second notices. It is much easier for people to lose or trash a mailed notice than it is to ignore you on the phone.

CALL TO COLLECT

When you call to collect money, be nice. People respond better to nice, firm requests for payment than they do to legal intimidation. You don't want to alienate the customer. You want to collect the money that is owed to you.

It is best to call the slow-paying individuals at their homes, not their jobs. Try calling during business hours. If that doesn't work, call in the late afternoon or early evening. Don't call in the middle of the night just to catch a deadbeat off guard. There are laws that pertain to when and how you can attempt to collect past-due accounts. If you violate these laws, you could lose your past-due account and you might have to pay cash fines or face other legal action. Check with your attorney about local laws that pertain to credit collections.

COLLECTION AGENCIES

Collection agencies can help you collect your bad debts, but they are going to take a percentage of everything they collect. Most agencies charge you only for the money they recover, and their fees can be any percent of the money to which the two of you agree. Before you hand your receivables over to an agency, read their contract closely. Verify how they intend to collect your money, how long they have exclusive rights to the collections, how much they will charge for their services, and so on.

Like plumbing businesses, some collection agencies are better than others. Ask for references and check them out. Make sure that the agency is reputable and efficient. If you hook up with a bad agency, your accounts will age for months before you can retrieve them and seek other collection methods.

COLLECTION ATTORNEYS

Collection attorneys are an alternative to collection agencies. Attorneys know the law well, and people are more intimidated when they talk to a lawyer than they are when they talk to a collection agency. Some attorneys don't do collection work; others concentrate on collections.

When past-due customers receive letters from an attorney, most of them will pay attention to the legal stationery. These individuals will feel more threatened than they would with letters from collection agencies. Seeing a request for payment on legal letterhead indicates a lawsuit is not far away. A few phone calls can turn up attorneys that will be willing to help with your collection problems.

MECHANIC'S LIENS

Mechanic's liens can be filed when you do work on a property and are not paid for it. These liens must be filed within a certain time period and in the proper manner. The liens don't automatically get your money for you, but they are a strong step in the right direction.

Mechanic's liens encumber a property and make it difficult for the property to be sold or refinanced. To be effective, mechanic's liens must be perfected through court action. If you use subcontractors, make sure they sign lien waivers when you pay them (FIG. 9-3 and FIG. 9-4). Consult your attorney for the facts pertaining to mechanic's liens in your state.

NEW BUSINESSES ARE VULNERABLE

When a business opens it needs customers. In the search to find customers, it is not unusual to wind up with some bad credit risks. New business owners are more concerned about finding customers than they are about qualifying them. This is a major mistake. Screen all customers to ensure proper payment for your time and materials. It won't do you any good to be busy if you are not being paid.

Short-Form Lien Waiver

Customer name: _____

Customer address: _____

Customer city/state/zip: _____

Customer phone number: _____

Job location: _____

Date: _____

Type of work: _____

Contractor: _____

Contractor address: _____

Subcontractor: _____

Subcontractor address: _____

Description of work completed to date: _____

_____

_____

_____

Payments received to date: _____

Payment received on this date: _____

Total amount paid, including this payment: _____

The contractor/subcontractor signing below acknowledges receipt of all payments stated above. These payments are in compliance with the written contract between the parties above. The contractor/subcontractor signing below hereby states payment for all work done to this date has been paid in full.

The contractor/subcontractor signing below releases and relinquishes any and all rights available to place a mechanic or materialman lien against the subject property for the above described work. All parties agree that all work performed to date has been paid for in full and in compliance with their written contract.

The undersigned contractor/subcontractor releases the general contractor/customer from any liability for non-payment of material or services extended through this date. The undersigned contractor/subcontractor has read this entire agreement and understands the agreement.

_____   _____
Contractor/Subcontractor   Date

9-3 Short form lien waiver

Long-Form Lien Waiver

Customer name: _____

Customer address: _____

Customer city/state/zip: _____

Customer phone number: _____

Job location: _____

Date: _____

Type of work: _____

The vendor acknowledges receipt of all payments stated below. These payments are in compliance with the written contract between the vendor and the customer. The vendor hereby states that payment for all work done to this date has been paid in full.

The vendor releases and relinquishes any and all rights available to said vendor to place a mechanic or materialman lien against the subject property for the described work. Both parties agree that all work performed to date has been paid for, in full and in compliance with their written contract.

The undersigned vendor releases the customer and the customer's property from any liability for non-payment of material or services extended through this date. The undersigned contractor has read this entire agreement and understands the agreement.

Vendor Name	Signature of Co. Rep.	Signature Date	Service Performed	Date Paid	Amount Paid
Plumber (Rough-in)					
Plumber (Final)					
Electrician (Rough-in)					
Electrician (Final)					
Supplier (Framing lumber)					

*This list should include all contractors and suppliers. All vendors are listed on the same lien waiver, and sign next to their trade name for each service rendered, at the time of payment.

9-4 Long form lien waiver

USE GOOD HABITS

Good organizational habits are essential to reducing bad debts. If you don't realize an account is past-due, you are not going to know to collect it.

You cannot monitor all aspects of your business while you are out plumbing all day. However, you cannot afford to allow issues like delinquent accounts to go unnoticed. If your business is set up on a computer, the computer can tell you when to send out reminder notices and when to take further action. An aging report run off the computer will tell you quickly what accounts are past due and how long it has been since you received money.

Whether you use a computer or an efficient filing system to stay on top of your bookkeeping, make sure you know where you stand on a weekly basis. Too many contractors look at their accounts on a monthly basis. When you go month by month, you allow time to pass that could be critical to the collection of your money. Get organized and don't neglect your accounts receivables.

If you don't have the personality or inclination to collect your own past-due accounts, seek professional help. Don't put off the collection process. You and your business need the money owed to you to survive.

I prefer to use attorneys to collect my past-due accounts, but collection agencies can be successful. You might prefer to hire a part-time credit manager to handle your receivables. Find a way that works for you, and do it.

10

Manage your money

Cutting the right expenses and projecting the future are integral parts of refining a business plan. No business can stand stagnate and survive. Times change, and businesses must change with them.

BEAT OVERHEAD EXPENSES

Overhead expenses are not related directly to a particular job. Examples of these expenses include rent, utilities, phone bills, advertising, insurance, office help, and so on. These expenses can be enough to drive you out of business. If you fail to investigate and rate your operating costs, you might find yourself looking for a job. Since this is such an important aspect of your business management, let's take a closer look at how you can get a handle on your overhead expenses.

Rent

If you work out of your home, you will not notice a new financial strain if you convert one of your rooms to a designated office.

If you rent commercial office space, you will be aware of increased money demands. Prime locations are expensive for an office of any size. While you might rent a small upstairs office in an average location for less than $400 a month, the same space in a fashionable part of town could cost upwards of $800 a month. If your business is located in a large, popular city, the cost of office space might be considerably more. The size of your office will also affect its cost.

Utilities

Utilities are expenses you can hardly do without. These expenses include heat, hot water, electricity, air conditioning, public water fees, and sewer fees. You might be able to make minor cuts in these expenses, but it will be difficult to slash the costs of these necessities.

Phone bills

Phone bills for a busy business might amount to hundreds of dollars each month. One way to reduce your expenses is to take advantage of all the discount programs offered by the many phone services. Another possibility is to make your long-distance calls after normal business hours. Reducing idle chit chat also can have a favorable impact on your phone bill. Don't be too quick to cut back on your directory advertising. You might lose more business than the savings is worth.

Advertising

You can make your advertising dollar stretch further by making your advertising more effective. Keep records on the pulling power of your ads. Track the number of responses that turn into paying work. Target your advertising to bring in the type of work that is the most profitable for your firm. Refine your advertising and it will pay for itself.

Insurance

Most business owners resent this expense, but you can't afford to be without it. There are two keys to controlling your insurance expenses. The first key is to avoid over insuring your company. There is no reason to pay premiums for more insurance than you need. The second key is to shop rates and services. Insurance is a volatile market. Rates change often and quickly. The insurance you had last month might need to be reassessed this month. Periodic evaluations and shopping will help you maintain maximum control over your insurance expenses.

Professional fees

Professional fees might not be incurred on a monthly basis, but they can amount to hundreds, possibly thousands of dollars a year. Engage professional help when you need it, but lower the cost of these services by doing some of the work yourself.

If you have a CPA do your taxes, and you probably should, you can save money by doing some preparation work. Organize and label all your documents and you will reduce the number of phone calls, visits, and time you spend with the professional. The time you save the accountant will result in a lower fee.

Attorneys should be consulted on legal matters and they should draft and review legal documents. If you draft an outline for the attorney to go by, you will save time for the lawyer. When you meet with your attorney, have your questions prepared, preferably in writing, and organized. The quicker you get in and out, the less you will have to pay.

Office help

Office employees can be one of your most expensive overhead items. Don't generate this type of overhead expense until your business can't function properly without it.

Office supplies

Office supplies might not seem like a large expense, but they add up. Reduce the cost of office supplies by buying them in bulk from wholesale distributors.

Office equipment and furniture

Every office needs some office equipment and furniture. You will need a desk, a chair, a filing cabinet, and a telephone. Before you buy anything, make sure you need it and that the cost is justified. Office equipment and furniture is an area where many business owners go overboard.

Every business has a need, from time to time, to make copies of documents. Some businesses do enough volume to justify buying or leasing a copier, but most small businesses don't. When you consider you can go to the local print shop and make copies for about 10¢ a piece, it will take a lot of copies to pay for owning or leasing a copier. Going out to make copies is inconvenient, but it can save you a considerable amount of money.

Unless you deal with a large number of commercial clients you probably don't need a fax machine. If you need a fax, go to the print shop and pay a few bucks per page to send your documents. Most of these pay-as-you-go fax places will allow you to use their fax number to receive incoming documents. To recoup the $400 to $1,000 purchase price of a fax, you will need to send a lot of documents from the print shop.

Don't get caught up in the gadget trap. How often will you use a globe of the world? Do you really need a binding machine to bind your reports and proposals? Can you live without an electric stapler? Before you spend precious money on items that will do little more than be in your way, consider what you are buying.

Vehicles

Company vehicles might be considered overhead expenses. While it's true you need transportation, you don't have to have the ultimate in automotive engineering. If you can do your job in a $7,500 mini pick-up truck, don't buy a full-size truck. Cutting your overhead is a matter of common sense and logic. Buy what you need; don't buy what you don't.

INVESTIGATE OTHER EXPENSES

Cutting the wrong expenses might be worse than not cutting any expenses. We have just finished looking at normal overhead expenses. What other expenses might you cut back on?

Field supervisors

If you have a field supervisor, ask yourself if you could do the field supervision and use that individual as an income producer. There are many advantages to being your own field supervisor. You will see, first hand, how your jobs are progressing. Customers will see you on the job and be more comfortable that you are doing a good job and giving them special attention. The cost of having an employee as a supervisor will be eliminated or reduced. Before you pay high wages to a field supervisor, consider doing the work yourself.

Left-over materials

Left-over materials are common in the contracting business. Since the quantity of these leftovers is usually minimal, many contractors put the material in storage. If the items will be used within a month, putting them in storage is not a bad idea. If you don't know when you will have an occasion to use the materials, return them to the supplier for credit.

Returning left-over materials keeps your money from being tied up in unneeded inventory, and you from needing a large storage area. It also reduces the cost of wages you pay and the time you lose handling the materials. When the materials are moved from the job to your storage facility, time is spent. When the materials are taken out of storage and transported to a job, more time is spent.

Most of your regular suppliers will be happy to pick up your left-over materials and credit your account. When you need the materials again, the supplier will deliver them for you. You save money both ways.

Travel expenses

Cut your travel expenses by keeping mileage logs for all your vehicles. When tax time comes deduct the cost of your mileage. The amount you may deduct is set by the government, but it is enough to make keeping a mileage log worthwhile.

Cash purchases

Most contractors have occasions when they purchase small items with cash. The items might be nails, photocopies, stamps, or any number of other business-related items. Keep the receipts for these items and they can become tax deductions. While a receipt for less than a dollar might not seem worth the trouble of recording, if you collect enough of them you will appreciate the savings (FIG. 10-1 and FIG. 10-2).

Testing your expenses

Decide what costs to cut by testing your expenses. The two examples I gave earlier on copiers and fax machines indicate one method of testing. Other ways to test your expenses are as varied as the expenses themselves. Before

Cash Receipt

Date_____

Time_____

Received of_____

Address_____

Account number_____

Amount received_____

Payment for_____

Form of payment_____

Signed_____

10-1 Cash receipt

Petty-cash record

Month_____

Year_____

Vendor	Amount	Item	Date	Job

10-2 Petty cash record

you incur or cut an expense, be sure you are doing the right thing. Taking action too quickly can result in costly mistakes. For example, taking your advertisement out of the phone directory will probably be a regrettable mistake. Dropping your health insurance might come back to haunt you. Scrutinize all of your expenses and cut only the ones that will not hurt you or your business.

CASH FLOW IS PARAMOUNT TO SUCCESS

Paper profits are nice, but they don't pay the bills. Have you ever heard about the person who is land rich and cash poor? Well, it's true. I've had tremendous financial statements and nearly no cash. Having a business with a high net worth is not worth much if you don't have enough money to pay your bills. Cash flow is very important to a healthy business.

I've seen a large number of businesses forced to the brink of bankruptcy, even though they had significant assets. These businesses held valuable assets, but couldn't convert the assets into cash. If a business becomes cash poor, it is handicapped. A business without cash is like an army without ammunition. The cash might be on the way, but if the enemy attacks before it arrives, the business cannot defend itself. Regardless of your assets and business strength, if you don't have cash, you are in trouble. As the old saying goes, "you've got to pay to play."

One of the biggest traps to avoid is bad jobs. Jobs that result in slow pay or no pay also can be your undoing. Don't get greedy. Greed is a major contributor to business failure. It is better to take a slow approach and reach your goals than it is to run full out, only to fail.

CUTTING THE WRONG EXPENSES CAN BE EXPENSIVE

If you cut the wrong expenses, you might lose more money than you save. Some of your actions might be difficult to reverse. For these reasons, use sound judgment when you make cuts in your business expenses. Let's look at some of the expenses you might not want to cut.

Directory advertising

Directory advertising in the phone book is one of the first expenses many business owners contemplate cutting. Before you cut this expense, remember that you will have to live with the change for a full year. If you reduce the size of your ad or eliminate it, you can't reverse your actions until the next issue is printed.

Directory advertising does work. It is a proven fact that people let their fingers do the walking. If you are a service business that caters to emergency calls, you must have an ad in the phone book.

I am sure you will get calls from your directory advertising, but the cost of the ad might be more than the calls are worth. Track your calls for a year and decide if you are getting your money's worth from the phone book. You might be wise to have a modest listing in the directory and spend the money you save on a more targeted form of advertising. The main thing is to not make radical changes in your directory advertising before you are sure they are justified. A year is a long time to live with a mistake that hurts your business.

Answering services

Human answering services are another frequent target of business owners looking to cut expenses. While some businesses do alright with answering machines, most businesses do better when a live voice answers the phones.

Most answering services can be terminated and picked back up the following month. If you are unsure of the value of your answering service, terminate it for a month and compare the number of leads you get for new work. If you don't notice a drop in business, you made a wise decision. If you are losing business, reinstate the answering service.

Health insurance

Health insurance is very expensive, and many business owners consider eliminating their coverage at one time or another. You take a big risk when you drop your health insurance. As expensive as the insurance is, if you have a major medical problem the insurance will be a bargain. Big medical bills could drive you into bankruptcy. If you feel you have to alter your insurance payments, look for a policy with a higher deductible amount. These policies will reduce your monthly premiums and still provide protection against catastrophic illness or injury.

Dental insurance

Dental insurance is not as important as health insurance, but it is still a comforting thing to have. If you have bad teeth, dental insurance can pay for itself. There are, of course, other types of dental services that will make your insurance premiums seem small. Try to avoid cutting out any of your insurance coverage.

Disability insurance

Disability insurance is not carried by all contractors, but probably should be. Disability insurance provides a buffer between you and financial disaster if you become disabled. You might get by without this type of coverage, but the gamble might not be worth the savings.

Inventory assets

Inventory assets often come under fire when money is tight. Stock your trucks with adequate supplies. If you cut back too far on inventory, your crews will waste time running to the supply house, and your customers will be frustrated by your lack of preparation.

Retirement funding

Retirement plans are frequently one of the first expenses cut by contractors. A short moratorium on retirement funding is okay, but don't neglect to reinstate your investment plans before it is too late.

Bid-sheet subscriptions

While these expenses are not monumental, they might appear to be an easy cut. If all you do with your bid sheets is glance at them and trash them, by all means cancel your subscription. If you bid work on the sheets and win some jobs, eliminating your subscription could be the same as turning away work.

Credit bureaus

Before you make the decision to do without credit reports on your potential customers, weigh the risk you are taking. Doing work for one customer that doesn't pay will more than offset the savings you make by eliminating the credit bureau fees.

Advertising

It is not wise to eliminate your advertising, but it is smart to target it. Do a marketing study to determine where and what to advertise, and then do it. If your marketing research is accurate, the cost of your advertising will be returned in new business.

Sales force

Even when sales people are paid only by commission, some business owners consider eliminating them. This makes no sense. If you have a sales force that only gets paid for sales made, why would you want to get rid of them? Unless you are going to replace the existing sales force with new, more dynamic sales people, the move to eliminate salespeople is senseless.

STRETCH YOUR MONEY

Learn to stretch your money and you can do more business. The more business you do, the more money you can make. There are many ways to stretch your dollars. Let's see how you can increase the power of your cash.

- Rent expensive tools until you know you need them.
- Don't give subcontractors advance deposits.
- Collect job deposits from homeowners whenever possible.
- Make the best use of your time.
- Forecast financial budgets and stick to them.

- Buy in bulk whenever feasible.
- Pay your supply bills early and take the discount.
- Put your operating capital in an interest-earning account.
- File extensions and pay your taxes late in the year.
- Don't overstock on inventory items.
- Keep employees working, not talking.
- Consider leasing big-ticket items.

These are only a few of the ways you can manage your money. Study your business and you will find other ways to maximize your profits.

11

Schedules, budgets, and job costing

With good planning and forecasting you have a better-than-average chance of having a profitable business. You must look ahead and plan. Having plans and goals can make the difference between survival and failure.

ESTABLISH PRODUCTION SCHEDULES

Production schedules allow you to plan and track your workload. Working out a viable schedule is not hard, and it doesn't take long to do. You can rough out your production schedules on a computer or on note paper. Start with just one job. Once you have a schedule for the first job, scheduling the remainder of your jobs will be easy.

Start by putting the job name and address on the schedule. Lay out the schedule with headings for each phase of work you will perform. Allow spaces to fill in dates for the various work phases. You will want space for many dates. The first space will contain your anticipated start date. Another space will contain the date work is actually started. You should have an entry for the estimated time needed to complete the task. Then you should have a spot to enter the date of actual completion. In addition to your start and finish dates, allow space to write in dates for material deliveries.

The production schedule should have provisions for listing the names and phone numbers of subcontractors and suppliers you will use. Write these names and numbers next to each work phase and delivery. Having the names and numbers on the schedule will make it easier to make follow-up confirmation calls. Now all you have to do is fill in the appropriate dates.

Staying on schedule is going to take effort. You cannot maintain a schedule without working at it. You will have to make confirmation calls, review the progression of your jobs, stay on top of subs and suppliers, and routinely monitor all aspects of your jobs.

ADJUST FOR UNFORESEEN OBSTACLES

After being in business for awhile you start to anticipate the unexpected. Seasoned contractors are so good at projecting problems that they rarely have them. As a new contractor you may suffer through some tough times and pay a price for your lack of experience, but organization will help.

Many people assume that because they know their trade, they know their business. Knowing how to do your job as a plumber is not the same as knowing how to run a business. You might be very competent at estimating the time you will need for the work you will do yourself. If you're not an experienced contractor, however, you may not know what allowances to make for subcontractors and suppliers. These two variables can destroy a schedule.

PROJECT YOUR BUSINESS BUDGET

Developing a business budget requires extensive thought. You must consider your immediate needs and project your future needs and goals. For example, if you want to retire in 20 years, you should make an allowance for this desire in your budget. Let's take a look at some of the factors you should incorporate into your business budget.

Salary

Many business owners don't pay themselves a set salary. They make as much money as they can and use the money they need. This works for some people, but it is not the way to make a business budget.

You need to establish a set amount for your salary. You might not always be able to take as much money for your salary as the budget reflects, but you need to plug in a number for your income. When you set your salary, don't forget your responsibility for income taxes. You have to look at your net-income needs and gross-income requirements.

Office expenses

Office expenses can cause your budget to balloon. Think about all the various expenses that you will incur to keep your office running. These expenses might include rent, utilities, phone bills, cleaning, equipment rentals, office supplies, furniture, and much more. The cost of running your office can account for a high percentage of your annual expenses. Check over your office expenses. You will likely find ways to save money.

Field expenses

Field expenses can be broken down into more specific categories and usually are. These costs include vehicles, fuel, field supervisors, signs, and other related expenses. For a number of contractors, field expenses are a large part of their annual budget.

Vehicle expenses

The cost of trucks, cars, fuel, tires, and similar expenses can amount to thousands of dollars. Of course, your vehicle expenses will be related directly to the size and structure of your business. If you rely on subcontractors for all of your field work, your vehicle expenses will be minimal. If you have a fleet of trucks and an army of employees, vehicle expenses can be astronomical.

Tool and equipment expenses

There are two types of tool and equipment expenses. There is the cost of initial acquisitions and the cost of replacement. Even if you have all the tools and equipment you need, you have to budget for replacement costs. Your hardware may be broken, stolen, or worn out. Sooner or later it will need to be replaced. If you are not prepared financially for these replacement expenses, you might find yourself unable to continue doing business. Take a look at your tools and equipment. Estimate the life expectancy of your hardware and put a figure in your budget for its replacement.

Employee expenses

When you look at employee expenses you have to look much deeper than the hourly rates earned by your employees. You must look at employee taxes and benefits. If you provide insurance benefits for your employees, you are spending serious money. Paid vacations are another major expense. Sick leave, paid holidays, and similar employee benefits can amount quickly to thousands of dollars.

If your business is top-heavy with employee expenses, you might do well to consider engaging independent contractors. If you have employees, don't neglect to include the cost of employee benefits in your budget.

Insurance expenses

Insurance expenses can run some businesses into the ground. All businesses need liability insurance. Workman's compensation insurance can be expensive if you have employees. Insurance to protect against theft and fire is another common business need. When a company is properly insured, the expense of the insurance can account for much of the total business budget.

Advertising expenses

Advertising expenses are one of the few expenses from which businesses see a direct gain. When used efficiently, advertising will pay for itself and then some. While you cannot be sure of the results of your advertising, you can project how much you are willing to spend to generate new business. Many companies dedicate a percentage of their gross sales to advertising. Most small companies pick a dollar amount rather than a percentage.

Whichever method you use, make sure to include your anticipated advertising costs in your business budget.

Loan expenses

Loan expenses might be overlooked when you build a budget. This is especially true if you will use short-term, interest-only loans. Don't forget to include the fees you will incur in your business budget.

Taxes

The impact of taxes can cause severe stress on a business. Unless regular tax deposits are made, the burden of coming up with enough money to satisfy the tax authorities can be overwhelming. To avoid being caught in a cash bind, include your estimated tax liabilities in your budget projections. If you are unable to forecast your taxes, consult a tax professional. You cannot afford to be left high and dry on tax day.

Growth expenses

Few businesses grow without a plan. Part of any growth plan will involve expansion capital. Consider your intent for company growth when you build your budget and include provisions for the cost of expansion.

Retirement goals

Retirement goals frequently get pushed to the back of the list. When money is tight it is hard to invest in retirement plans. The impulse is to fight the fires of today and worry about retirement later. Unfortunately, age and retirement creep up on all of us, often sooner than we plan.

As you build your business budget you may discover other items for which you should account, but this list of routine expenses will get you started in the right direction.

MAINTAIN YOUR BUDGET

Having a budget will do you little good unless you have the discipline and skills to maintain it. It helps to have a natural ability to stay within budget constraints, but if you don't, you can learn the skills and discipline. Most of us have some weak areas in our self discipline. Your job as a business owner is to find your weak areas and reinforce them.

If you find the deals on tools in mail-order catalogs irresistible, you may discover you are spending far too much on tools. When you are infatuated with having the most high-tech office equipment available, you may be investing too much money on the wrong items. The list of potential weaknesses could go on, but you get the idea.

All of these potential weaknesses must be evaluated. If you are quick to give in to impulse buying, set rules for yourself. Make yourself wait for a reasonable period of time before you buy that new tool or office equipment. Wait and see if you need the item or if you only want the item.

Look into every aspect of your business habits. Are you going to lunch at expensive restaurants on a regular basis? If you are, you may be spending enough to pay for a more justified business expense.

Document all of your spending for the next two weeks. Include even small cash purchases. At the end of the two weeks, go over your list of expenditures. Compare these expenses to your budget. How many of your recent expenditures are not reflected in your budget? My guess is that you will find several areas where you spent money that wasn't budgeted. This is a danger signal. You can't allow yourself to run rampant with your company's financial resources. If you do, your business will fail.

After tagging all the unbudgeted expenses, decide if you will continue to make similar purchases. If you come to the conclusion that your expenses are justified, include them in your budget. If the spending habits are not necessary, eliminate them. Periodically repeat the two-week test. By monitoring and refining your budget, you can stay within its framework.

As you work with your business, there will be other factors to consider when you plan for a long and successful business career. The key is to always tend to today and look to tomorrow.

PREPARE ACCURATE TAKE-OFFS

A take-off is a list of items needed to do a job. Take-offs are the result of reading blueprints or visiting the job site. Some estimators are wizards with take-offs, and others have a hard time trying to project all of their needs. If you can't discipline yourself to learn how to do an accurate take-off, your venture into contracting is going to be a rough road.

To make sound bids, you must be adept at preparing accurate take-offs. It doesn't matter if you use a computerized estimating program or a pen and paper, get your facts straight. If you miss items on the take-off, you will lose money. If you overestimate the take-off, your price will be too high. An accurate take-off is instrumental to winning a job.

Use take-off forms

You can reduce your risk of error by using take-off forms (FIG. 11-1). If you use a computerized estimating program, you might want to customize the generic form. Whether you are using stock computer forms or making your own forms, be sure they are comprehensive.

Take-off forms should list every item you might use for various jobs. In addition, there should be places on the form where you can fill in blank spaces with specialty items.

As a plumber you might have several types of take-off forms. You might have one for doing the rough-in plumbing on a new house. You could also have one for the finish work in the house. It's conceivable that you would have a different form to list materials for underground plumbing and the

Job Name:		
Job Address:		
Item	Quantity	Description
2" Pipe	100'	PVC
4" Pipe	40'	PVC
4" Clean-out w/plug	1	PVC
2" Quarter-bend	4	PVC
2" Coupling	3	PVC
4" Eighth-bend	2	PVC
Glue	1 quart	PVC
Cleaner	1 quart	PVC
Primer	1 quart	PVC

11-1 Take-off form

water service and sewer. Of course, you could have all phases of your work on one form, but that might get confusing.

When the time comes to figure your material requirements to install a sewer, you can go down your form and fill in the quantities of each item you will need. For instance, you might need 70 feet of 4-inch pipe and 3 clean-out assemblies. You might also need some wyes, eighth-bends, and caps. If you are working with plastic pipe, you will need glue and probably a cleaner. The list could go on, but you get the idea.

The advantage to using take-off forms is that you are prompted on items you might otherwise forget. However, don't get into such a routine that you only look for items on your form. It is very possible a job might require something that you haven't yet put on the form. Forms help, but there is no substitute for thoroughness.

Keep track of what you've already counted

Doing a take-off on a large set of plans can be tedious. The last thing you need is to lose your place or forget what you've already counted. To avoid this problem, mark each item on the plans as you count it.

Build in a margin of error

If you think you are going to need 1,000 feet of pipe, add a little to your count. How much you add will depend on the size of the job. A lot of estimators build in a float figure of between 3 and 5 percent. Some contractors add 10 percent to their figures. Unless the job is small, I think a 10-percent add-on might cause you to lose the bid.

Much of your cushion for mistakes will depend on your ability to make an accurate take-off. If you are good with take-offs, a small percentage for oversights will be sufficient. If you always seem to run short of materials, you will need a higher slush pile.

Keep records

Don't throw away your take-off. When the job is done, compare the material actually used with what you estimated on your take-off. This will help you see where your money is going and make you a better estimator. Track your jobs and compare final counts to original estimates and you will refine your bidding techniques and win more jobs.

USE JOB COSTING

Job costing is the act of adding up all the costs incurred to complete a job. Depending upon your methods, job costing may only account for labor and materials. In more sophisticated reports, the numbers will include the cost of overhead and operation expenses.

Your routine business expenses must be factored into the cost of jobs, but you don't have to include it in individual job-cost reports. Instead, use a percentage of your on-job profit to defer your overhead costs. Let's see how each of these methods might be used.

SIMPLE JOB COSTING

Simple job costing might include all expenses incurred for a specific job, excluding overhead expenses such as office rent and utilities, general insurance, advertising, and so forth. To do a simple job cost, you need nothing more than pencil, paper, and information (FIG. 11-2). First, list all the materials you used on the job. Then price the materials based on what you paid for them. Next, calculate all the cost of all the labor that went into the job. Soft costs, such as permit fees, will be your next category.

Once you have listed all the job costs, check over the list for omissions. When you are sure you haven't forgotten anything, add up the total of the costs. Subtract the total of your costs from the money you received for doing the job to get your gross profit.

Let's say you sold the job for $5,000. The total of your on-job expenses was $3,500. This means your gross profit was $1,500 or 20 percent. Does this mean you made a profit of $1,500 on the job? No; the gross profit of $1,500 doesn't reflect your overhead expenses. These expenses must be subtracted from the gross profit.

Let's say that you had four jobs of equal value and equal effort running at the same time. For this example, assume that you started and finished all four jobs in one month. Further, let's say that your overhead expenses average $2,000 a month. In this simple example you would divide your overhead expenses by four to obtain the percentage of these expenses that should be charged to each job.

In this case, your overhead expenses equal $500. Twenty-five percent of your overhead was attributed to the job in question. After doing this math, you find that your net profit on the job was $1,000 or 20 percent of the total job cost. You could also say it was two-thirds of your gross profit.

In real life, it is not easy to account for overhead expenses. It is not un-

Job Cost Log

Job name _____

Mechanic _____

Truck _____

Date _____

Item	Quantity	Size

11-2 Job cost log

common to have several jobs running at once and many jobs overlapping each other. This complicates the division of overhead between jobs. Some businesses project a percentage of their overhead and apply it to every job. Other businesses use complex methods to detail the exact cost of their overhead to each job. How you do your job costing is up to you, but you must allow for overhead expenses to get a true accounting of your profit margin. Let's see how a job-costing report might be done using a blanket percentage for overhead expenses.

PERCENTAGE JOB COSTING

Percentage job costing is a common method used to determine profits and losses. To perform this task, duplicate the example given for simple job costing. Once this is done, subtract a percentage of the contract price for the job. The percentage you subtract will represent your overhead expenses.

Using the same numbers as in the earlier example, let's see how this math works. In your first step, you determined a gross profit of $1,500, excluding overhead expenses. The job sold for $5,000. Let's say that after testing, you estimate your overhead factor to be 10 percent. So, find 10 percent of the contract price and deduct it from the gross profit. In this case, 10 percent is $500. When you subtract $500 from $1,500, you arrive at a net profit of $1,000.

What percentage should you use? The percentage you should apply for overhead will depend on your business structure. Some businesses carry heavy overhead expenses; others are streamlined to maximum efficiency. You will have to experiment with your personal circumstances to determine what percentage will cover your overhead expenses.

ADJUST YOUR PRICES

Adjusting your prices will be much easier when you work with the results of accurate job-costing reports. If you review the job-cost reports from three similar jobs and find a pattern, you will be able to determine if you are charging enough, too much, or not enough. For example, let's say you replace a high volume of water heaters and well pumps. Which of these jobs is the most profitable for you? All you have to do is review job-cost reports for several similar jobs and you can determine which type of job is most lucrative.

This is only one way of using job-cost reports to adjust your pricing. You might find that you need to raise your prices. The key is being able to determine how your business is doing in the area of net profits. Once you have concrete facts, you can adjust your prices to satisfy your goals.

It is likely your prices for labor and materials will change frequently. You must routinely monitor your competition and market trends. If the price of copper drops and stays low for months, you will probably have to lower your prices for copper materials to remain competitive. Never assume you will not have to alter your pricing more than once or twice a year. Keep informed about current pricing trends. Keep your prices at acceptable, and profitable, levels.

12

Price your labor and materials

Determining the price of your labor and materials is key to a profitable business. If your prices are too low, you might be busy but your profits will suffer. If your prices are too high, you will be sitting around hoping for the phone to ring. Somewhere between too low and too high is the optimum price for your products and services. The trick is finding those prices. This chapter is going to help you put the right price on your labor and materials.

MAKE YOUR PRICES ATTRACTIVE

Call competitive plumbers and ask what they charge for an hourly rate. This method will be more useful if the plumbers you call are unaware that you are about to become their newest competitor. This is simple research. All you have to do is go through the phone book and call the other contractors. When they answer, ask them their hourly rates. In less than an hour you can know what the majority of your competitors charge for their services.

Some newcomers to the contracting business make a serious mistake by pricing their services far below the crowd. Setting extremely low prices can be the same as setting a trap for yourself. If you set your prices far below your competitors, you will alienate yourself from the competition and customers might be afraid to use your services. As a new company, with low overhead, it's fine to work for less than the well-established companies, but don't price yourself into a deep hole.

When it comes to picking attractive prices, look below the surface. There are many factors that control what you are able to earn. Let's take a look at what is considered a profitable mark up.

WHAT IS A PROFITABLE MARK UP?

Some contractors feel a 10-percent mark up is adequate. Others try to tack 35 percent onto the price of their materials. Which group is right? Well, you can't make that decision with the limited information I have given you. The contractors that charge a 10-percent mark up may be doing fine, especially if they deal in big jobs and large amounts of materials. The 35-percent group might be justified in their mark up, especially if they are selling small quantities of lower-priced materials.

Mark up is a relative concept. Ten percent of $100,000 is much more than 35 percent of $100. For this reason, you cannot blindly pick a percentage of mark up to be your firm figure. The figure will need to be adjusted to meet the changes in market conditions and individual job requirements. You can, however, pick percentage numbers for most of your average sales.

If you are in the repair business and typically sell materials that cost around $20, a 35-percent mark up is fine if the market will bear it. If you are doing large jobs, a 10-percent mark up on materials should be sufficient. To some extent, you have to test the market conditions to determine what price consumers are willing to pay for your materials.

If you are selling common items that anyone can go to the local hardware or building supply store and price out, you must be careful not to inflate your prices too much. Customers expect you to mark up your materials, but they don't want to be gouged. If you install a flapper in a toilet and charge twice as much for it as the homeowner could have bought it for in the store, you are likely to wind up with an irate customer. Even though the amount of money involved in the transaction is puny, the principle of being charged double for a common item still exists.

If you typically install specialty items, increase your mark up. People will not be as irritated paying a marked up, but reasonable price for an unusual product. A mark up of 20 percent will almost always be acceptable on average residential jobs. When you decide to go above the 20-percent point, do so slowly and test the response of your customers.

HOW CAN YOUR COMPETITORS WORK FOR SUCH LOW PRICES?

There always seems to be some company that has a knack for winning bids and beating out the competition. If you know low prices are winning the bids, you can't help but wonder how the winner of the bids can do it.

Low prices can keep companies busy, but that doesn't mean the low-priced companies are making a profit. Gross sales are important, but net profits are what business is all about. If a company is not making a profit, there is not much sense to operating the business.

Companies that work with low prices fall into several categories. Some companies work on a volume principle. The company makes less money on each job, but makes a profit by doing many jobs. This type of company is hard to beat.

Some companies sell at low prices out of ignorance. Many small business owners are not aware of the overhead expenses involved with being in business. For example, a plumber that is making $16 an hour at a job might think that going into business independently and charging $25 an hour will be great. The plumber might even start by charging only $20 an hour. From the plumber's perspective, he is making at least $4 an hour more than he was at his job. Is he really making $4 an hour more? Yes and no, he is being paid an extra $4 an hour, but he is not going to get to keep much of it.

When this low-priced plumber comes into the business world, he might take a lot of work away from established contractors. Experienced contractors know they can't make ends meet by charging such small fees. But the inexperienced business owner doesn't know all of his expenses. Once the overhead expenses start eating away at what the plumber thought was a great profit, the deal may not look so good.

This businessman will soon learn that overhead expenses are a force with which to be reckoned. Insurance, advertising, call backs, self-employment taxes, and a mass of other hidden expenses will erode any profits the plumber thought he was making.

This type of inexperienced businessperson will either quickly go out of business or adjust his prices for services and materials. For established contractors competing against newcomers, being able to endure the momentary drop in sales will be enough to weather the storm. In a few months the new business will either be gone or up into a reasonably competitive range.

PRICE YOUR SERVICES FOR SUCCESS

It can be difficult to decide on the right price for your time and material. There are books that give formulas and theories about how to set your prices, but these guides are not always right. Every town and every business will add different factors to the prices the public is willing to pay. There are many methods you might use to find the best fees for your business to charge. Let's look at some of them.

Pricing guides

Most estimating guides provide a formula for adjusting the recommended prices of labor and materials in various regions. For example, a 52-gallon water heater might be listed with a labor-and-material estimate of $485. While the job might be worth this in Virginia, it might be worth less in Maine and more in California. The formulas used to make this type of adjustment are usually a number that is multiplied against the recommended price. By using the multiplication factor, a price can be derived for services and materials in any major city.

The idea behind these estimating guides is a good one, but there are flaws in the system. I have read and used many of these pricing books. From my personal experience, the books have not been accurate for the type of work I did. I don't say this to mean the books are no good. There are many times when the books are accurate. I never have been comfortable depending solely on a mass-produced pricing guide. I use pricing guides to compare my figures and to ensure I haven't forgotten items or phases of work. Most bookstores carry some form of estimating guides in their inventory.

Research

Research is one of the most effective ways to determine your pricing. When you look back at historical data, you will find answers to many of your questions. You will see how prices have fluctuated over the years, and you can start to project the curve of the future.

Newspaper ads can sometimes give you a feel for what your competitors are doing, but be careful. Advertising can be deceiving. When you look at an ad offering to install plumbing for a complete basement bath for $1,500, there is usually a catch or an angle. Unless you can see all the details of the job listed in the ad, you have to make assumptions. When you begin making assumptions, you set yourself up for trouble.

Combining methods is the best way to set your prices. Do as much research and consult as many resources as possible before you set your fees. Once you feel comfortable with your rates, test them. Ask customers to tell you their feelings. There is no feedback better than that of the people you serve.

EFFECTIVE ESTIMATING TECHNIQUES

To develop effective estimating techniques, you can learn the technical aspects of estimating by reading. Your estimating skills can be further perfected by referring to estimating handbooks and pricing guides. Much of what you learn will come from experience. Learning from your mistakes can be expensive, but you don't soon forget these costly lessons.

One of the most important factors in effective estimating is organization. When you are well organized, you are more likely to complete a thorough estimate (FIG. 12-1). Let's take a quick look at some ways to improve your estimating style.

Keeping notes

If you are sitting in your office and can't remember if the house had a 3-inch drain or a 4-inch drain, you are in trouble. It is necessary for you to address and evaluate every aspect of a job. When you can't remember details, your estimate is unlikely to be a good one. Your price will either be too high to compensate for what you can't remember, or too low because you didn't have the facts you needed. Keep notes on all your potential jobs and your estimates will be more accurate.

Look closely

If you fail to notice that the building drain is too small to accommodate an additional toilet, you might have to absorb the cost of installing new pipe. As a professional, it is your responsibility to know what needs to be done

Phase	Labor	Material	Total
Rough-in	$900	$875	$1475
Final	$350	$850	$1200
Permit			$60

12-1 Cost projections

to complete the job. Not all customers are going to be willing to pay for extras that come up after the job is started. Look closely at existing conditions, plans, and specifications.

Listen to the customer

Listen to the customer when you estimate a job. Not only will the customer appreciate your interest, you might gain valuable information. If the customer is talking about roughing in plumbing for a future installation, make a note of it. Later, solicit the customer for the additional work.

Keep copies

Keep copies of all your estimates. Some contractors fail to keep copies and become extremely embarrassed when they can't remember what they proposed to their customers. Keep copies of your notes and formal proposals. You never know when they will be needed.

Make files

Make files for each of your estimates. Don't pile them on your desk, or you might lose the estimate information. If a would-be customer calls to go over an estimate, you don't want to scramble through a stack of papers to locate the right estimate. It is much easier to open the file drawer and quickly and professionally produce the estimate.

Sell from the start

Good estimators begin selling from the moment they make contact with a customer. Many good sales people can talk the customer into adding additional features to their proposed plans. This technique can serve you well in two ways. First, you get more work. Second, if you can get the customer to change the description of the work, you eliminate the validity of any other estimates. This gives you a better shot at getting the job.

THE FEAR FACTOR CAN SELL JOBS

If you prepare yourself with some stories to tell, you can increase your in-home sales. People are often nervous about the dependability, ability, and performance of contractors. This nervousness stems from fear created by the media. When people read a news story about how a homeowner was cheated out of money by an unscrupulous contractor, they become concerned. This type of news can hurt business, but it can also be your ace in the hole.

Once you have developed a portfolio of contracting-related horror stories, use the fear factor to sell more jobs. People generally assume you wouldn't be educating them in the risks that are present with contractors if you are one of the bad guys. When you begin warning the consumer, you build the image of being one of the good guys.

After telling your stories, tell the customer how you operate in order to put their mind at ease. By showing the consumer what could happen, and why it won't—if they work with you—you're on your way to signing a new deal.

13

Equipment and inventory needs

Equipment, vehicles, and inventory will account for most of your start-up costs. These same items also will consume a large portion of your operating capital. There is no question that buying an $18,000 truck can put a dent in your bank account. Even with a 10-percent down payment and a 5-year loan at 10-percent interest, you are going to have to shell out $1,800 in cash and about $344 a month for payments. Add to this the cost of registration, taxes, and insurance, and you have a major expense.

Depending upon the type of business you have, you also might have to buy equipment. Hand tools are expensive and power tools are even worse. As for inventory, a service plumber can easily pay $10,000 for in-truck inventory. With these types of expenses, your savings account might need a transfusion.

A large number of businesses are forced to close each year because of purchases made for equipment, vehicles, and inventory. Some business owners decide to lease vehicles. This saves up-front money and the payments are usually less. But if the vehicles have excessive mileage or body damage when the lease is up, the end costs might exceed those of purchasing the vehicle.

Not only is the cost of acquiring inventory steep, keeping employees from stealing it can be a problem. Somewhere among the maze of options in these three big-ticket items is a happy medium. This chapter is going to help you find your way through the perilous maze, to financial safety and success.

LEASING vs. PURCHASING

Most business owners contemplate the advantages of leasing versus purchasing. It makes a lot of sense to rent tools that you only use a few times a year, and leasing vehicles can save you money and provide tax advantages. So what should you do? Well, let's find out.

Renting tools

Renting expensive tools can be a smart move for a new business. When you start out, money can be especially tight, and you might not have a real handle on what tools you need. Rent what you need, when you need it, and you will derive several advantages. You can try a tool before you buy it, evaluate how badly you need the tool, and determine how much extra money you can make with the tool.

When I started my first plumbing business I couldn't afford to buy a large electric drain cleaner. My plumbing business was centered around remodeling and new construction. I didn't get a lot of call for cleaning drains, but I hated referring the calls I did get to other plumbers. I decided to try renting the tool. I rented a drain cleaner for about six months. This gave me time to evaluate how often I used it and how much money I made with it. It became obvious that I could increase my profits by buying such a tool. I bought a good drain cleaner and it paid for itself in a matter of months. After that, all the money I made with it was gravy. It was inconvenient having to run to the rental center to pick up the snake, but the process enabled me to make a wise buying decision. You can do the same type of experiment.

Buying specialty tools

If you buy a bunch of tools you don't use very often, you will deplete your cash for a lost cause. For example, I used to do a high volume of basement bathrooms. Installing these basement baths required the use of a jackhammer. I started out renting a hammer and wound up buying one. For me, this was a good move. However, it might have been a superfluous expense for some plumbers.

Before you buy specialty tools, make sure you need them. The best way to assess your needs for specialty tools is to rent them when you need them, and keep track of how they affect your business. If your profits increase, consider purchasing the tool. If you find you only rent the tool a few times a year, continue to use rental tools.

Leasing vehicles

The good points of leasing are minimal out-of-pocket cash, normally lower payments, possible tax savings, and possible short-term commitments. The disadvantages are no equity gain, more concern for the condition of the vehicle, and possible cash penalties when the lease expires.

Most auto leases only require the first month's rent and an equal amount for the down payment. In other words, if the vehicle is going to cost you $250 a month, you will need $500 for the down payment and first month's rent. To purchase the same vehicle, you might need $1,000 to $2,000 for a down payment.

The monthly payments on leased vehicles are usually lower than the payments on a purchased vehicle. The savings will add up. However, remember you don't own the vehicle and at the end of the lease you will have no equity in the truck or car.

Leases can usually be obtained for any term, ranging from one to five years, and sometimes more. Two-year leases are popular, as are four-year leases. By leasing a vehicle for a short time, like two years, your company fleet can be renewed frequently. This keeps you in new vehicles and presents a good image. However, if a vehicle is not in good shape at the end of the lease, you will pay a price for the abuse.

Most leases allow for a certain number of miles to be put on the vehicle during the term of the lease. When the lease expires, if the mileage is higher than the allowance you will have to pay so much per mile for every mile over the limit. This can get expensive. Additionally, if the vehicle is beat up you can be charged for the loss in the vehicle's value. This can also amount to a substantial sum of money.

Then there are the tax angles. Since I'm not a tax expert, I recommend you talk to someone who is. It is likely that leasing will be more beneficial to your tax consequences than buying, but check it out.

Purchasing vehicles

When you purchase your vehicles you build equity in them. If you abuse the vehicle, you will lose money when you sell or trade it, but you won't be penalized by a lease agreement. If your trucks will lead a hard life, purchasing them is probably a good idea.

SEPARATE NEEDS FROM DESIRES

Before you buy expensive equipment, vehicles, or inventory, separate your needs from your desires. Too many contractors get caught up in having the best and most expensive items available. This is not only unnecessary, it can kill your business. If you can do the job with a $15,000 van, don't buy a $20,000 truck.

Let's start our look at needs and desires with inventory items. Most new business owners often wind up being overstocked. This results in tied up cash and sometimes lost money. Before you buy your inventory items, figure out what you need, not what you want.

Let me give you an example of how bad inventory purchases can shackle your business legs. I consulted with a plumbing company a few years ago. This particular company had eight service plumbers on the road and a ton of unneeded inventory. The business owner couldn't understand why he was short on cash. When I assessed the business, I found several faults, but inventory was one of the major problems with the company's cash flow.

Being a master plumber and a business owner for many years, I know what a plumber needs on a service truck. When I looked inside this company's trucks, I was amazed. Instead of having one box of copper ells, these trucks had as many as five. This is a frequently used fitting, but you don't need five boxes of them on a service truck.

My inspection turned up countless items, in multiple quantities, that were unlikely to be used in a year's time. After we streamlined the trucks to a viable rolling inventory, the company returned the excess items and received a credit from the supplier for over $12,000. And that was just truck stock! We went through the back storage room and eliminated several more thousands of dollars in inventory. By reducing the inventory to what was needed, not what was wanted, the company generated close to $20,000, after paying restocking fees.

FINANCIAL JUSTIFICATION

Financial justification is the key to making a wise buying decision. Some people are able to justify buying anything they want. I suppose if you work at it long enough, you can convince yourself of just about anything. However, justifying a purchase isn't enough. You must justify the purchase financially by proving your need for the item and determining the payback period for it. I gave a brief example earlier about how I rented a drain cleaner before buying one. Let's look at the steps I went through to justify that purchase financially.

I started renting the tool whenever I had a need for it. I rented the tool for about six months. During this time I kept track of the number of times I used the equipment, what I paid in rental fees, the money and time I lost picking up and returning the unit to the rental center, and how much money I grossed on the use of the snake.

When I sat down and ran the numbers to evaluate this tool, I saw clearly that it would be a good investment for my company. The new tool, with accessories, cost about $1,200. The rental fee for the unit was about $20. During normal business hours I charged $65 for the machine and a mechanic to operate it. My normal hourly fee was $30, so I was essentially charging $35 for the use of the machine. Out of this $35 I paid the rental store $20. Still, I was getting work I couldn't get without the machine.

The cost of paying a plumber to pick up and return the machine ate up the money I was making off the equipment rental, though I still made my normal profit from the service call. I deduced that if I owned the machine, I would have no lost time and my profit per call would increase by $35. Of course, I would first have to pay for the machine in order to see this additional profit.

I averaged six calls a week for the drain cleaning machine. With this volume of activity it made sense to buy my own drain cleaner. If the demand continued, as it had for the six months during my test period, the machine would pay for itself in about six weeks. After the machine was paid for I would enjoy higher net earnings for the remaining life of the machine.

I bought the machine and my plans worked out perfectly. In less than two months the machine was paid for and I continued to see increased revenue from its use. This is a prime example of how you financially justify a buying decision.

HOW MUCH INVENTORY SHOULD YOU STOCK?

Inventory requirements vary with different types of businesses. Where a service plumber might need a rolling stock of $7,000, a new-construction plumber might get by with an inventory of less than $2,000. To establish your inventory needs you must assess your customers' buying trends.

Planned jobs

Planned jobs don't require much inventory because you can order a specific amount of material for the job when it starts. You will want some inventory to make up for any items you might forget in the big order, but on-truck inventory needs for this type of work are minimal.

Impulse buying

If one of your plumbers is at a house fixing a kitchen sink, the homeowner might ask the plumber to install a new lavatory faucet while he's on the job. The customer knows this will save travel time and money. If your plumber's truck has an acceptable lavatory faucet on it, you've made a sale. If the plumber has to go get the faucet, the customer will probably put off the expense and trouble of swapping the faucet. If you will be doing work where the customer is likely to ask you to do more work, stock some standard impulse items.

Time savers

If you are on the job and need an extra 50 feet of pipe, you will save time and money by having it on the truck. It is a good idea to carry a rolling stock of your most frequently used items. But don't get carried away, a service truck doesn't need 5 boxes of copper ells.

Shop stock

Limit shop stock to what you will use in a two-week period. As you use the material, order new stock. This keeps your inventory fresh and your money turning over.

CONTROL INVENTORY THEFT

This is a problem that can hit any company that has employees. Whether you have 1 employee or 100 employees, you might be getting ripped off. Lost inventory is lost money. Take steps to ensure that your employees are honest and that the material is being used for legitimate jobs.

The best way to reduce inventory pilfering is to keep track of your inventory on a daily basis (FIG. 13-1). Have your workers complete and turn in forms for all material used each day. Let employees know, in a nice way, that you check inventory disbursement every week. This tactic alone will greatly reduce the likelihood of employees stealing from you.

Another way to control the loss of shop stock is to issue all stock yourself. If you don't allow employees access to your inventory, they can't steal it. Rolling stock is harder to account for, but if your employees know you

Inventory Control for Trucks

Item	Quantity	Job Name	Employee	Truck#	Date

13-1 Inventory control log for trucks

keep daily records of your stock, they will be less likely to empty your truck. It never hurts to do surprise inspections and inventories on the trucks. Make sure the employees see you inspecting the trucks. The fact that you go on the truck and audit the inventory will reduce your losses.

STOCK YOUR TRUCKS EFFICIENTLY

Service vehicles should be set up with everything they need and nothing they don't. Keep your rolling stock to a minimum. You never know when the truck will be broken into or stolen. If the inventory on your trucks is collecting dust, get rid of it and don't reorder it.

A good way to establish your truck-stock needs is to keep track of the materials you use off the truck (FIG. 13-2). If you track your material usage, you will be able to stock your truck with materials that you will use. If you have got some slow moving items on the truck, don't replace them when they are sold. Conversely, if you have some hot items, keep them on the trucks.

Stocking your trucks efficiently will take a little time. Start small and work your way up. After you have been in the trade for awhile you will have a good idea of your inventory needs.

Truck Inventory

Truck number: _____

Driver: _____

Item	Size	Color	Brand	Quantity

Inventory taken on the _____th of _____, 19_____

13-2 Truck inventory log

14

Choose your product lines

Carefully choose your product lines. If you pick the wrong products, your business will fizzle. The proper products will sell themselves. As a business owner you can use all the help you can get, so carry products that the public wants.

Decide on what products to carry by doing some homework. Read magazines that appeal to the type of people you want as customers. For example, if you want to concentrate on kitchen and bathroom remodeling, read magazines that cater to this type of work. Pay attention to the ads in these magazines and you will get a good idea of the products your customers will want.

Walk through local stores that carry products you will be selling or competing with. Take notes as you cruise the aisles. Pay attention to what is on display and the cost of each item. This type of research also will help you target your product lines.

The most direct way to determine what customers want is to ask them. If you think you can't ask customers what they want until you have customers, you're wrong. As a matter of fact, you shouldn't wait until you have a strong customer base to establish your product lines.

How do you walk up to a stranger and ask them what type of faucets they like best? You can go door to door and do a cold-call canvassing of a neighborhood. You will experience a lot of rejection, but you will also get some answers. If you don't like knocking on doors, use a telephone. You can even have a computer make the phone calls and ask the questions for you.

If you don't want to use face-to-face techniques or telephones, use direct mail. Mail a questionnaire to potential customers. Done properly, your mailing will look like you have a sincere interest in what the consumer wants. It will appear this way because you do have a sincere interest. Direct mail is easy to target, and it's fast and effective. While mailing costs can get steep, the results can overcome the costs.

The answers to your questionnaire will tell you what products to carry. You can improve the odds of having the pieces returned by self addressing the response card. You should also pick up the tab on the return postage. This can be done by purchasing a permit from the local post office and printing it on your cards. If you don't like that idea, you can affix postage stamps to the cards, but this will cost more. With the permit from the post office you pay only for the cards that are returned and the permit fee. If you use postage stamps, you will pay for postage that might never be used.

To convince people to fill out your questionnaire, you might provide an incentive. One idea for an incentive is a discount from your normal fees. This idea might work, but it will look very commercial. A better idea might be to make the questionnaire look more like research. If you design the piece to look like a respectable research effort, more people will respond to your questions.

AVOID DELAYS IN MATERIAL DELIVERIES

If your materials are delayed, your jobs will be delayed. If your jobs are delayed, your payments will be delayed. If your payments are delayed, your cash flow and credit history might falter. If your cash flow dries up, your business is in trouble. Extended delays can result in the loss of your good credit rating or even your business. You can eliminate some of these potentially dangerous situations by avoiding delays in your material deliveries.

DEALING WITH SUPPLIERS

Dealing with suppliers is not as simple as placing an order and waiting. It is up to you to set the pace for all of your business dealings. This is not to say that you should be a radical dictator, but you should call the shots (FIG. 14-1 through FIG. 14-3).

It is wise to establish a routine with your suppliers. If you are going to use purchase orders, use them with every order. If you want job names written on your receipts, insist that they are always included. Are you going to allow employees to make purchases on your credit account? If so, set limits on how much can be purchased. Make sure everyone at the supply house knows which employees are authorized to charge on your account.

Get to know the manager of the supply house. Without a doubt there will come a time when you and the manager will have a problem to solve. At these times, it helps to know each other.

When you start using a new supplier, make sure you understand the house rules. What is the return policy? Will you be charged a restocking fee? Will you get a discount if you pay your bill early? What is your discount percentage? Will the discount remain the same, regardless of the volume you purchase? These are just some of the questions you should ask.

If all goes well, you will be doing a lot of business with your suppliers. Since each of you depends on the other to make money, you should develop the best relationship possible.

Your Company Name
Your Company Address

Dear Sir:

I am soliciting bids for the work listed below, and I would like to offer you the opportunity to participate in the bidding. If you are interested in giving quoted prices on <u>material</u> for this job, please let me hear from you, at the above address.

The job will be started in _____ weeks. Financing has been arranged and the job will be started on schedule. Your quote, if you choose to enter one, must be received no later than
_____.

The proposed work is as follows:

_____

_____

_____

Plans and specifications for the work are available upon request.

Thank you for your time and consideration in this request.

Sincerely,

Your name and title

14-1   Form letter for soliciting material quotes

EXPEDITE MATERIALS

Material handling accounts for much of the time contractors lose on a daily basis. If a worker has to leave the job to pick up materials at a supply house, time and money are lost. Inaccurate take-offs and deliveries that are poorly managed can cost you thousands of dollars. Is there anything that can be done to reduce these losses? Yes, expedite materials and you will save time and money.

Most contractors don't have an employee with the sole responsibility of getting materials on the job like some large companies do. These contractors must do their own material acquisitions and handling. When a person has to tend to multiple tasks, it is easy for some part of the job to be neglected. The expediting of materials is often pushed aside to make room for more pressing duties.

All too many contractors call in a material order and forget about it. They don't make follow-up calls to check the status of the material. It is not

Material Order Log

Supplier: _____

Date order was placed: _____

Time order was placed: _____

Name of person taking order: _____

Promised delivery date: _____

Order number: _____

Quoted price: _____

Date of follow-up call: _____

Manager's name: _____

Time of call to manager: _____

Manager confirmed delivery date: _____

Manager confirmed price: _____

Notes and Comments

_____

_____

_____

_____

_____

_____

_____

_____

_____

_____

_____

14-2 Material order log

Material Specifications

Phase	Item	Brand	Model	Color	Size
Plumbing	Lavatory	WXYA	497	White	19"×17"
Plumbing	Toilet	ABC12	21	White	12" rough
Plumbing	Shower	KYTCY	41	White	36"×36"
Electrical	Ceiling fan	SPARK	2345	Gold	30"
Electrical	Light kit	JFOR2	380	White	Standard
Flooring	Carpet	MISTY	32	Grey	14 yards

14-3 Material specification list

until the material doesn't show that these contractors take action. By then, time and money is lost.

A large number of contractors never inventory materials when they are delivered. If 400 feet of pipe was ordered, they assume they got 400 feet of pipe. Unfortunately, mistakes are frequently made with material deliveries. Quantities are not what they are supposed to be. Errors are made in the types of materials shipped. All of these problems add up to more lost time and money.

If you want to make your jobs run smoother, take some time to perfect your control over materials. When you place an order, have the order taker read the order back to you. Listen closely for mistakes. Call in advance to confirm delivery dates. If a supplier has forgotten to put you on the schedule, your phone call will correct the error before it becomes a problem.

When materials arrive, check the delivery for accuracy. Ideally, this should be done while the delivery driver is present. If you discover a fault with your order, immediately call the supplier. You can reduce your losses by catching blunders early.

Keep a log of material orders and expected delivery dates. One glance at the log will let you know the status of your orders. When you talk to various salespeople, record their names on your log. If there is a problem, it always helps to know who you talked to last. Get a handle on your materials and you will enjoy a more prosperous business.

15

Office space

For some businesses, location is vital to success. However, most plumbing businesses can function from a low-profile location. This is not to say that office space is not needed or is not important. Whether you work from your home or a penthouse suite, your office has to be functional and efficient if you want to make money.

HOME VS. COMMERCIAL SPACE

Most people will know if they have a need for commercial office space. I have worked from home and from commercial offices. My experience has shown that the decision to rent commercial space is dictated by your self discipline and the type of business you operate. Let's explore the factors you should consider before you decide where to set up shop.

Self discipline

If you are not able to make yourself stick to your work, you will find yourself out of business. It is easy to get caught up sitting around the breakfast table or taking a stroll around your farm. Working from home is very enjoyable, but you have to set rules and stick to them.

Storefront requirements

Some businesses have storefront requirements. Your plumbing business might need to display the fixtures it sells. If you need a storefront window, you probably can't work from home. But many plumbing companies do a brisk business without showrooms and window displays. Storefront space is expensive; if you don't need it, why pay for it?

Home office

A home office is a dream of many people. Putting your office in your home is a good way to save money, if it doesn't cost you more than you save. Home offices can have a detrimental effect on your business. Some people will assume that if you work from home you are not well established and might be a risky choice as a contractor.

I work from home now, and I have worked from home at different times for nearly 20 years. I love it. I am also very disciplined in my work ethic, and even though my office is in the home, it is set in professional style. When clients come to my home office, it is obvious that I am a professional. I will talk more about setting up a home office a little later, but take your home office seriously.

Commercial image

A commercial office can give you a commercial image. This image can do a world of good for your business, but the cost can be a heavy weight to carry. Before you jump into an expensive office suite, consider all aspects of your decision.

ASSESS YOUR OFFICE NEEDS

Before you decide where to put your office, assess your office needs. This part of your business planning will be instrumental to your success. Can you imagine opening your business in a fancy storefront and then, say six months later, having to move out of the expensive retail space? Not only would that situation be potentially embarrassing, it would be bad for business. Once people get to know your business and where it is located, they expect it to stay there or to move up. A downward move, like the scenario described, would alarm present customers and scare off a percentage of future customers. This is only one reason why office selection and location is important.

How much space do you need?

If you are the only person in your business, you might not need a lot of space in the office. The type of business you operate will determine the size office you will need. For example, an average plumbing business can be run with minimal office space. Instead, storage space is needed for pipe, fittings, fixtures, and such. Some plumbing companies, the ones that bid big commercial work, might need an elegant office environment to entertain general contractors. A plumbing company that concentrates on drain cleaning will have little need for an expansive office or storage space. Tailor your office to your business.

When you consider your space requirements take time to sketch out your proposed office space. It helps if you make the drawing to scale. How many people will you meet with at any given time? How many desks will be in the office? I'm now a one-man business, not counting subcontractors, but I have two desks and a sorting table in my primary office. In addition, I have another room designated as my library and meeting room, another space set up as a darkroom, and a photography studio in my basement. My barn stores my tools, equipment, and supplies. You see, even a small business can need large spaces.

As you design your office, consider all your needs. Desks and chairs are only the beginning. Will you have a separate computer work station? Do you need a conference table? Where will your filing cabinets go? Where and how will you store your office supplies? How many electrical outlets will you need? The more questions you ask and answer before you make an office commitment, the better your chances are of making a good decision.

Do you need a storefront?

Almost any business can do better with commercial visibility, but the benefits of this visibility might not warrant the extra cost. If you are out in the field working every day, and you don't have an employee in the office, what good will it do to have a storefront? A person looking for a replacement plumbing part is not going to come back to your store hours later if the store is closed. That individual is going to find a store that is open and has the part, unless you are the only game in town. If your business allows you to remain in the office most of the time, a storefront might be beneficial. You might get some walk-in business that you wouldn't get working out of your home. In general, if you can't be there to mind the store, you don't need the store.

Do you need warehouse space?

If you have to keep large quantities of supplies on hand or deal in bulky items, warehouse storage might be essential. A popular solution for office and storage space is a unit that combines both under the same roof. These office/warehouse spaces are efficient, professional, and normally not outrageously expensive.

If you don't need fast access to the materials you put in storage, renting a space at a private storage facility might be the best financial solution. At one time, I ran a medium-sized plumbing company from a small office and a private storage facility. This arrangement was not convenient, but it was cost effective, and it worked.

Where will you be located?

If you provide in-home service to customers in the city, living in the country can be inconvenient. It also can cause you to lose customers, especially if you charge extra for travel time. Having an office where you are allowed to display a large sign is excellent advertising and builds name recognition for your company. If your office is in a remote section of the city, people might not want to come to it. If you work from your home, and your home happens to be out in the boonies, customers might not be able to find you, even if they are willing to try.

Aside from the prestige angle of office location, you must consider the convenience of your customers. If your office is at the top of six flights of steps, with no elevators available, people might not want to do business with you. If there is not adequate parking in the immediate vicinity of your office, you might lose potential customers. All of these location factors play a part in your public image and success.

What public image do you need?

Public opinion is fickle, but important. If your business is perceived to be successful, it probably will become successful. On the other hand, if the public sees your business as a loser, look out. The location of your office probably has nothing to do with the quality of your service but the public thinks it does. For this reason, you must cater to the people you hope will become your customers.

If you are dealing with a business where a downtown office is expected, plan to work your way into a downtown office. If you don't, a time will come when your customer base will peak and stagnate. There are only so many people that will deal with you when your business is unconventional.

How much office can you afford?

When you look at your office expense budget, you must consider all the costs related to the office: heat, electricity, cleaning, parking, snow removal, and other expenses. These incidental expenses can add up to more than the cost to rent the office.

If you rent an office in the summer, you might not think to ask about heating expenses. In Maine, the cost of heating an office can easily exceed the monthly rent on the space. When you determine your office budget, take all related expenses into account. Come up with a budget number with which you are comfortable. Then make sure you keep your office rent and related expenses within your budget.

When you begin shopping for an office outside of your home, ask lots of questions. Who pays for trash removal? Who pays the water and sewer bill? Who pays the taxes on the building? Some leases require you, the lessee, to pay the property taxes. Who pays the heating expenses? Who pays for electricity? Who pays for cleaning the office? Does the receptionist in the lower level of the building cost extra? If there is office equipment in a common area, like a copier for example, what does it cost to use the equipment? Your list of questions could go on and on.

Ask all the questions and get answers. If you are required to pay for routine expenses, like heat or electricity, ask to see the bills for the last year. These bills will give you an idea of what your additional office expenses will be.

Before you rent an office, consider the ups and downs in your business cycle. If you are in a business that drops off in the winter, will you still be able to afford the office? Do you have to sign a long-term lease, or will you be on a month-to-month basis? It usually costs more to be on a month-to-month basis, but for a new business a long-term lease can spell trouble. If you sign a long lease and default on it, your credit rating can be hurt. What happens if your business booms and you need to add office help? If you are in a tiny office with a long-term lease, you've got a problem. If you do opt for a long-term lease, negotiate for a sub-lease clause that will allow you to rent the office to someone else if you have to move.

It can be easy to fantasize about how a new office will bring you more business. It's fine to enjoy this thought, but don't put yourself in a trap. When you project your office budget, base your forecast on your present workload and be conservative in your projections for the future.

Many new business owners get carried away with their offices. They look for space with marble columns, fancy floors, wet bars, and all the glitter depicted in offices on television. Well, unless you are independently wealthy, these lavish work spaces can rob you of your profits. Not only will the cost of the office drain your cash flow, you might lose business because of your expensive taste. That's right, you might lose business by renting a great office.

Consumers aren't stupid. It doesn't take long to figure out that if a company has high office overhead, the customers are paying for it. The flashy office might be fun, and it might be impressive, but it also might be bad for business. Of course, this will depend on the type of business you have and your clientele, but don't assume that an expensive office is going to get you higher net earnings.

ANSWERING SERVICE OR ANSWERING MACHINE

When the pros and cons of answering services are compared to answering machines, you might find many different opinions. Most people prefer to talk to a live person, rather than a cold, electronic machine. However, as our lives become more automated, the public is slowly accepting the use of electronic message storage and retrieval.

When you shop for services, which do you prefer, an answering service or an answering machine? Do most of your competitors use machines or live people to answer their phones? This is easy to research, just call your competitors and see how the phone is answered. It's pretty well accepted that the use of an answering machine can cause you to lose business, but that doesn't mean that you should not consider the use of a machine.

Answering machines are relatively inexpensive and most machines are dependable. These two points give the answering machine an advantage over an answering service. Answering services are not cheap, and they are not always dependable. But more callers will leave a message with an answering service than will on a machine. This point goes in favor of the answering service. Answering services also can page you to give you important and time-sensitive messages; answering machines can't. Are you confused yet? Don't worry, we'll sort it all out.

To determine which method you should use, let's make a list of the advantages and disadvantages of each.

Qualities to look for in an answering machine

Look for an answering machine that lets you check your messages remotely from any phone. Choose a machine that allows the caller to leave a long message. These machines are voice activated and will cut off only when the caller stops speaking. Pick a machine that will allow you to record and use a personal outgoing message. If you buy an answering machine that meets all of these criteria, you should be satisfied with its performance.

What should you look for in an answering service?

Price is always a consideration, but don't be too cheap; you might get what you pay for. Find an answering service that answers the phone and takes messages in a professional manner. You want a dependable service that will see that you get all of your messages. Ask if you can provide a script for the operators to use when they answer your phone. Some services answer all the phones with the same greeting, but many will answer your line any way you like.

Ask what hours of the day you will get coverage. Most services provide 24-hour service, but it generally costs extra. Ask if the service will page you for time-sensitive calls; most will. Determine if your bill will be a flat rate or if it will fluctuate based on the number of calls you get. Inquire about the length of commitment you must make. Some answering services will allow you to go on a month-to-month basis; others will want a long-term commitment.

If you decide to use an answering service, periodically check on their performance. Most services provide a special number for you to call to pick up your messages, especially if they base your bill on the number of calls taken on your phone line. Even if you have to pay when you call in on your own line, do it every now and then. You will get first-hand proof of how they handle your calls. Have friends call and leave messages. The operators won't recognize the voices of these people and will treat them like any other customer. This is the best way to check the performance of human answering services.

Which way should you go?

If callers expect fast service from your business, go with an answering service. When people with emergency repair needs call and get a machine, they will call around to find another plumber. If you have a business that doesn't require immediate response, such as new-construction plumbing, a machine might serve your needs. You will lose some business, but you will also save some money.

I think the business you lose with an answering machine is more valuable than the money you save. If you can hire a human answering service, I think you should. I have had my phones answered each way and I am convinced that human answering services are the best way to go.

16

Computers and software

Computers and software have made a monumental impact on the way modern business is conducted. A computer is likely to be one of your equipment purchases. With the use of computers and the associated peripherals that go with them, a business can do almost any office task faster and in most cases, better.

Modems send documents over the phone lines from one computer to another. Credit checks can be flashed on a monitor in a matter of moments. Bookkeeping can be done by people who would never attempt such a task without the aid of computers and software. Scanners can put hand-drawn sketches into the computer for modification. Estimating programs can take the guesswork out of job quotes. Computers are truly remarkable.

Many people are intimidated by computers and will never learn to benefit from modern technology. When you compete against this group of people, computers can give you a competitive edge.

COMPUTERS ARE A WAY OF LIFE

Most businesses that have used computers for any length of time wouldn't know how to operate without them. Dependency starts with a word-processing software package. You see how much easier it is to prepare your contracts and correspondence on the computer. You no longer need correction tape for the old typewriter. Saving forms on your computer disk makes it fast and easy to turn out proposals, letters, and much more.

The next step is spreadsheet software. You start playing the what-if game and get excited about the potential of your company. Suddenly, forecasting the future and tracking your budget is fun. Your software can produce graphs and charts to track your production and predict the future (FIG. 16-1 through FIG. 16-3). You are starting to get hooked.

Then, you experiment with database programs. Mailing lists were never so easy to accumulate and use. Marketing is much easier with your new,

151

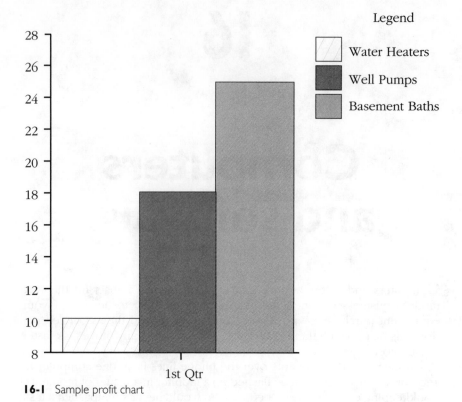

Legend
- Water Heaters
- Well Pumps
- Basement Baths

16-1 Sample profit chart

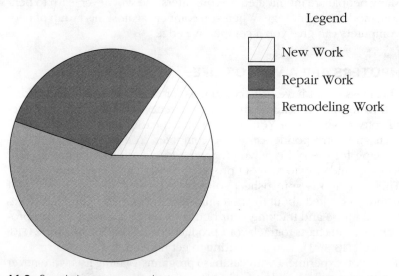

Legend
- New Work
- Repair Work
- Remodeling Work

16-2 Sample income source chart

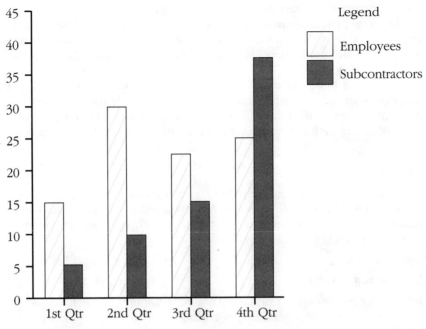

16-3 Labor comparison graph

computerized customer base. Checking inventory is a snap, and storing historical data is a breeze.

With a little more time you get into accounting programs and automated payroll. A little playful study and you find you can do what you've been paying other people to do for you. For the one-time cost of your software, you eliminate a routine overhead expense.

If you don't like the idea of using computers, you might find this scenario hard to believe, but don't be surprised to find yourself in a similar situation.

WILL A COMPUTER HELP YOUR BUSINESS?

A computer can help your business in a myriad of ways. You can perform almost any clerical or financial function on a computer. You can draw riser diagrams on a computer. Marketing and advertising will be easier when you utilize the help of a computer. Inventory control and customer billing will almost take care of themselves on a computer. When you take the time to look, you will see that there are dozens of ways for your business to benefit from the use of computers.

Marketing

Marketing can be done more efficiently with a computer. You can build a database file of all your customers and potential customers. Then you can print mailing labels for all of these names. If you use telemarketing, you can use computers to conduct your cold-calling surveys.

Drawing programs enable you to create logos and flashy flyers. By using the creative options available with your computer and drawing program, you can attract attention to your business and cut down on your outside printing costs.

Following historical data is easy with a computer. With just a few keystrokes you can see what water heaters were selling for two years ago. A few more taps on the keys will display your most profitable type of work. Computers can definitely make your marketing more effective and faster.

Payroll

If you have employees on the payroll, you will enjoy the automated features available on payroll software. After you enter a minimal amount of data, the computer will run your payroll for you. This is a real timesaver for companies with several employees.

Job-costing results

Job-costing results can be printed out of your computer files in minutes. Not only will computer-generated job-costing numbers come about more quickly, they will probably be more accurate.

Tracking your budget

You can boot up the computer and see where you stand at anytime during the year. This is not only convenient, it can keep you from busting your budget.

Projecting tax liabilities

If you are wondering how much money you will need at tax time, just ask the computer. Without hesitation the computer will give you the information you need to plan for your tax deposits.

Computerized estimating

There are systems available that almost do estimates for you. Of course, you have to give the machine a little help, but not much. Move a pen across the blueprints, and you can have take-offs done before you could get started manually.

Word processing

With built-in spell checkers and thesauruses, today's word-processing software takes the drudgery out of writing a letter. If your grammar skills are rough around the edges, incorporate grammar software to correct your writing.

Databases

Databases are used to store information on any subject. Whether you want to know the cost of a well pump or when your trucks are due for service, a database file can do the job. Design the database file to include as much or as little information as you like. Sorting these electronic files is much easier than digging through an old filing cabinet.

Checks and balances

If you don't like writing checks or keeping track of your bank balance, let the computer do it for you. There are dozens of programs and forms available for paying your bills. As a side benefit, the computer will make adjustments to your bookkeeping records as it goes.

Customer service

Customer service can be improved with the use of computers. When you receive a warranty call you can quickly determine if the job is still covered under warranty. When your customers are having a birthday, your computer can remind you to send out a birthday card. If your customers require routine maintenance, like charging their water-treatment equipment, the computer can send out reminders to the customers of their service needs.

Inventory control

Inventory control is made faster and more efficient with the use of a computer (FIG. 16-4). As your stock is depleted, the computer can tell you what to order. At the end of the year you won't have to spend hours going into the back room to count your inventory. All you have to do is ask the computer to print a report, and in moments your inventory will be done.

Personal secretary

With a memory-resident program, your computer becomes a personal secretary. The machine will beep to let you know it is time for your next appointment. You can store phone numbers in the computer and have it dial your calls for you via a modem. The right software will all but replace your old appointment book. With the touch of a hot key you can scan all of your appointments, as far in advance as you like.

The fact is, computers and software can tackle about any job you throw at them. I'm not suggesting that people should be replaced with machines, but there is definitely a place for computers in your business.

BUILD CUSTOMER CREDIBILITY

Computers can lend an air of distinction to your company. In some circumstances, the credibility will be gained as a result of customers having direct contact with the computer. In other cases, the confidence is built by what

Inventory Log

Item	Quantity	ID Number	Checked By	Date

16-4 Inventory log

the computer allows you to do. Let's see how these two different approaches work.

Direct-contact approach

The direct-contact approach is the method most often recognized. An example might be when customers come into your office and comment on your computer system. There is no doubt that the visual effect of the hardware impresses customers.

Another means of building credibility through direct contact might come from demonstrating the power of your computerized system. For example, assume you have a young couple come to your office to discuss their plans for remodeling their bathroom. The couple has a rough sketch of what they want, but it is not drawn to scale. Other contractors they have visited made photocopies of the sketch and let it go at that. But you are going to be different; you are going to make a lasting impression on this young couple.

When the couple produces their well-worn line drawing, you look it over. Then you get up and put it on your flat-bed scanner. The couple watches, at first thinking you are making a normal copy of the drawing. When they see their sketch come up on your computer screen, they are amazed. But the show's not over.

Now you take your mouse, a computer drawing aid, and begin drawing lines on the monitor. In less than 15 minutes you have converted the rough sketch into a scale drawing of the couple's dream. As you talk to the potential customers you make adjustments to the on-screen drawing, moving the lavatory bowl down the counter to create space for a make-up area. In less than an hour you have a viable plan drawn for the anxious customers.

Now tell me, which contractor would you hire to remodel your bathroom? The one who made a photocopy or the one that took the time and had the technology to produce a professional drawing? I think the answer is obvious. Even if the computerized contractor wanted more money for the same job, you would probably assume he was worth it. As you can see, with a little thought you can use computers as sales tools.

The indirect approach

The indirect approach relies not on what the system looks like, but what you do with it. Assume for a moment that you are a homeowner. You are soliciting bids for a new basement bath. During your search you narrow the field of plumbers down to two. The two contractors are evenly matched in their prices, references, and apparent knowledge of plumbing and remodeling. Who will you choose? You start your reconsideration by going back over the bid packages.

The first contractor, Bill's Basement Bathrooms, Inc. has submitted a bid package similar to the other contractors. You received a fill-in-the-blank proposal form, the type available in office supply stores. The proposal had been typed, but it is obvious the preparer was not a typist. Bill's references checked out, even if they were handwritten on a piece of yellow legal paper. The plans Bill submitted were drawn in pencil. The graph paper was stained, probably from coffee. While there was a spec sheet in the package, it was vague. In general, Bill's bid package was complete, but it wasn't professional.

Bill's competitor, Pioneer Plumbing, Ltd., submitted essentially the same information, but the method of presentation was considerably different. The contract from Pioneer Plumbing was clean and neatly printed with a laser printer. The paper the contract was printed on was of a heavy, high-quality stock. The accompanying specification sheet was thorough. It listed every item and specified the items in complete detail.

The reference list supplied by Pioneer was printed with the same quality as the contract, and the references were all satisfied customers. The plans were drafted on a computer and showed the new bathroom in great detail.

The bid package from Pioneer Plumbing, Ltd. was compiled in an attractive binder. It exuded professionalism. Since all factors seem equal, except the bid packages, you decide to give the job to Pioneer.

If this were a true story, which contractor would you have chosen? I believe you would have picked Pioneer Plumbing, Ltd. Sometimes all it takes to win the job is a good presentation. Computers can help you make fantastic presentations.

SPREADSHEETS, DATABASES, AND WORD PROCESSING

Spreadsheets, databases, and word-processing software applications are what the majority of business owners use most. You can buy each of these programs as stand-alone software, or you can buy a software package that incorporates all of these features into one package. Most of these combo packages are called integrated packages.

Should you buy an integrated package or stand-alone programs? Both types of software are good, but the answer to the question depends on your needs and desires. If you are new to computers, an integrated package might be your best choice. Many stand-alone programs are more complex than the individual modules in integrated packages.

You don't have to spend a fortune for software. Once you get into the computer scene you will find a flood of inexpensive software. Some of this bargain-basement software is great, and some of it leaves a lot to be desired. For less than $5 you can test drive the software with a demo disk before you buy the package.

You can find almost any software combination you want. If you opt for a major-brand software you might need some time to get acquainted with your purchase. There are some excellent reference books available to help you learn these software applications. If you go for the inexpensive, generic software, you will have more trouble finding after-market resource directories.

Let's take a look at some of the pros and cons of each type of software.

Spreadsheets

Choosing the best spreadsheet for your business needs will require some research. There are dozens of programs that can get the job done. Some of these programs cost hundreds of dollars and others can be had for about $50.

One of the most popular spreadsheet programs has spawned a low-cost, generic competitor. The name-brand program will cost upwards of $250; the clone will run about $50. Other than one function, a financial function that deals with depreciation, I haven't found any substantial difference between the two, other than the price.

Databases

Think of database software as your opportunity to file and retrieve any information you want. Sorting and retrieving information in a database is easy. Printing reports and mailing labels is no problem when you have a database program. If you would keep it in a filing cabinet, you can keep it in a database.

Word processing

Word processing is probably the most frequently used type of software available. This type of software is great! You can write and store form letters. You can merge names into the form letters to achieve a personalized mailing. If you make a mistake in your typing you don't need correction tape or correction fluid. With word-processing software, you simply type over your mistakes. Word-processing programs can be used for all your correspondence needs.

Integrated programs

Integrated programs combine spreadsheet, database, and word-processing software into a single software package. These combo programs are efficient and relatively inexpensive. While most integrated programs are not full-featured software, they can satisfy the needs of many small- to average-sized businesses.

Computer-aided-drafting programs

If you deal in floor plans, riser diagrams, or any other type of technical drawings, you can benefit from a computer-aided-drafting (CAD) program. CAD programs allow people who can't free-hand draw to produce professional plans and diagrams.

HARDWARE DECISIONS

While some people buy computer equipment to satisfy their curiosity or their got-to-have-it impulses, selecting the hardware for your computer is serious business. What should you look for in computer hardware? Let's find out.

Desktop computers

Desktop units are available in many configurations and speeds. No matter what your needs are, there is a desktop computer available to meet them. Desktop computers can be purchased for less than $1,000, or you can spend upwards of $10,000. The difference in price is determined by many factors. One factor is name recognition. Other factors include speed, memory, features, and more.

Laptop computers

Laptop computers are taking the market by storm. These mini powerhouses are capable of the same tasks as many desktop units. The compact size and portability of laptops make them especially desirable for busy people on the move.

You might think you have to give up features for portability, but you don't. It is possible to find as many features in a laptop as you will find in the average desktop unit. It is not uncommon to find laptops with huge hard drives and blazing clock speeds. Couple these features with a VGA screen and the freedom of battery-operated power, and you've got a winner.

Notebook computers

Notebook computers resemble laptop computers, but are typically smaller and lighter. For this size advantage, you normally will have to sacrifice some features. Notebook computers are fine as a second computer, but I wouldn't recommend one for a primary computer.

Computer memory

Older computers operated with 512 kilobytes (K) of random-access memory (RAM). There are still many computers available with 512K of memory. This is adequate memory for running most software, but much of the newer software requires more RAM. If you don't want to be restricted in software, buy a computer with 640K of memory. Additional memory can be added to most desktop and many laptop units. One megabyte of memory is not uncommon and memory expansion can go much higher.

If you will be doing a lot of CAD work, you will probably want at least two megabytes of memory and possibly more. If your computer doesn't have enough memory, complex drawings will not be able to load from the files into the computer's memory. This means you will not be able to get the drawing on your monitor.

Computer speed

How fast is fast enough? Some applications will be painfully slow with older, slower computers. If you are doing CAD work, a slow computer will drive you crazy. In the time it takes a slow computer to redraw your drafting project, you can get a cup of coffee, open your mail, and pace around the computer. If you plan to use CAD programs, get the fastest machine you can afford.

If you will use your computer primarily for word processing, its speed and memory are not as important. Almost any computer will allow you to use word-processing software.

Database work is more enjoyable with a fast computer, but high speed is not essential. Your memory requirements will depend on the type of database software you have, but most programs will work with minimal memory.

How do you judge the speed of a computer? The first way is by name: an XT computer is slower than an AT computer. You also can get an idea of a computer's speed by its number designation. A 486 machine is extremely fast, a 386 machine is very fast, and a 286 machine is fast.

To determine the exact speed of individual computers, you must look at the megahertz (MHz) rating. The higher the number in the megahertz rating, the faster the machine. For example, not all 386 machines run at the same speed. You might find one 386 with a speed of 16 MHz and another with a speed of 20 MHz. The machine with the 20-MHz rating is the faster of the two machines.

Hard drives

Hard drives or hard disks are storage devices found inside a computer. Not all computers have hard disks. Some computers operate on floppy-disk drives. Many software programs require a hard drive because of the size of the software files. If you are planning to do serious work on your computer, you will want a hard drive. Hard drives are faster and more convenient than floppy drives.

Hard drives come in many sizes. The size determines how much data can be stored. For example, a 20-megabyte hard drive will hold only half as much data as a 40-megabyte drive. What size hard drive do you need? At a minimum you should have a 20-megabyte hard drive. A 40-megabyte drive will allow you more room for expansion. If you are planning to store a high volume of graphic and CAD files, you will need a much larger hard drive.

Floppy-disk drives

Floppy-disk drives can be mounted in the housing of a computer, or they can be independent units that connect to the computer with a cable. Not long ago, many computers depended on floppy-disk drives for their operation. Today, hard drives are taking over. Even when computers have hard drives, they usually have floppy drives, as well. Common floppy-disk drives come in two sizes: 5¼" and 3½". The most popular size is 3½".

CGA monitors

CGA monitors are color monitors at the low-end of the price spectrum. If you will be using your computer for short periods of time, a CGA monitor will do fine. If you will be spending hours staring at the screen, you owe it to your eyes to get a better monitor. If you will be doing graphic work, you will want a more expensive monitor. Before you buy any monitor, make sure it is compatible with your computer. Not all monitors work with all computers.

EGA monitors

EGA monitors are a step up from CGA monitors. If you want more than a CGA monitor, however, I recommend moving up to a VGA monitor.

VGA monitors

VGA monitors are much easier on your eyes than the less expensive monitors. If you are doing graphic work, you almost have to have a VGA monitor. When you spend your whole day in front of the monitor, a VGA is much easier on your eyes.

Laser printers

Laser printers are considered the best printers you can buy. They turn out beautiful work, and offer creative options not available with other printers. If you plan to do graphics and CAD work, a laser is well worth the expense. For letters and reports, a dot-matrix printer will get the job done.

Letter-quality printers

Letter-quality printers produce documents that appear to have been typed on a typewriter. These printers do neat text, but they are dreadfully slow.

Dot-matrix printers

A dot-matrix printer might serve most of your needs. These impact printers are fast. When you want to check your job cost, you can run off a report, in draft-mode, before you can walk across the office. If you want your text to be dark and pretty, you can switch to the near-letter-quality mode. In this mode the printer prints at about half the speed it would in draft-mode, but it is still faster than a letter-quality printer.

The quality of the text produced with a dot-matrix printer can't compare with that of a laser or letter-quality printer, but it is fine for most business applications.

Other printers

There are, of course, other types of printers. There are thermal printers and printers that spray ink on the paper. With a little shopping you can see all of the available printers. The printers I detailed are the most popular.

Modems

Modems are devices that allow computers to talk to each other over telephone lines. Some modems are inside computers and others sit outside the computer and attach with a cable. You can add a modem at any time, and you probably won't need one in the beginning.

Mouse

A mouse, in computer terms, is a device used for drawing on the computer and for clicking on commands. If you will be doing graphic work, you will want a mouse. For everyday office work you should be able to get by without one.

17

Customer relations

Customers give your business value. How you treat existing customers will influence the long-range success of your business. If you alienate customers, they won't give you return business or referrals. It is much less expensive to keep good customers than it is to find them. Once you have established a customer base, work hard to maintain it.

MEET CUSTOMERS ON THEIR LEVEL

When you work with people, you want them to be as comfortable as possible. For this reason, you have to be able to change clothes and personalities. The most successful sales people are the ones who are chameleons. These gifted people can move up and down the social ladder to serve any prospect who comes along. This flexibility is an advantage the average salesperson doesn't possess. Being able to assume the personality of a customer makes it easier to close a deal.

Fitting in, with what you wear and drive, is another key to sales success. This might mean wearing a suit in the morning and jeans in the afternoon. You might find it advantageous to switch from your family car to your pickup truck. The more effort you put into blending in with your customers, the more sales you will make.

GAIN THE CUSTOMER'S CONFIDENCE

To get the confidence of your customer, you have to spend time talking. Talk about the customer's children, grandchildren, hobbies, car, or anything else that seems appropriate. You can get a good idea of how to start the conversation by looking at the pictures in the customer's home. If you see pictures of horses, talk about horses. If you see pictures of flowers, talk about flowers. Always allow the customer to lead the conversation. You can't afford to take a chance on saying the wrong thing.

After you have talked with the customer for awhile, talk a little business. If you seem to be losing the customer, go back to talking about a friendly subject. Tell stories about your life. Let the customer get to know you. Once you have settled in with the customer, getting the sale will be much easier.

SIMPLE SALES TACTICS SELL MORE JOBS

When you respond to a request for an estimate, how do you handle the situation? Do you get to know the potential customer? Do you look over the job and then call back with a price or do you mail the estimate? Do you follow up on your estimate to confirm its status? How you handle estimates can affect your sales percentages.

All contractors are salespeople of a sort. You need sales to stay in business. By incorporating simple sales tactics into your day-to-day life, your business can enjoy more success.

Professional sales people spend time getting to know their prospects. Call it breaking the ice, probing, or whatever you want, but you will be more successful if you show an interest in your prospects. Whenever possible, arrange a meeting to go over your estimate with potential customers. If you mail or call in the price of a job, you have little opportunity to pitch the advantages of your company. A sit-down meeting will always produce more sales.

Following up on your estimate is also important. Most contractors don't check the status of their estimates. If you make a follow-up call, you have a second chance to sell the customer. Even if you don't get the job, you can get feedback on why you didn't get it. If you find out what you are doing wrong, you can amend your tactics and build a better business.

BEFORE-AND-AFTER PHOTOS SELL JOBS

When you have the opportunity, take photos of your jobs before, during, and after your work. These photos build credibility and can be used as a part of your reference package. Photographs are also good for giving new customers ideas.

Create an album of all your before-and-after shots. Take the album with you on all of your sales calls, and don't hesitate to show it to potential customers. You can use the photos to point out methods you use that your competition doesn't.

PROFESSIONAL PROPOSALS SELL JOBS

When you present your proposal, arrange for all the buying power to be present. This normally means having husband and wife both at the table. You don't want to have your closing of the sale blocked by the old line, "I'll talk it over with my spouse and get back to you."

Set the meeting for a time and place where the customer will be at ease. The customer's home is a good place to meet. Pick a time that will be conducive to an uninterrupted meeting. Don't set the meeting too close to dinner time. Allow up to two hours to close large sales. I've found that if I can stay in front of the buying power for between one and two hours, I'll get the sale.

When you present your proposal, pitch your good points. Tell the prospect how your work is better than average. Don't name names and criticize specific competitors. This is a cheap shot and will not be respected by most prospects. Study sales techniques and practice your presentation skills. When you become competent in sales methods, your business will grow.

CLOSE THE SALE

Closing a sale might not be the first consideration in your job description, but without sales, you will not have a job. Like it or not, you must be sales orientated. If you don't have the ability or inclination to make sales, hire sales professionals. But one way or another, you need sales.

The easiest way to close a sale is to ask the customer for the sale. You might be surprised how many contractors are afraid to ask for a "yes." If you aren't willing to ask the customer to commit to your offer, you won't get many jobs. Customers expect you to ask for the sale, so you might as well accommodate them.

Not all closings are easy. I have spent hours closing sales. I have been asked to leave as many as three times and still made the sale. Over the years I have developed many sales skills. I learned how to sell by reading how-to books and through on-the-job experience. I don't think I could have been as successful without both of these learning opportunities. The books gave me ideas and formulas. The real-world experience allowed me to refine what I read and to develop my own style.

Back when I was keeping track, I had a closing ratio of 65 percent. That means that I was selling more than half of the jobs I went out to estimate. You might think I was giving the jobs away, but I wasn't. Many times my prices were higher than other bids. I won the jobs with my sales skills, and you can too.

Until you learn to close sales, your business will not work to its maximum production. Take some time to study books on sales techniques and don't be afraid to try them out. Even if you are not a master at sales tactics, you will be ahead of most of your competition. Never underestimate the power of marketing, advertising, and sales skills.

SATISFY YOUR CUSTOMERS

To learn how to keep your customers satisfied, you must look at each customer individually. There will, of course, be similarities between customers, but each person will have at least a slightly different opinion of what is required of you. There are some basic principles to follow when you work with customers, they are:

- Keep your promises.
- Promptly return phone calls.
- Maintain an open and honest relationship.

- Be punctual.
- Listen to the requests of your customers.
- Do good work.
- Don't overcharge consumers.
- Stand behind your work.
- Be professional at all times.
- Don't take your customers for granted.
- Put priority on warranty work.
- When feasible, give customers what they want.
- If possible, give customers more than they expect.

If you follow the basic rules of customer satisfaction, you should have a high ratio of happy patrons. There will, of course, be some customers you can't satisfy. Some of these people don't know themselves what it will take to make them happy. When you run into this type of client, grin and bear it.

Even if a customer is being irrational, go to extremes to please him. One angry customer will spread more word-of-mouth advertising than 10 satisfied customers. You don't want the type of publicity a disgruntled customer will give you.

If you reach a point where you can't deal with an unreasonable person, end the connection as quickly and professionally as you can. Avoid name calling and arguments. If the customer is dead wrong, defend your position. If the circumstances are questionable, cut your losses and get out of the game. Avoiding conflicts and striving for customer satisfaction will do you more good than standing on a soapbox, screaming to the world that someone is a jerk.

BUILD A REFERENCE LIST

As you probably know, building a reference list from existing customers is an excellent way to produce new business. Ask your customers to give you a letter of reference or to complete a performance-rating card and you will compile a valuable stack of ready references.

Asking customers for the names and phone numbers of friends or relatives is another way to get new business. For example, assume you are nearing completion of a bathroom remodeling job. You might ask the customer for the names and phone numbers of her neighbors. That evening, call the neighbors and introduce yourself as the plumbing contractor working on Mrs. Smith's remodeling project. Explain to the neighbors that the Smith job is nearing completion, and that you wanted to see if they had any work that needed to be done before you pulled your crews and equipment out of the area. Further explain how you can offer special pricing and discounts for any work they want done now, since your people and equipment are already working in the neighborhood.

You have a good chance of starting a conversation when you know the neighbor's name. By giving Mrs. Smith's name as a reference, you have a good chance of keeping the conversation going. Your offer to discount your services sounds viable, and you might be surprised how many neighbors will take you up on your offer.

LEARN TO DEFUSE TENSE SITUATIONS

If you choose not to work on ways to handle difficult situations, you will have a tough time in business. All business deals have the potential to turn into tense situations. It doesn't take much to make a good deal turn sour. Many times jobs will run smoothly until the last few days of the project. For some reason, the end of the job seems to be the most difficult hurdle to get over.

When a job is nearly complete, you have expended a lot of time, money, and energy to get and keep a happy customer. If you lose control at the end of the job, all of your previous efforts will be wasted. Normally, talking through a bad time will solve the problem.

Sometimes just being a good listener is enough to resolve disputes. Some people get anger out of their systems by yelling and screaming. Some people deal with anger by beating their bed. When a human being is consumed with anger, the results are unpredictable.

Most on-the-job confrontations don't elevate to extreme limits. Generally, work-related disputes can be resolved with open communication and occasionally, compromise. Every angry customer will react a little differently. It might be necessary to step away from the argument and look at the real reasons why the blow up has occurred. The best you can do is remain calm and reasonable.

CALM DISGRUNTLED CUSTOMERS

Calming a disgruntled customer is similar to defusing a tense situation, but it might not always be the same. A customer can be dissatisfied without being physically upset. In fact, the calm customer who is displeased can be more difficult to work with than the customer who is shouting in rage.

When you have an unhappy customer on your hands, find a remedy that will appease the client. If you are able to carry on a normal conversation with the consumer, resolving the problem shouldn't be too difficult.

Ask your customer why he is dissatisfied. Before making a rebuttal, consider the other person's position. Does he have a legitimate gripe? If he does, take action to rectify the situation. If you disagree with the customer's opinion, discuss the problem in more depth.

Before you start a debate, put the customer at ease. Assure him that you are willing to be reasonable, but that you need more facts to understand his position fully. Start this way and the customer should remain calm and businesslike. On the other hand, if you open your defense aggressively, the situation might escalate to a tense and unpleasant shouting match.

It is usually best to attempt a settlement of disputes in a relaxed atmosphere. If your crews are banging pipe and buzzing saws or drills, ask the customer if the two of you can find a more suitable place to discuss your differences. This accomplishes two goals—you get the customer in a congenial setting, and your workers will not witness the disagreement.

After relocating, ask the client to repeat his grievance. Pay close attention, and see if the story remains the same. If the customer comes up with additional complaints or a great variance from the initial comments, you might have some additional trouble. This behavior might indicate a person that is going to be hard to please. However, if the complaint is essentially the same as it was when you first heard it, you have a good chance of ending your discussion in concurrence.

Think before you speak. If you are good at thinking on your feet, you will do better than people who must meditate before coming to a conclusion. Your customer is going to expect answers now, not next week. Once you know what you want to say, say it sincerely and with conviction. Let the customer know you believe strongly in your position, but that you are willing to compromise.

You might find that you and your customer will exchange several opinions and offers before you reach an amicable decision. Once the two of you agree on a plan, put the plan in writing. Write a change order for the compromise to seal the deal and reduce the risk of having to negotiate it further at a later date.

AVOID ON-THE-JOB DECISIONS

When you make snap decisions you are likely to make some mistakes. These mistakes might run the gamut from upsetting the homeowner to causing you extra work. When possible, give yourself some time to consider your decisions. Of course, there will be times when you have to shoot from the hip, but avoid quick decisions when you can.

There are, of course, dozens of other potential pitfalls you might encounter in the plumbing business. Pay close attention to your business at all times, and always be ready and willing to make changes. If you are judicious in your decisions and projections, your business should last a lifetime.

18

Work sources

Building business clientele is one of your most important jobs as a business owner. Learning how to win bids is one of the most effective ways to build your business clientele. Many contractors never figure out how to win bids successfully. This chapter is going to show you how to win bids and build up your business.

WORD-OF-MOUTH REFERRALS

Word-of-mouth referrals are the best way to get new business. Every time you get a job, work that customer for referrals that will lead to more work. Getting referrals from existing customers is not only the most effective way to generate new business, it's the least expensive. If you can turn up new work from talking with existing customers, you eliminate the cost of advertising.

If you do good work and take care of your customers, referrals will be easy to get. People will sometimes give your name and number to friends, and they occasionally write nice letters. However, to make the most of word-of-mouth referrals, you have to ask for what you want. Let's see what it takes to get the most mileage out of your existing customers.

Lay the ground work

Make your first contact with the customer professional and maintain this image to the end. Many contractors start off on the right foot, only to stumble before the job is done. I have seen many jobs go sour in the final days of their completion.

One of the largest mistakes I have seen contractors make is not responding promptly to warranty calls. If you are in business for the long haul, you don't want to alienate customers, even after the job is done. Old customers often become repeat customers. If you don't respond to callbacks, you won't be called when there is new, paying work to be done.

During the job

Cater to the customer. Most contractors don't have a problem with this aspect of customer satisfaction, but there is more to making customers happy than doing good work. You have to fulfill your promises, be punctual, be respectful, and be professional.

At the end of the job

When you complete a job, ask your customer to fill out and sign a reference form. Do it on the spot. Once you are out of the house, getting the form completed and signed will be more difficult. If you design a simple form (FIG. 18-1), almost all satisfied customers will complete and sign it.

As you begin building a good collection of reference forms, don't hesitate to show them to prospective customers. Use an attractive three-ring

---

Customer Reference Report

Date:

Job Name:

Job Address:

Quality of workmanship	Poor	Good	Great
Quality of materials	Poor	Good	Great
Dependability	Poor	Good	Great
Overall satisfaction	Poor	Good	Great
Would recommend to others	No	Maybe	Yes

Comments

_____

_____

_____

_____

Customer signature

18-1 Job performance report

binder and clear protective pages to store and display your hard-earned references. When you get enough reference letters, you have strong ammunition to close future deals.

BID SHEETS

Reach out to a new customer base through bid sheets. Bid sheets are open to all reputable contractors. The jobs put out for formal bids are almost always done. Unlike common residential estimates, where customers change their minds, formal bid sheets are rarely changed. This type of work is very competitive. The percentage of profit is usually low, but bid work can pay your bills.

Where do you get bid sheets?

Bid sheets can be obtained by responding to public notices in newspapers and by subscribing to services that provide bid information. If you watch the classified section of major newspapers, you will see advertisements for jobs going out for bid. You can receive bid packages by responding to these advertisements. Normally, you will get a set of plans, specifications, bid documents, bid instructions, and other needed information. These bid packages can be simple or complicated.

What is a bid sheet?

A bid sheet is a formal request for price quotes. There is a difference between a bid sheet and a bid package. The bid sheet will give a brief description of the work available. A bid package gives a complete detail of what will be expected from bidders. Most contractors start with a bid sheet and if they find a job of interest, order a bid package. Bid sheets are usually provided free of charge. Bid packages often require either a deposit or a nonrefundable fee.

Bidder agencies

Bidder agencies are businesses that provide listings of bid opportunities. These listings are normally published in newsletter form. The bid reports are generally delivered to contractors on a weekly basis. Each bid report may contain 5 jobs or 50 jobs. These publications are an excellent way to get leads on all types of jobs.

What types of jobs are on bid sheets?

All types of jobs appear on bid sheets, from small residential jobs to large commercial jobs. The majority of the jobs are commercial. The size of the jobs range from a few thousand dollars to millions of dollars.

Government bid sheets

Government bid sheets (FIG. 18-2) are another source of abundant work. Like other bid sheets, government bid sheets give a synopsis of the job description and provide information on how to obtain more details. Government jobs can range from replacing faucets to building a commissary.

Government jobs are a safe bet for getting your money. The money might be slow in coming, but it will come. The paperwork involved with government jobs can be excessive, so if you are not willing to deal with mountains of paperwork, stay away from government bids.

ARE YOU BONDABLE?

Performance and security bid bonds are a necessity for many major jobs. If you order a bid sheet or package, you will almost certainly see that a bond is required. It is common for bid requirements to be tied to the anticipated cost of the job. The bigger the job, the more likely it is a bond will be required.

There are three basic types of bonds: bid bonds, performance bonds, and payment bonds. Each type of bond serves a different purpose. A bid bond is put up to assure the person receiving bids that the bidding contractor will honor the bid if a contract is offered.

Performance bonds prevent contractors from abandoning a job and leaving the customer in dire financial straits. If a contractor reneges on completing a job, the customer may hold the performance bond for financial damages.

Payment bonds are used to guarantee payment to all subcontractors and suppliers used by a contractor. These bonds eliminate the risk of mechanic's and materialman liens being filed against the property where work is being done.

When you put up a bond, the value of the bond is at risk. If you default on your contract, you lose your bond to the person that contracted you for the job. If you use the equity in your home for collateral to get a bond, you could lose your house. Bonds are serious business. If you can get a bond, you have an advantage in the business world, but don't ignore the risks involved.

Before you try bidding jobs that require bonding, check to see if you are bondable. The requirements for being bonded vary. Check in your local phone book for an agency that does bonding, and call to inquire about the requirements.

BIG JOBS EQUAL BIG RISKS

There are risks in all jobs, but big jobs carry big risks. Should you shy away from big jobs? Maybe, but if you go into the deal with the right knowledge and paperwork, you should survive and possibly prosper.

Cash-flow problems

Unlike small residential jobs, big jobs don't generally allow contractors to receive cash deposits. If you tackle these jobs, you will have to work with your own money and credit. For a new business, the money needed to get

SOLICITATION MAILING LIST APPLICATION

1. TYPE OF APPLICATION	2. DATE	FORM APPROVED OMB NO.
☐ INITIAL ☐ REVISION		3090-0009

NOTE—Please complete all items on this form. Insert N/A in items not applicable. See reverse for Instructions.

3. NAME AND ADDRESS OF FEDERAL AGENCY TO WHICH FORM IS SUBMITTED (Include ZIP code)	4. NAME AND ADDRESS OF APPLICANT (Include county and ZIP code)

5. TYPE OF ORGANIZATION (Check one)

☐ INDIVIDUAL ☐ NON-PROFIT ORGANIZATION

☐ PARTNERSHIP ☐ CORPORATION, INCORPORATED UNDER THE LAWS OF THE STATE OF:

6. ADDRESS TO WHICH SOLICITATIONS ARE TO BE MAILED (If different than Item 4)

7. NAMES OF OFFICERS, OWNERS, OR PARTNERS

A. PRESIDENT	B. VICE PRESIDENT	C. SECRETARY
D. TREASURER	E. OWNERS OR PARTNERS	

8. AFFILIATES OF APPLICANT (Names, locations and nature of affiliation. See definition on reverse.)

9. PERSONS AUTHORIZED TO SIGN OFFERS AND CONTRACTS IN YOUR NAME (Indicate if agent)

NAME	OFFICIAL CAPACITY	TELE. NO. (Include area code)

10. IDENTIFY EQUIPMENT, SUPPLIES, AND/OR SERVICES ON WHICH YOU DESIRE TO MAKE AN OFFER (See attached Federal agency's supplemental listing and instructions, if any)

11A. SIZE OF BUSINESS (See definitions on reverse)	11B. AVERAGE NUMBER OF EMPLOYEES (Including affiliates) FOR FOUR PRECEDING CALENDAR QUARTERS	11C. AVERAGE ANNUAL SALES OR RECEIPTS FOR PRECEDING THREE FISCAL YEARS
☐ SMALL BUSINESS (If checked, complete items 11B and 11C) ☐ OTHER THAN SMALL BUSINESS		$

12. TYPE OF OWNERSHIP (See definitions on reverse) (Not applicable for other than small businesses)

☐ DISADVANTAGED BUSINESS ☐ WOMAN-OWNED BUSINESS

13. TYPE OF BUSINESS (See definitions on reverse)

☐ MANUFACTURER OR PRODUCER ☐ REGULAR DEALER (Type 1) ☐ CONSTRUCTION CONCERN ☐ SURPLUS DEALER

☐ SERVICE ESTABLISHMENT ☐ REGULAR DEALER (Type 2) ☐ RESEARCH AND DEVELOPMENT

14. DUNS NO. (If available)	15. HOW LONG IN PRESENT BUSINESS?

16. FLOOR SPACE (Square feet)

A. MANUFACTURING	B. WAREHOUSE

17. NET WORTH

A. DATE	B. AMOUNT
	$

18. SECURITY CLEARANCE (If applicable, check highest clearance authorized)

FOR	TOP SECRET	SECRET	CONFIDENTIAL	C. NAMES OF AGENCIES WHICH GRANTED SECURITY CLEARANCES (Include dates)
A. KEY PERSONNEL				
B. PLANT ONLY				

CERTIFICATION — I certify that information supplied herein (Including all pages attached) is correct and that neither the applicant nor any person (Or concern) in any connection with the applicant as a principal or officer, so far as is known, is now debarred or otherwise declared ineligible by any agency of the Federal Government from making offers for furnishing materials, supplies, or services to the Government or any agency thereof.

19. NAME AND TITLE OF PERSON AUTHORIZED TO SIGN (Type or print)	20. SIGNATURE	21. DATE SIGNED

NSN 7540–01–152–8086
PREVIOUS EDITIONS UNUSABLE

129-106

STANDARD FORM 129 (REV. 10-83)
Prescribed by GSA
FAR (48 CFR) 53.214(c)

18-2 Form used to get on government bid lists U.S. Government Printing Office

to a draw disbursement on a big job can be the undoing of the company. It's wonderful to think of signing a $250,000 job in your first year of business, but that job could put your business into bankruptcy court.

Before you dive into deep water, make sure you can get to the other side. Some lenders will allow you to use your contract as security for a loan, but don't bet your business on it. If you want to take on a big job, first get your finances in order.

Slow pay

Large jobs are notorious for slow pay. It's not that you won't get paid, but you might not get paid in time to keep your business going. New businesses are especially vulnerable to slow pay. When you move into the big leagues, be prepared to hold your financial breath for awhile. The check you thought would come last month might not show up for another 90 days.

No pay

Slow pay is bad, but no pay is worse. Just as new contractors can get in trouble with large jobs, developers and general contractors can get into financial difficulty with big jobs. Most of the people spearheading big jobs don't intend to stick their subcontractors, but sometimes they do.

If subcontractors don't get paid, suppliers don't get paid. The ripple effect continues. Anyone involved with the project is going to lose. Some will lose more than others. Generally, when big jobs go bad the banks or lenders who hold the first mortgage on the property will foreclose.

For subcontractors, filing mechanic's liens is the best course of action. If a contractor hasn't been paid for labor or materials, a mechanic's lien can usually be levied against the property where the labor or materials were invested. If you have to file a lien, make sure you follow the rules to file and perfect a lien. You can file your own liens, but I recommend working with an attorney on all legal matters.

Even after you file and perfect your lien, you might not get your money. If you get any money, it will likely be a settlement for a reduced amount. You can never quite get the sour taste of bad jobs out of your mouth.

Completion dates

Completion dates can also wreak havoc with inexperienced contractors. Big jobs often include a time-is-of-the-essence clause. Along with this clause is usually a penalty fee that must be paid if the job is not finished on time. The penalty is normally based on a daily fee. For example, you might have to pay $200 per day for every day the job runs past the deadline.

Penalty fees and the possible loss of your bond can ruin your business. Contractors with limited experience in big jobs are often unprepared to project solid completion dates. Don't sign a contract with a completion date you are not sure you can meet.

ELIMINATE YOUR COMPETITION

There is no shortage of competition in the field of plumbing. There are, however, often shortages of work. With the combination of limited work and unlimited competition, a new business, or any business for that matter, can get discouraged. But don't, there are ways to thin out the competition.

Beating the competition with bid sheets

Unless you have a track record and are well-known, money will talk. Low prices are what most decision makers look for in bids that are the result of bid sheets. Being the low bidder can get you the job, but don't bid a job too low. It doesn't do you any good to have work if you're not making money.

How can you improve your odds in mass bidding? If you can get bonded, you have an edge. A lot of bidders can't get bonded. This fact alone can be enough to cull the competition. When you prepare your bid package for submission, be meticulous. All you have going for you is your bid package. If you want the job, spend the time to prepare a professional bid packet.

In-person bids

If you are dealing with in-person bids, follow the guidelines found throughout this book: dress appropriately, drive the right vehicle, be professional, be friendly, get the customer's confidence, produce photos of your work, show off your letters of reference, and follow up on all your bids.

19

Your
public image

The type of business image you present might mean the difference between success and failure. Does it really matter if you don't have a logo? Yes. People quickly learn to associate a logo with its owner. Logos can do a lot for you in all your display advertising.

How important is the name you choose for your company? Some names are easier to remember than others. A name can conjure a mental picture of the image you want for your business. If you have any plans to sell your business in the future, the company name should not be too personalized; the new owner might not like owning a business with your personal name as part of the company name.

A company image can affect the type of customers the business attracts and the rates you will be able to charge for business services. How you shape your business image might set you apart from the crowd and eliminate the normally heavy competition. Your image will have many facets. Your tools, trucks, signs, advertising, and uniforms will all have a bearing on your company image.

The value of a public image is hard to determine. While it might be almost impossible to set a monetary value on your company image, it is easy to see how a bad image will hurt your business.

HOW DOES THE PUBLIC PERCEIVE YOUR BUSINESS?

If you give your customers the impression of a successful business, you probably will be successful. On the other hand, if you don't take an active interest in building a strong public image, your business might sink into obscurity. There are many factors that contribute to how the public perceives your business.

Take your truck as an example. If a contractor came to your house to give an estimate, how would you feel if the company truck was an old, battered pick-up with bald tires and a license plate hanging from baling wire?

Would you rather do business with this individual or a person pulling up in a late model, clean van that had the company name professionally lettered on the side? Which truck points to the most company success and stability? Most people would prefer to do business with a company that gives the appearance of being sound financially. This doesn't mean you have to have flashy new trucks, but they should be modern and clean.

Is it important to have your company name on the business vehicles? You bet it is. The more people see your trucks around town, the more they will remember your name and develop a sense of confidence in your business. It is acceptable to use magnetic signs or professional lettering, but don't letter the truck with stick-on letters in a haphazard way. Remember, you are putting your company name out there for all the world to see.

Designing your ad for the phone directory is another major step. As people flip through the pages of the directory, a handsome ad will stop them in their tracks. An eye-appealing ad can get you business that would otherwise be lost to competitors.

Any professional salesperson will tell you that to be successful you must always be in a selling mode. It doesn't matter where you are or what you're doing, you must be ready to cultivate sales. Compare this fact to your public image. Your image is being made and presented every day and in every way. You can't afford to let your business image slip.

If your company image is strong enough, customers will come to you. They will see your trucks, job signs, and ads, and call you. When a customer calls a plumber, they are usually serious about having work done. Whether your company does the work or one of your competitors gets the job will depend upon many factors. Your company image is one of those factors. Build and present the proper image and you will be half way to making the sale.

SET YOURSELF APART FROM THE CROWD

In order to make your business better than average, you must set yourself apart from the crowd. How do you do that? You do it with your company name, logo, company colors, slogans, and any other marketing tools that are appropriate for your business. Let's look at some ways to give your company a unique identity.

Company names

Company names say a lot about the business they represent. For example, High-Tech Heating Contractors might be a good name for a company specializing in new heating technologies and systems. Solar Systems Unlimited might be a good name for a company that deals with solar heating systems. Authentic Custom Capes might make a good name for a builder that specializes in building period-model Cape Cods. How about a name like Jim's Plumbing? It's alright, but it doesn't say much. A better choice might be, Jim's 24-Hour Plumbing Service. Now the name tells customers that Jim is there for them, 24 hours a day. See how a name can influence public perception of your business?

The more you can tie the name of your business to the type of business you are in, the better off you will be. If you can include descriptive words, like 24-hour service, your name will tell customers more about your business.

When you choose a name for your company it also helps to find words that flow smoothly together. How does Pioneer Plumbing sound to you? Both words start with a "P," and the words work well together. A name like Can-Do Commercial Plumbing sounds good and so does a name like Dependable Drain Cleaning, Inc. In contrast, a name like Englewood Plumbing & Heating is not bad, but it is not as good as the others. A name like Septic Suckers flows well and might be fitting for a company that pumps out septic tanks. The name might not generate business, but the more I think about it, the more I like the name. It might generate enough talk around town to keep your phone ringing for months.

Logo

A logo (FIG. 19-1) can be as important as your company name. Logos, the symbols that companies adopt to represent their business, play an important role in marketing and advertising. While people might not remember a specific ad or even a company name, they are likely to remember a distinctive logo. If you put your mind to it, I'll bet you can come up with at least 10 logos that stick in your mind.

Your logo doesn't have to be complex. In fact, it might be nothing more than the initials of your company name. Then again, you might have a complex logo that incorporates an image of what your business does. One of my favorite logos was used by a real estate company. The logo was a depiction of Noah's ark, complete with animals. In the ad featuring the ark were the words, "Looking For Land?" The business was selling land, and the ark logo was humorous and fitting for the occasion.

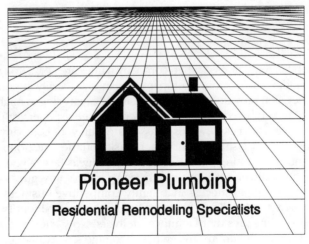

19-1 Example of a company logo

Company colors

Company colors are one way to attract attention and become known all over town. There are consultants who specialize in colors. These professionals work with companies to develop company colors that influence their consumers. Different colors affect how people think, the mood they are in, and what they do. We've all heard that bulls will charge a red flag. Well, I don't think the flag has to be red to attract a bull's attention, but if I were forced to enter the pasture wearing either red pants or green pants, I'd choose green. You see, whether the color of the flag makes a difference or not is not as important as our mental image of the color.

Choosing the right colors for your company is important. How seriously would you take a plumber who pulled up in a pink van with painted flowers? The color and decoration of the plumber's van has no bearing on the technical ability of the plumber, but it does cast an immediate impression. Choose your company colors with care.

The color of your trucks might be dictated by the color of the truck you presently own. It is more impressive to see a fleet of trucks that are uniform in color and design than it is to see a parade of trucks that include various makes and colors. A unified fleet gives a better impression. Color also is important in your truck lettering and job-site signs. If your truck is dark blue, white letters will show up better than black letters. If the truck is white, black or blue letters would be fine.

Colors also are important on your business stationery. It would generally be considered inappropriate to use fluorescent orange for your letters and lime green for your envelopes. Certainly these colors would attract attention and be remembered, but the impression likely would not be the one you wanted to create. For most businesses tan, ivory, light blue, or off-white are acceptable stationery colors.

For job signs, it is important to pick a background color and a letter color that contrast well. You want the sign to be easy to read. When you talk with your sign painter or dealer, review samples of how different colors work together.

Slogan

Slogans are often remembered when company names are not. If you will be advertising on radio or television, a company slogan is especially important. Since radio and television provide audible advertising, a catchy slogan might make its mark and be remembered. When you advertise in newspapers or other print ads, slogans give readers key words to associate with your company.

I want you to try a simple test. When I ask you the question in the next sentence—no fair peeking—think of one company as fast as you can. What pizza company delivers? If you thought of Domino's, my guess was right. Domino's has had great success in a highly competitive business. The logo on their box is a domino. They have the Noid character to identify with, and one of their slogans says that Domino's delivers. Now a lot of pizza places deliver, but if you live in an area where Domino's is available, you can't think of pizza delivery without thinking of Domino's. This fact is no accident. I'm sure the brains behind Domino's have spent huge sums of money to develop this image.

Thinking of a slogan for your business might take a while, but it's worth the effort. If you need inspiration, look at other successful companies. Examine their slogans to gain ideas for yours, but never use someone else's slogan.

If your mind is not at its best when it comes to creative images and marketing, consult with a specialist in the field. Choosing the proper name and logo is important enough to warrant investing some time and money. Of course, you know your financial limitations, but if you can swing it, get a professional to design your company image.

YOUR IMAGE AND FEE SCHEDULE

Image might not be everything in business, but it is a big part of your success. People have become afraid of contractors. The public has read all the horror stories of ripoffs and contractor con artists. Unfortunately, much of what has been printed about unscrupulous contractors is true, and the public does have a right to be concerned. With the growing awareness of consumers, image is more important than ever before. Let's take a quick look at how your image affects your business.

The visual image

In our first example, a plumber goes on an estimate in well-worn work clothes, driving a truck that has seen better days. While this image will not offend or alienate some customers, it will surely turn off many customers.

In our second example, you drive up in an expensive luxury car and go into the home wearing a suit that costs more than the first contractor's truck. A select group of homeowners will relate and respond well to your image, but most consumers will resent your financial flaunting. They will assume you charge far too much because you can afford such expensive clothing and transportation. You might also intimidate or embarrass the customer with your assumed financial standing. Your fancy suit also might make the statement that you don't know the first thing about hands-on work and are only a sales professional, about to take the homeowner's hard-earned money to pay for more suits and a more expensive car.

If you dress neatly in casual clothing, and drive a respectable, but not lavish vehicle, your odds of appealing to the masses improve. Wear clothes that allow you to crawl into the attic or under the sink, and you will give the impression of someone who knows the plumbing business.

The same basic principles apply to your office. If your office is little more than a hole in the wall with an answering machine, an old desk, and two chairs, people will be concerned about the financial stability of your business. If your office is staffed with several people, decorated in expensive art and furnishings, and in the high-rent district, customers will assume your prices are too high. It generally works best to hit a happy medium with your office arrangements.

Fee factors

To a large extent, people feel that they get what they pay for. While this might be a misconception, it is a popular belief. The image you present has a direct effect on your fees. If you convince potential customers you are a professional, the customers will be willing to pay professional fees. Extend your image by making the customers feel safe when doing business with you, and you have leverage for higher fees. When you become a specialist, you can demand even higher fees. Think about it, who gets a higher hourly rate, your family doctor or a heart specialist? When you convince the customer that nobody knows plumbing better than you, you build a case for higher fees.

For years I specialized in kitchen and bath remodeling. My crews did nothing but kitchen and bathroom remodeling. When you do the same type of work day in and day out, you get good at it. With my experience in this specialized field of remodeling, I could anticipate problems and find solutions that most of my competitors might not. This specialized experience made me more valuable to consumers. I could snake a 2-inch vent pipe up the wall from the kitchen to the attic without cutting the wall open. I could predict, with great accuracy, how long it would take to break up and patch the concrete floor for a basement bath.

I became known as a competent professional in a specialized field. I could name my own price, within reason, for my services. You can do the same thing. If you have a special skill and can show the consumer why you are more valuable than your competitors, the consumer is very likely to pay a little extra for your expertise. Building a solid image as a professional that specializes in a certain field has its advantages.

CHANGING YOUR IMAGE

Let's say you started your business without much prior thought. You picked a name out of thin air and never got around to designing a logo. Now you realize that you have hurt your business prospects. What should you do? You must make changes to correct your identified mistakes.

If you want to change the name of your company, do a direct-mail campaign to your existing customer base. Send out letters to all of your customers advising them of your new company name. Explain that you are changing the name of your company to reflect its growth and expansion. Impress upon the existing customers that the company has not been sold and is not under new management, unless you have a bad image to overcome. Then the new-management announcement might be a good idea, if it's legitimate.

Start running new advertisements with your new company name and logo. Build new business under your new name and convince past customers to follow you in your expansion efforts. Take this approach, and you will get a new public image without losing the bulk of your past customers. While this approach will work, it is best to create a good image when you begin your business. It is always easier to do the job right the first time than it is to go back and correct mistakes.

20

Marketing and advertising

Marketing and advertising strategies might well be the most important lessons for new business owners. While it is true that marketing and advertising alone will not make a business a success, they are critical elements for a thriving business. If you don't do a good job with your marketing and advertising, you won't have much of a business. This chapter is going to immerse you in the world of professional marketing and advertising.

THERE IS NO BUSINESS WITHOUT SALES

To get the opportunity to make sales, most businesses must advertise. Without advertising, the average business will not get many customer inquiries. If no one knows your business exists, how will they contact you for service? Since public exposure is paramount to the success of your business, so is a strong marketing plan and effective advertising.

Advertising is the act of putting your message in front of consumers. You can advertise in newspapers, on radio, on television, by direct mail, or in many other ways. Marketing is the reading of the business climate. When you track your advertising results, design your ads, develop sales strategies, and define your target market, you are performing marketing functions.

Marketing is much more complicated than advertising. Advertising your business requires little more than the money needed to pay for your ads. Marketing demands an extension of the normal senses. You must be able to read between the lines and determine what the buying public wants. There are many books available on marketing, professional seminars teach marketing techniques, and community colleges offer courses in marketing. With enough effort and self study, you can create efficient marketing strategies. If you want a business with a long life, expend your energy to develop marketing skills.

WHERE SHOULD YOU ADVERTISE?

Advertising is a powerful business tool. In skilled hands, advertising can produce fantastic sales results. Consider this, you are about to move to a new city, what real estate brokerage in the new city will you call for relocation help? I would guess you would call the brokerage where all the brokers and agents wear gold coats. There we go again with company colors, but the gold-coat brokers get a lot of visibility on television, radio, and in print ads. Once you hear a hundred times how they are the best real estate team around, you might start to believe it.

Advertising plants the seed that the brokerage with the gold coats mean success. If you buy into the advertising, you are likely to call these brokers. If the broker doesn't make a good personal impression, you might choose another brokerage, but at least you called the gold team. This same strategy can work for you.

The list of possible places to advertise is limited only by your imagination. Some advertising media are better than others. Let's take a close-up look at some specific examples.

The phone directory

The phone directory is an excellent place to have your company name advertised. The size of your ad, however, will depend on the nature of your business and the type of work you want to attract. Being listed in the phone book adds credibility to your company. Whether you have a line listing or a full-page display ad, get your company name in the phone book as soon as possible.

The size of your ad in the directory should be determined by the results you hope to achieve. Large display ads are expensive, and they might not pay for themselves in your line of work. If you are a plumbing company that offers emergency repair service, a large ad is beneficial. People with a basement that is flooding or a toilet that is running over in the upstairs bath are in a hurry to find a plumber. Most phone directories place the larger ads in the front section of the category heading. Being the first plumbing company a panicked homeowner comes to can be a real advantage.

If your business is plumbing new houses, a large display ad probably isn't necessary. When people are shopping for this type of plumber they are not normally in a hurry. An ad that is one column wide and an inch or two in length can pull just as many calls under these circumstances. A quick look at how your competition advertises can give you a hint as to what you should do. If all the other new-construction plumbers have large ads, you might do better with a large ad.

Over the years I have tried many experiments with directory advertising. At one time I was running a half-page ad for my plumbing business. I thought I could save money by going to a smaller ad. I did pay less for my new ad, but my business suffered. I had a noticeable drop in phone requests for service.

As I became more knowledgeable about business, marketing, and advertising, I continued to test the results of various directory ads. During my test marketing, I found that for remodeling and new-construction work, big ads were not as important as they were for service and repair work.

Newspaper ads

Newspaper ads provide quick results: you either get calls or you don't. As a service contractor, my experience has shown that most respondents to newspaper ads are looking for a bargain. If you want to command high prices, I don't think newspapers are the place to advertise. But when you are new in business, the newspaper can produce customers for you quickly.

Handouts, flyers, and pamphlets

These methods seem to generate calls quickly, but the callers are usually looking for low priced services. Many businesses consider this form of advertising degrading. I don't know that I would agree with that opinion, but I don't think you will receive the money you are worth with these low-cost advertising methods.

Radio advertising

Radio advertising is expensive, but it is a good way to get your name into the ears of listeners. I believe the key to radio advertising is repetition. If you can budget enough money for several radio spots, for a few weeks, you will gain name recognition. If you can't afford to sustain a regular ad on the radio, I would advise against using this form of advertising. Most people are not going to hear your ad and run to the nearest phone to call you.

Television commercials

Television commercials can be very effective. Unlike radio, where people only hear your ad, television allows viewers to see your ad. People associate television advertisers with success. With the many cable channels available, television advertising can be an affordable and effective way to get your message out to the community.

I have used ads on cable television very effectively, and I know other plumbing contractors that have been successful with this type of advertising. Whether you are selling a $30 service call or a $5,000 remodeling package, television ads can increase your sales.

Direct-mail advertising

Direct-mail advertising is not always cost effective. The cost for direct-mail advertising can easily run into thousands of dollars. Most people who use this form of advertising are happy if only 1 percent of the people they mail to become customers. If you are selling services for less than $50, direct mail probably won't work for you. If you are selling major bathroom and kitchen remodeling jobs, direct mail might be great for your business.

Direct-mail advertising allows you to reach a targeted market. If you want to advertise to people with incomes in excess of $50,000, you can rent a mailing list of just those people. If you want to mail to recent home buyers, mailing lists are available. You have complete control over who sees your advertisement.

Most mailing lists are available for about $75 for each 1,000 names you receive. Many list brokers require a minimum order of 3,000 names. The names can be supplied to you on stick-on labels.

If you want to reduce your mailing costs, your local postmaster can set you up with a bulk-rate permit. To use the bulk-rate service, you must mail a minimum of 200 pieces of mail at a time. The cost for this type of mailing is much less than first-class postage, but there are one-time and annual upfront fees. Talk with your local post office for full details.

Creative advertising methods

You might want to rent space on a billboard to advertise your business. Perhaps you will cut a deal with a local restaurant to have your company highlighted on their menu. Providing uniforms for the local little league can get your name in front of a large audience. If you put your mind to it, there is almost no end to the possibilities for creative advertising.

BUILD NAME RECOGNITION

We have already talked about building name recognition through advertising, but now we are going to learn how it's done. You want people to see or hear your company name and feel like they know your company. To accomplish this goal, you must use repetitive advertising.

Repetitive advertising can be used in all forms of advertising. Take radio advertising for example. When you hear radio commercials, you normally hear the company name more than once. Pay attention the next time you hear ads on the radio. You will probably hear the company name or the name of the product being sold at least three times.

Television uses verbal and visual repetition to ingrain a name or product in your mind. Watch a few television commercials and you will see what I mean. During the commercials you will see or hear the company name or product several times.

Not only should your name be used often in the ad, the ad should be run regularly. If you advertise in the newspaper, don't run one ad and stop. Run the same ad several times. Use your logo in the ad, and place the ads on a regular schedule. This type of repetition will implant your company name into the subconscious of potential customers. When these potential customers are ready to become customers, they will think of your company.

GENERATE DIRECT SALES

For a service business, generating direct sales is possible with direct mail, radio, television, print ads, telemarketing, and other forms of creative marketing. Telemarketing and direct mail are two of the fastest ways to generate sales activity.

Telemarketing is a job for thick-skinned people. Calling people you don't know and asking them to use your services, buy your product, or allow you into their home for a free inspection, estimate, or whatever is not much fun. However, if you can live with rejection and are not afraid to call 100 people to get 10 sales appointments, cold calling will work.

When your motive for advertising is to generate sales activity, it helps to make your offer on a time-restricted basis. Offer a discount for a limited time only. Create a situation where people must act now to benefit from your advertising. Turning up the heat with time-sensitive ads can generate activity quickly.

REPEAT SALES TO EXISTING CUSTOMERS

Repeat sales to existing customers are a good way to get extra value from your advertising. Getting a customer can be an expensive proposition. If you were to calculate how much time and money you invest for each customer you have, the results might shock you. Once you get these hard-earned customers, don't let them get away. First, take good care of your customers, and keep them happy. Second, don't let them get away with just a single sale. Sell to your existing customers over and over. Use existing customers to generate leads on new customers.

Most customers that buy from you once will buy from you again. Send a mailing to each of your customers on a routine basis. Newsletters are often mailed quarterly to existing customers to maintain contact and generate sales opportunities. Don't overlook the value of your customer base. Always keep your name fresh in the minds of your customers, and never stop selling.

WHAT IS YOUR RATE OF RETURN?

The response to your advertising will depend on your marketing plan and the execution of your advertising. If you are advertising in the local newspaper, you might expect about a .001 response. In other words, if the paper has 25,000 subscribers, you might get 25 responses to your ad. This projection is aggressive. In most cases your response will be much lower. If you only get 10 calls, don't be surprised.

Advertising a contracting business on the radio or television might seem like a waste of money. It is not uncommon for these ads to run without generating calls, but that doesn't mean the ads are not effective. Television and radio advertising builds name recognition for your company. This form of advertising works best when it is used in conjunction with some type of print advertising. If you are running ads in the paper, distributing flyers, or doing a direct-mail campaign when the television and radio ads air, you should see a higher response than you would without the radio and television ads.

Direct-mail advertising often provides fast results. People receiving ads by mail either trash them or quickly act on them. A 1-percent response on direct-mail advertising is generally considered good. For example, if you mail to 1,000 houses, you should be happy if you get 10 responses. Due to the low response rate of bulk mailings, direct mail is not effective for low-priced services. If you are selling big-ticket items, direct mail can work very well.

If you target your direct-mail market, you should do much better on your rate of return. Pick a list based on demographics, and you can be sure you reach the type of customer you want. Demographics are statistics that tell you facts about the names on your mailing list. You can rent a mailing list that is comprised of specific age groups, incomes, and so forth. These statistics can make a big difference in the effectiveness of your advertising.

Determining the effectiveness of advertising is a task all serious business owners must undertake. To learn what ads are paying for themselves, you need to know which ads are generating buying customers. Some ads generate a high volume of inquiries, but don't result in many sales. Other ads produce less curiosity calls and more buying customers. You need to track the results of your advertising.

For example, assume you placed four advertisements in four different publications. You phone starts ringing. Business is good, but it could be better. Before you ran the ads, business was slow. You know the ads increased your business, but do you know which ad worked best or which publication was responsible for the highest number of responses?

You would know which ads were productive if you had keyed each ad. For example, run the first ad with the box number 1029-A. The second ad might carry the box number 1029-X. The third ad might be keyed as box number 1029-P. If you key the ads, you will be able to identify the source of the customer response. This allows you to rule out publications that don't produce profitable results and to increase advertising in the publications with the most pull.

As a service business, where most work is requested by phone, keying your ads with a box number is not effective. You have to come up with another way of identifying your customer source. Try using a variation of your name. One ad might tell the reader to ask for John. The next ad could instruct the caller to ask for Mr. Woodson.

Offering a discount to the customer for mentioning the ad is another way to keep track of your advertising results. It is not uncommon to see an ad that offers a 10-percent discount to anyone mentioning the ad.

Putting a coupon in the ad is another way to find out the source of your business. Have your ad tell the reader to present the coupon at the time of service for a discount. This method is effective and gives clear evidence of where the customer got your name.

There is also the direct approach. Ask the customer where they learned of your business. Most people will be glad to tell you where they heard of you and why they called you. This type of information is valuable. It enables you to refine your marketing plan and increase your business, while saving money that would be wasted on the wrong media.

USE PROMOTIONAL ACTIVITIES

Promotional activities are an excellent way to get more sales and to build name recognition. Use special promotions to capture public attention and create an opportunity for additional sales. Let me give you an example of how you could stage a promotional event.

For this example, assume you are a contractor who specializes in kitchen and bath remodeling. Talk to your local material supplier and develop a seminar. Have the material supplier allow you to come into the store and give a remodeling seminar to shoppers. Tell the supplier how the seminar will be good for the store's image and increased material sales. Advertise the free seminar for about two weeks prior to the date of your talk. The supplier might be willing to pay a portion of the ad costs; after all, the store is gaining publicity from this promotion as well.

When people begin gathering around you in the store, be sure you have your business cards, rate sheets, before-and-after photos, and other sales aids out where the shoppers can see them. After your seminar, field questions from the audience. This type of promotion can create the image of you being an expert in your field.

If it is legal in your area, give away a door prize. Have the audience fill out cards with their names, addresses, and phone numbers for a prize drawing. The prize could be a discount on remodeling services, a small appliance, or just about anything else. After the seminar, you have a box full of names and addresses to follow up on for work. This type of idea can increase your business dramatically.

JOIN CLUBS AND ORGANIZATIONS

Whether you like it or not, as a business owner you must also be a salesperson. When you join local clubs and community organizations you meet people. These people are all potential customers. By becoming visible in your community, your business will have a better chance of survival. If you support local functions, children's sports teams, and the like, you will become known. You can use these local opportunities to build your business. When citizens see your company name on the uniforms of the local kids' baseball team, they remember you. Further, they respect you for supporting the children of the community. You can take this type of approach to almost any level.

21

Employees

Employees could easily be the biggest unsolved mystery of the business world. Most business owners want employees until they have them, then they often wish they didn't need them. There is no question that employees will complicate your life. However, the right employees will make you more money than you could make alone. So how do you decide what to do about the issue of employees? This chapter is going to show you the ropes of finding, hiring, managing, and terminating employees.

DO YOU WANT EMPLOYEES?

This a simple question, and you shouldn't need any help answering it. You either do or don't want employees. If you want employees, you know it. Assuming that you do want employees, let's examine a few justifiable questions.

Why do you want employees?

Owners might be quick to say they want employees, but they often can't express why they want them. Before you begin to build a list of employees, decide why you are hiring them. It is easy to hire employees, but it is not as easy to get rid of them. Don't hire people until you need them and know why you are hiring them.

To make more money?

Most employers will give this as their reason for hiring employees. There is a belief, true or false, that the more employees you have, the more money you will make. While this theory can hold true, it can also be dead wrong.

From personal experience I have seen both sides of this coin. There have been times when I had several employees and made less in net profits than I did without them. Then there have been occasions when employees have been good for my financial health. What caused the differences? There were many factors in my personal experiences.

The cycles of the economy have been a factor in my experience with employees. In my early years, poor management contributed to my failings with employees. My selection of employees has definitely made a difference in the success and failure of the relationship. Don't get the idea that more is always better. A lot of contractors do better financially with small crews than they do with large work forces.

To cast a brighter public image?

It is true that the public often associates the success of a company with the number of employees in it. But this is not reason enough to hire employees. Hire employees for profitable reasons, not for public opinion.

To make you feel more important?

Most people won't admit to this, but many of them do feel more important when they have employees. This is not a good reason to hire people. There are less costly ways to improve your self appreciation.

To be more successful?

People measure success with different measuring sticks. Some people consider themselves successful when they have a lot of money. Having a number of employees can spell success for others. Family health and happiness is a measurement of success for some business owners. How you measure success is up to you, but don't lean too heavily on employees to find happiness. Unless you are satisfied providing jobs for others, while you get by on meager profits, employees can be a mistake.

Does it sound like I'm against hiring employees?

I'm not against employees, but I do want to show you both sides of the issue. Many business owners never take the time to consider the bad points of hiring employees. Since I assume you have dozens of reasons why hiring employees is great, I want to expose you to some other possibilities.

EMPLOYEES vs. INDEPENDENT CONTRACTORS

There are limitations to what any one individual can do without help. However, you might be able to accomplish your goal with independent contractors, eliminating the need for regular employees. Independent contractors might seem more expensive than employees when their rates are first reviewed, but further investigation might prove the independent professionals to be less expensive. Let's look at the pros and cons of employees versus independent contractors.

Hourly rates

The hourly rates of independent contractors will normally be higher than the wages you would pay an employee to perform the same function. This is to be expected, but it might not be as it seems. Since independents often work for multiple employers, they do not depend on you for their entire income. You pay only for what you need and for what you get.

Employees, on the other hand, rely on you to pay their salaries for the whole year. While you might be paying a lower hourly rate to your employees, if you are paying them for time when you don't need them, you might be wasting money.

Insurance costs

Independent contractors pay for their own insurance costs, which can amount to a substantial sum of money. You might have to pay liability insurance, health insurance, dental insurance, worker's comp insurance, and disability insurance for your employees, but you won't have these same expenses with subcontractors. You will still want liability insurance, but the rest of the coverages can be avoided.

Transportation

Subcontractors are responsible for their own transportation. If you hire employees, you will probably have to furnish company vehicles for field personnel. When you consider the cost of acquiring, insuring, and maintaining vehicles, the subcontractors who provide their own transportation are desirable options.

Payroll

Payroll for companies with many employees can be a full-time job. If you have to pay a full-time employee just to handle the payroll for your other employees, you will have additional overhead that will have to be recovered in the price of your services. Subcontractors eliminate the need for payroll and payroll records. You will still have to write checks to the subs, but this procedure is less labor intensive than doing payroll.

Payroll taxes

Payroll taxes are another expense you eliminate by using subcontractors. With employees you will have to make additional payroll tax deposits. This is nonexistent when independent contractors are utilized.

Paid vacations

Most employees expect to receive paid vacations. If you give the average plumber a 2-week paid vacation, you will lose over $1,000 a year. If you have 10 plumbers, you will lose over $10,000 a year by being a nice boss. Subcontractors don't expect you to give them a paid vacation.

Sick leave and other benefits

Sick leave and other benefits can be compared to paid vacations. Most employees expect these benefits, but subcontractors don't.

Convenience

If convenience is a factor, employees might have an edge over subcontractors. Subcontractors can be difficult to control; that's why they are called independent contractors. If you want people at your fingertips, employees are generally more reliable than subs.

Competition

Many contractors fear that their subcontractors will become direct competition. These contractors assume the independents are using them to get to their customers. While some subcontractors will attempt to steal your customers, most won't.

Employees are not generally looked upon as competition, but they might pose more of a threat than subcontractors. Subcontractors are already in business and already have customers. Employees might be looking to go into business for themselves. They might try to take some of your customers with them. Either group is a possible threat, but I would be more concerned about employees.

Comparisons

Comparisons between employees and subcontractors are not hard to make. Before you dash out and hire employees, consider the advantages to using subcontractors. You might find that you are happier and more prosperous with independent contractors.

COMMISSIONED SALESPEOPLE

Commissioned salespeople can make a dramatic difference in your business. On the plus side of the deal, commissioned salespeople can generate a high volume of gross sales. Since you are paying the sales staff only for what they sell, an army of sales associates can be mighty enticing. A high volume of sales also can create numerous problems. You might not have enough help to get the jobs done on time. You might have to buy new trucks and equipment. The increased business might tie you to the office and cause your field supervision to suffer. There are many angles to consider before you bring a high-powered sales staff online.

The benefits of a sales staff

If you find the right people to represent your company, you can enjoy increased sales. With commissioned salespeople you don't have the normal overhead of employees, and you only pay for what you get. Good salespeople will hustle up deals that would otherwise never come your way. A person who can close deals will make jobs happen on the spot, so you have quick sales and no downtime.

Sales professionals can take a simple estimate and turn it into a major job for your plumbers. With the right training and experience, sales professionals can get more money for a job than the average contractor. It is clear that for some businesses a sales staff is a powerful advantage.

The drawbacks to commissioned salespeople

The drawbacks to commissioned salespeople might outweigh the advantages. Some salespeople will tell a customer anything to get a signature on a contract. As the business owner, you will have to deal with this form of sales embellishment at some point. The customer might tell you that the salesperson assured her she would get a shower door with her new shower, when you had not figured a door into the cost of the job. The salesperson might have promised that the job could be done in two days, when in reality the job will take a week. This type of sales hype can cause serious problems for you and your workers.

Most sales associates are not tradespeople. They don't know all the ins and outs of a job. They know how to sell the job, not how to do it. A salesperson might tell a prospect that putting a bathroom in the basement is no problem, when in fact such an installation requires a sewer pump that adds nearly $800 to the cost of an average basement bath. There are many times when an outside sales staff undersells a job. Sometimes they sell the job cheap to get a sale. Other times the wrong price is quoted out of ignorance. In either case, you as the business owner have to answer to the customer.

Getting too many sales too quickly can be as devastating as not having enough sales. If the salesperson you put in the field is good, you might be swamped with work. This can lead to problems scheduling work, with quality of the work turned out, field supervision, cash flow, and a host of other potential business killers.

Sending the wrong person out to represent your company can have a detrimental effect on your company image. If the salesperson is dishonest or gives the customer a hard time, your business reputation will suffer.

Deciding if and when to use commissioned salespeople is your decision. But let me tell you, don't take the decision lightly. There is no question that the right salespeople can make your business more profitable. There is also little doubt that the wrong sales staff can drive your business into the ground. If you decide to use commissioned salespeople, I suggest you go with them on the first few sales calls.

When you interview people to represent your company, remember they are sales professionals. These people will be selling you in the interview with the same tenacity they will use on prospects in the field. Go into the relationship with your eyes wide open. Don't take anything for granted. Check the individuals out for integrity and professionalism.

FINDING GOOD EMPLOYEES

Business owners of all types struggle to find good employees. Before you can hope to hire good employees, you must understand what makes a good employee. Define the qualities you want in your staff, then try to find employees with these qualities that are available for work.

Classified ads

Classified ads are the quickest way to get applications, but they generally are not the best way to find prime candidates for your opening. Classified ads can produce top-notch people. If you go into your employee search with the knowledge you will have to sift through a mass of unqualified applicants to find one good worker, classified ads might be worthwhile.

Employment agencies

Employment agencies are known for their work with executives and professionals. Generally, the agency will contact the business owner and go over the traits of a prospective employee before the employee knows who the employer is. Then if you are interested in talking with the applicant, the agency will arrange an interview.

Some agencies charge applicants when they locate a job for them. Most agencies charge employers for finding acceptable applicants. Before you deal with an agency, be sure of what you are getting. If you are asked to sign a contract or engagement letter, read it carefully and consider consulting your attorney before you sign the document. The fees charged by some agencies are ridiculously high.

Employment agencies are geared more towards white-collar positions than they are to blue-collar jobs. If you are looking for people in the trades, agencies might not be of much help.

Word-of-mouth

Word-of-mouth referrals for job applicants are a good way to find the best employees. If you put the word out that you are looking for help, you might drum up some applicants through your existing employees or friends. When a person applies for a job because a friend has recommended your company, you have the advantage of built-in credibility.

Unemployment office listings

Unemployment offices carry listings of job opportunities. If you have a job to fill, notify the local unemployment office. They will put your opening in their computers and on their bulletin boards. This type of listing service is free and can produce quick results.

Hand picking

Hand picking employees is one of the best ways to get who you want. However, you must remain ethical in your procedures as you select and solicit individuals. Stealing employees from your competition is frowned upon. Let's look at how you should and shouldn't go after specific employees.

First, let's look at an example of the wrong way. Years ago I was a project superintendent on a townhouse project. I was in charge of all the plumbers and their support people. The economy was good and all good plumbers had jobs. Most plumbing companies needed more plumbers to keep up with the rapid building trends.

There were companies that showed no remorse when stealing good plumbers from the competition. During this project I saw representatives from competitive companies come onto my job site and offer my plumbers more money, right in front of me!

The plumbers knew they could get work anywhere, and many of them would change jobs for an extra 25¢ an hour. When these people raided my job, they often left with my plumbers in the back of their trucks. The plumbers didn't give any notice; they just left to follow the higher hourly wages. Some plumbers even tried to get me and the other company's representative into bidding wars.

You can imagine the ill will that formed between companies under these circumstances. One company would steal a plumber on Monday. On Friday another company would take the plumber away to a new job. This endless turnover of plumbers hurt everyone in the business. You don't want to use these techniques when you hand pick employees.

There are many ways to make employees aware that you are interested in offering them a position. One excellent way is to run into them at the supply house. While the two of you are standing around, start a conversation that leads to your need for help. Stress how you are looking for someone just like the person to whom you are talking. If the other person is interested in pursuing employment with your company, you should get some signals.

If you have your eye on a particular person for your position, don't hesitate to call or write the individual. If you don't want to look too obvious, ask the person if he knows of anyone with qualifications like his that is looking for work. This approach allows you to give all the details you want about the position, without making a direct solicitation of the individual.

There are many tactful ways to get your point across to people that are presently employed. You don't have to stoop to going public with your attempt to take the employee away from the existing employer. Be discreet and keep your dealings fair.

KEEPING GOOD EMPLOYEES

After you have hired your people, you will need to keep them. If employees are worth having, someone else will want them. Many factors will influence employees to stick with your company. Some of these factors are:

- Comfortable wages
- Health insurance
- Dental insurance
- Paid vacations
- Sick leave
- Company vehicles

- Retirement plans
- Good working conditions
- A friendly atmosphere
- Competent co-workers
- Fair supervisors
- Pride in the company

If you establish a good environment for your employees, they will have no reason to leave your employ. Bonus plans and other incentives can even remove much of the risk of having the employees go into business for themselves. It will be up to you to communicate with your employees and to create circumstances to keep them happy. If you have valuable employees, they are worth the extra effort.

EMPLOYEE POINTERS

Let me give you a few employee pointers to provide a starting point for obeying employment laws. Don't take these pointers as legal or tax advice or the last word, and don't consider them conclusive. Look upon them as a guide to the questions you should ask your attorney and tax professional.

Employment applications

All prospective employees should complete an approved employment application. These applications tell you about the people you are considering hiring, and they provide a physical record for your files. Be sure the application forms you use are legal and don't ask questions you are prohibited from asking.

W-2 forms

W-2 forms (FIG. 21-1) are used to notify employees of what their earnings were for the past year and how much money was withheld for taxes. The forms must be mailed or given to employees no later than the last day of January, following the taxable year.

W-4 forms

W-4 forms are government forms that must be completed and signed by all employees. These forms tell the employer how much tax to withhold from an employee's paycheck. Once the form is filled out and signed, keep it in the employee's employment file. New W-4 forms should be completed and signed by employees each year.

1 Control number	22222	For Official Use Only ▶ OMB No. 1545-0008								

2 Employer's name, address, and ZIP code			6 Statutory employee ☐	Deceased ☐	Pension plan ☐	Legal rep. ☐	942 emp. ☐	Subtotal ☐	Deferred compensation ☐	Void ☐

7 Allocated tips	8 Advance EIC payment
9 Federal income tax withheld	10 Wages, tips, other compensation

3 Employer's identification number	4 Employer's state I.D. number	11 Social security tax withheld	12 Social security wages
5 Employee's social security number		13 Social security tips	14 Medicare wages and tips
19a Employee's name (first, middle initial, last)		15 Medicare tax withheld	16 Nonqualified plans
		17 See Instrs. for Form W-2	18 Other

19b Employee's address and ZIP code

20	21	22 Dependent care benefits	23 Benefits included in Box 10
24 State income tax	25 State wages, tips, etc.	26 Name of state	27 Local income tax	28 Local wages, tips, etc.	29 Name of locality

Copy A For Social Security Administration   Cat. No. 10134D   Department of the Treasury—Internal Revenue Service

21-1 W-2 Wage and Tax Statement Department of the Treasury, Internal Revenue Service

I-9 forms

I-9 forms are employment-eligibility-verification forms. These forms must be completed by all employees hired after November 7, 1987. I-9 forms must be completed within the first three days of employment.

Employers are required to verify an employee's identity and employment eligibility. Employees must provide the employer with documents to substantiate these facts. Some acceptable forms of identification are birth certificates, drivers licenses, and U.S. passports. If an employer fails to comply with the I-9 requirements, stiff penalties might result.

1099 forms

1099 forms (FIG. 21-2) are used to report money you pay to subcontractors. These forms must be completed and mailed at the end of each year. You will send one copy to the subcontractor, one copy to the tax authorities, and you will retain a copy for your files.

Since subcontractors come and go, they can be difficult to locate when the time comes to send out the 1099 forms. Insist on having current addresses for all your subcontractors at all times.

Employee tax withholdings

Employee tax withholdings cannot be ignored. When you do payroll, you must withhold the proper taxes from an employee's check. The Internal

```
            ٩595    □ VOID    □ CORRECTED
```

PAYER'S name, street address, city, state, and ZIP code	1 Rents $	OMB No. 1545-0115	**Miscellaneous Income**
	2 Royalties $	19**92**	
	3 Prizes, awards, etc. $		
PAYER'S Federal identification number / RECIPIENT'S identification number	4 Federal income tax withheld $	5 Fishing boat proceeds $	**Copy A For Internal Revenue Service Center**
RECIPIENT'S name	6 Medical and health care payments $	7 Nonemployee compensation $	**File with Form 1096.** For Paperwork Reduction Act Notice and instructions for completing this form, see
Street address (including apt. no.)	8 Substitute payments in lieu of dividends or interest $	9 Payer made direct sales of $5,000 or more of consumer products to a buyer (recipient) for resale ▶ □	
City, state, and ZIP code	10 Crop insurance proceeds $	11 State income tax withheld $	**Instructions for Forms 1099, 1098, 5498, and W-2G.**
Account number (optional)	2nd TIN Not. □	12 State/Payer's state number	

Form **1099-MISC**   Cat. No. 14425J   Department of the Treasury - Internal Revenue Service

21-2 1099 form Department of the Treasury, Internal Revenue Service

Revenue Service (IRS) will provide you with a guide to explain how to figure the income tax withholdings.

In addition to withholding for income taxes, you will also have to deduct for Social Security (FICA). Again, you can use a tax guidebook, available from the IRS, to figure the deductions.

Once you have computed the income and FICA withholdings, deduct them from the gross amount due the employee for wages. After doing this, enter the amount of withholdings in your bookkeeping records. While the money withheld is still in your bank account, it doesn't belong to you. Don't spend it.

As an employer you must contribute to the FICA fund for your employees. Your contribution will be equal to the amount withheld from the employee. This is just another hidden expense to having employees. Your portion of the funding will do you no good, it is only to benefit the employee.

Employer ID number

When you establish your business, apply to the IRS for an employer ID number. Some small business owners use their social security numbers as employer ID numbers, but it is better to receive an ID number for your business. You will use this identification number when you make payroll-tax deposits.

Payroll-tax deposits

Payroll-tax deposits are required of companies with employees. The IRS will provide you with a book of deposit coupons for making these deposits. The deposits can be made at your local bank.

Remember the money you withheld from your employee's paycheck, well, that's the payroll-tax deposit. The requirements for when these deposits are made fluctuate from business to business. Consult your CPA for precise instructions on how to make your payroll-tax deposits.

As a business owner, you can be held personally responsible for unpaid payroll taxes. If you sell or close your business and leave payroll taxes unpaid, the tax authorities can come after your personal assets to settle the debt. Don't play around with the money owed on payroll taxes.

Federal unemployment tax

The Federal Unemployment Tax is also know as FUTA. Your requirements for making FUTA deposits will depend on the gross amount of wages paid in a given period of time. Talk to your accountant for full details on how FUTA will affect your business.

Self-employment tax

As a self-employed individual, your Social Security tax rate might be nearly double. This is done to make up for the fact that you don't have an outside employer contributing to your portion of the Social Security fund (FIG. 21-3).

State taxes

State taxes are another consideration. Different states have various tax requirements. To be safe, check with your CPA or local tax authority to establish your requirements under local tax laws.

Labor laws

The labor laws control such areas as minimum-wage payments, overtime wages, child labor, and similar requirements. As an employer you must adhere to the rulings set forth in these laws. A phone call to the Department of Labor will get details mailed to you.

OSHA

The Occupational Safety and Health Act (OSHA) controls safety in the workplace. Your business might be affected in many ways by OSHA. To learn the requirements of OSHA, contact the Department of Labor.

Terminating employees

With so many employee rights that might be violated, you must be careful when you fire an employee. Since you never know when termination will be your only option, you should assume all employees are possible targets for termination. By this I mean you should create and maintain a paper trail on each employee's activities.

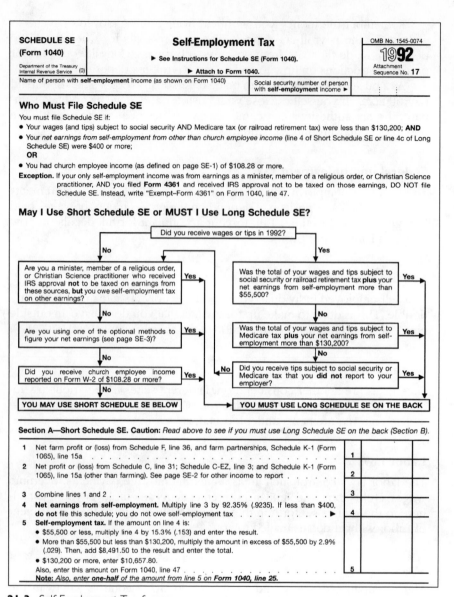

SCHEDULE SE
(Form 1040)

Department of the Treasury
Internal Revenue Service (0)

Self-Employment Tax

▶ See Instructions for Schedule SE (Form 1040).

▶ Attach to Form 1040.

OMB No. 1545-0074

1992

Attachment
Sequence No. **17**

Name of person with **self-employment** income (as shown on Form 1040)

Social security number of person with **self-employment** income ▶

Who Must File Schedule SE

You must file Schedule SE if:

• Your wages (and tips) subject to social security AND Medicare tax (or railroad retirement tax) were less than $130,200; **AND**

• Your *net earnings from self-employment from other than church employee income* (line 4 of Short Schedule SE or line 4c of Long Schedule SE) were $400 or more;
    OR

• You had church employee income (as defined on page SE-1) of $108.28 or more.

Exception. If your only self-employment income was from earnings as a minister, member of a religious order, or Christian Science practitioner, **AND** you filed **Form 4361** and received IRS approval not to be taxed on those earnings, DO NOT file Schedule SE. Instead, write "Exempt–Form 4361" on Form 1040, line 47.

May I Use Short Schedule SE or MUST I Use Long Schedule SE?

Did you receive wages or tips in 1992?

No

Yes

Are you a minister, member of a religious order, or Christian Science practitioner who received IRS approval **not** to be taxed on earnings from these sources, **but** you owe self-employment tax on other earnings? — **Yes** ▶

Was the total of your wages and tips subject to social security or railroad retirement tax **plus** your net earnings from self-employment more than $55,500? — **Yes** ▶

No

No

Are you using one of the optional methods to figure your net earnings (see page SE-3)? — **Yes** ▶

Was the total of your wages and tips subject to Medicare tax **plus** your net earnings from self-employment more than $130,200? — **Yes** ▶

No

No

Did you receive church employee income reported on Form W-2 of $108.28 or more? — **Yes** ▶

◀ **No**

Did you receive tips subject to social security or Medicare tax that you **did not** report to your employer? — **Yes** ▶

No

| **YOU MAY USE SHORT SCHEDULE SE BELOW** | ▶ | **YOU MUST USE LONG SCHEDULE SE ON THE BACK** |

Section A—Short Schedule SE. Caution: *Read above to see if you must use Long Schedule SE on the back (Section B).*

1	Net farm profit or (loss) from Schedule F, line 36, and farm partnerships, Schedule K-1 (Form 1065), line 15a	**1**
2	Net profit or (loss) from Schedule C, line 31; Schedule C-EZ, line 3; and Schedule K-1 (Form 1065), line 15a (other than farming). See page SE-2 for other income to report	**2**
3	Combine lines 1 and 2	**3**
4	**Net earnings from self-employment.** Multiply line 3 by 92.35% (.9235). If less than $400, **do not** file this schedule; you do not owe self-employment tax . . . . ▶	**4**
5	**Self-employment tax.** If the amount on line 4 is:	
	• $55,500 or less, multiply line 4 by 15.3% (.153) and enter the result.	
	• More than $55,500 but less than $130,200, multiply the amount in excess of $55,500 by 2.9% (.029). Then, add $8,491.50 to the result and enter the total.	
	• $130,200 or more, enter $10,657.80.	
	Also, enter this amount on Form 1040, line 47	**5**
	Note: *Also, enter* **one-half** *of the amount from line 5 on* **Form 1040, line 25.**	

21-3 Self-Employment Tax form Department of the Treasury, Internal Revenue Service

As soon as you hire an employee, start an employment file on the individual (FIG. 21-4). The file will grow to contain all documentation you have on the employee. Examples of the file contents might include tax forms, employment application, income records, performance reviews, attendance records, and disciplinary actions and warnings. If a time comes when you must dismiss an employee, these records will come in handy.

Before you lose your temper and fire an employee, consider the costs you will incur replacing the worker. Give yourself time to think about the

Name of person with **self-employment** income (as shown on Form 1040)	Social security number of person with **self-employment** income ▶	

Section B—Long Schedule SE

A If you are a minister, member of a religious order, or Christian Science practitioner AND you filed **Form 4361**, but you had $400 or more of **other** net earnings from self-employment, check here and continue with Part I . . . . . ▶ ☐

B If your only income subject to self-employment tax is church employee income and you are **not** a minister or a member of a religious order, skip lines 1 through 4b. Enter -0- on line 4c and go to line 5a.

Part I	**Self-Employment Tax**		
1	Net farm profit or (loss) from Schedule F, line 36, and farm partnerships, Schedule K-1 (Form 1065), line 15a. **Note:** *Skip this line if you use the farm optional method. See requirements in Part II below and on page SE-3*	**1**	
2	Net profit or (loss) from Schedule C, line 31; Schedule C-EZ, line 3; and Schedule K-1 (Form 1065), line 15a (other than farming). See page SE-2 for other income to report. **Note:** *Skip this line if you use the nonfarm optional method. See requirements in Part II below and on page SE-3*	**2**	
3	Combine lines 1 and 2	**3**	
4a	If line 3 is more than zero, multiply line 3 by 92.35% (.9235). Otherwise, enter amount from line 3	**4a**	
b	If you elected one or both of the optional methods, enter the total of lines 17 and 19 here . .	**4b**	
c	Combine lines 4a and 4b. If less than $400, **do not** file this schedule; you do not owe self-employment tax. **Exception.** If less than $400 and you had church employee income, enter -0- and continue . ▶	**4c**	
5a	Enter your church employee income from Form W-2. **Caution:** *See page SE-1 for definition of church employee income*	**5a**	
b	Multiply line 5a by 92.35% (.9235). If less than $100, enter -0-	**5b**	
6	**Net earnings from self-employment.** Add lines 4c and 5b	**6**	
7	Maximum amount of combined wages and self-employment earnings subject to social security tax or the 6.2% portion of the 7.65% railroad retirement (tier 1) tax for 1992	**7**	55,500 00
8a	Total social security wages and tips (from Form(s) W-2) and railroad retirement (tier 1) compensation	**8a**	
b	Unreported tips subject to social security tax (from Form 4137, line 9)	**8b**	
c	Add lines 8a and 8b	**8c**	
9	Subtract line 8c from line 7. If zero or less, enter -0- here and on line 10 and go to line 12a ▶	**9**	
10	Multiply the **smaller** of line 6 or line 9 by 12.4% (.124)	**10**	
11	Maximum amount of combined wages and self-employment earnings subject to Medicare tax or the 1.45% portion of the 7.65% railroad retirement (tier 1) tax for 1992	**11**	130,200 00
12a	Total Medicare wages and tips (from Form(s) W-2) and railroad retirement (tier 1) compensation	**12a**	
b	Unreported tips subject to Medicare tax (from Form 4137, line 14)	**12b**	
c	Add lines 12a and 12b	**12c**	
13	Subtract line 12c from line 11. If zero or less, enter -0- here and on line 14 and go to line 15 .	**13**	
14	Multiply the **smaller** of line 6 or line 13 by 2.9% (.029)	**14**	
15	**Self-employment tax.** Add lines 10 and 14. Enter the result here and on Form 1040, line 47 . **Note:** *Also, enter one-half of the amount from line 15 on* **Form 1040, line 25.**	**15**	

Part II	**Optional Methods To Figure Net Earnings** (See **Who Can File Schedule SE** on page SE-1 and **Optional Methods** on page SE-3.)		

Farm Optional Method. You may use this method **only if (a)** Your gross farm income[1] was not more than $2,400 **or (b)** Your gross farm income[1] was more than $2,400 and your net farm profits[2] were less than $1,733.

16	Maximum income for optional methods	**16**	1,600 00
17	Enter the **smaller** of: two-thirds (⅔) of gross farm income[1] or $1,600. Also, include this amount on line 4b above	**17**	

Nonfarm Optional Method. You may use this method **only if (a)** Your net nonfarm profits[3] were less than $1,733 and also less than 72.189% of your gross nonfarm income,[4] **and (b)** You had net earnings from self-employment of at least $400 in 2 of the prior 3 years. **Caution:** *You may use this method no more than five times.*

18	Subtract line 17 from line 16	**18**	
19	Enter the **smaller** of: two-thirds (⅔) of gross nonfarm income[4] **or** the amount on line 18. Also, include this amount on line 4b above	**19**	

[1] From Schedule F, line 11, and Schedule K-1 (Form 1065), line 15b.
[2] From Schedule F, line 36, and Schedule K-1 (Form 1065), line 15a.
[3] From Schedule C, line 31; Schedule C-EZ, line 3; and Schedule K-1 (Form 1065), line 15a.
[4] From Schedule C, line 7; Schedule C-EZ, line 1; and Schedule K-1 (Form 1065), line 15c.

*U.S. GPO: 1992-315-191

21-3 Continued

offense. Is it really necessary to fire the individual? If the circumstances demand termination, do so with care. Consult your attorney in advance to be certain of your responsibilities.

EXERCISE QUALITY CONTROL

By exercising quality control over employees you can build a better business (FIG. 21-5). Quality control is just what it sounds like—controlling qual-

Employee-File Checklist

Employee name: _____

Employee ss # _____

Item	In file	Need	Notes
I-9 Form			
W-4 Form			
Application			
Tax Info			
Insurance Info			
Reviews			
Warnings			
Attendance			

21-4 Employee-file checklist

Weekly Work History

Employee: _____

Payroll number: _____

Date	Work phase & Job name	Time in	Time out	Total time

21-5 Weekly work history

ity. The qualities most business owners are interested in controlling are:

- Punctuality
- Work habits
- Customer service
- Work quality
- Dependability
- Loyalty

There are other qualities you might wish to keep in check. You might request your employees to participate in continuing education programs. Having your employees expand their capabilities into other work areas could be one of your pet projects. Once you know what you want from your employees, work with the employees to meet your goals.

TRAIN EMPLOYEES TO DO THE JOB

Training employees to do the job used to be standard procedure, but not today. Today, most employers are looking for experienced people that can step into a position and be productive. The days of training apprentices are all but gone.

Why has this shift in the workplace occurred? One reason is money; it costs money to train employees. Even if you do the training yourself, it costs money. The time that you spend away from your routine duties is lost income. To train employees, you must look upon the training as an investment.

In the old days, employees stuck with their employers for a long time. If an employer trained an employee, the business owner could be reasonably confident the employee would stay with the company. Today, employees change jobs in the blink of an eye. Employers know this and are reluctant to train employees that will run to another employer if an opportunity arises. It is sad, but the traditional values that once existed have been eroded with the increased demand for the mighty dollar.

The quest for money is not only in the minds of employees. Many employers don't want to hire inexperienced help because they know new employees will not make as much money for them as an experienced employee. With everyone being in a hurry to grab the brass ring, no one has time to build a stable business or career. Everyone seems to take the shortest path they can find to potential riches.

These circumstances are changing the business world. Since the old masters are not passing their knowledge down to apprentices, the crop of qualified tradespeople is shrinking. In time, if this pattern continues, the artful craftsmanship of the past will be only a memory.

Should you hire experienced help or train new people to do the job your way? I guess it makes more sense to hire people that can jump out there and start turning a dollar. But if you do train employees to produce the type of work you want, you might be happier. You might gain a certain satisfaction from watching a rookie mature into a journeyman. The choice is yours, but be advised, trainees are likely to look for a higher-paying job once you have trained them.

TRAIN EMPLOYEES TO DEAL WITH CUSTOMERS

I believe training employees to deal with customers is the responsibility of every business owner. Every business is run differently, and even experienced plumbers have to be taught to treat customers the way you want them treated. Your customers are your business. If you alienate them, you lose your business. Employees are representatives of your company. If they act improperly around customers, it will be a reflection on your business.

It is a good idea to develop a policy manual on how you want customers treated. Issue the manual to each of your employees and require them to commit it to memory. If necessary, test the employees' knowledge of the manual. Before you put people in touch with your customers, make sure they will behave in a suitable manner.

ESTABLISH THE COST OF EMPLOYEES

There are many hidden costs involved with employees, and each employee will have a different set of circumstances. Before you set your prices, know what each of your employees is costing you.

The most obvious cost is the hourly wage, but there are other factors. Some employees will receive more benefits than others. If one employee gets a two-week paid vacation and another employee gets one week of paid vacation, the cost of the employees will be different by an amount equal to the extra week of vacation pay.

As employees build seniority, they normally gain additional benefits. You must consider all of these costs when you determine the overall cost of an employee. Whether it is health insurance, dental insurance, or paid leave, you must factor the cost into your projections.

Bonus pay is another item that can influence the cost of your employees. If you are in the habit of giving each employee a bonus during the holiday season, add this money to the cost of the employee.

Don't overlook any part of your employee expenses. Once you have all the figures, chart the hourly differences. When you bid a job, bid it based on your most expensive employees. Then if you can put employees that cost less on the job you will make more money. But if your least expensive labor is not available, you will not lose anything by putting your top-paid people on the job.

DEAL WITH PRODUCTION DOWN TIME

You have already seen how you can lose money if your crews must stop to run for materials, but that is not the only way you can lose money to down time. Some causes for these losses will be beyond your control, but many of them can be avoided with strong management skills.

Bad weather

Bad weather can often shut a contractor down. While you can't control the weather, you can plan for its effect on your business. If you have a business that involves inside work, try to save this work for days when the weather won't allow your normal outside operations.

If you start a job where the weather might cause delays, plan on ways to circumvent the lost time. This might involve using tarps to cover the work area or renting heaters to keep the job site comfortable. Look for ways to keep production up during any weather conditions.

When the circumstances cannot be overcome, use your best judgment when deciding what to do with your employees. Most employers will send the employees home without pay. On the surface this saves money, but it might cause you to lose your employees. Good employees are hard to find, and a turnover in employees is expensive. You might be money ahead to create some busy work for your crews, even if it is not cost effective.

Some ideas for busy work include counting inventory, taking trucks in for service, or performing maintenance on equipment. While these tasks might not warrant the use of highly paid personnel, they must be done. If it keeps your employees in place, you might be better off.

Past-due deliveries

There will be times when a delivery isn't made and you must find work for your crews. Be prepared for these times with some back-up plans. If you send the crews home, they might not be happy. On the other hand, maybe they would enjoy having the day off, even if they aren't getting paid. Give them the option of taking the day off or doing fill-in work.

Code-enforcement rejections

It is difficult to think of a suitable excuse for this type of down time. If you or your field supervisors are supervising the work, there should be no excuse for a failed inspection. If you start to have recurrent problems of this nature, you need tighter control over your field supervisors.

Disabled vehicles

Every contractor is going to have problems with disabled vehicles from time to time. The most you can do to prevent these problems is regular maintenance. When a truck breaks down and is going to be out of service for an extended time, try to double up your crews. There isn't much else you can do.

A lull in work

Sooner or later, a lull in your workload will cause you down time with your crews. There are times of the year when these lulls can be projected. Typical times include holidays, summer vacation seasons, tax seasons, and school start-up seasons.

Proper preparation can help you overcome these slow periods. Line up work in advance for the slow times. Advertise aggressively and offer discounts, if necessary, to keep your people busy. Avoid laying your people off. Once they are gone, you might not get them back.

REDUCE CALL BACKS AND WARRANTY WORK

Reduce employee call backs and warranty work and you will increase your profits. Customers will not pay you to do the same work twice, but you will have to pay your employees for their time. This can get expensive fast. If you have sloppy workers who frequently cause call backs, you must take action.

Everyone is going to make mistakes, but professionals shouldn't make many. Call backs are generally the result of negligence: the mechanic did the job too quickly, too poorly, or didn't check the work before leaving. You can and must control this type of behavior.

Call backs and warranty work hurt your business in two big ways. The first hurt is financial. You lose money on this type of work. The second problem is the confidence your customers lose in the quality of your work. You cannot afford either of these results. There are several options available for controlling these costly occurrences. Let's look at some of the ways that have worked for others and that might work for you.

Call-back boards

Call-back boards (FIG. 21-6) can reduce your call backs when you have multiple employees. Hang a call-back board in a part of your office that all employees can see. When a mechanic has a callback, the mechanic's name is put on the board. The board is cleared each month, but people with call backs must see their name on the board for up to a full month.

Employee	Call-Back	Date
Fred	Jackson Job	6-4-93
Joyce	Dunn Job	6-18-93
Bud	Wilson Job	6-22-93

21-6 Call-back board

Generally, there is a certain competitiveness among plumbers. If a mechanic's name is on the call-back board, he will probably be embarrassed. This simple tactic can have a profound effect on your call-back ratio.

Employee participation

Employee participation in the financial losses of call backs is another option. However, your employees must agree to this plan without being pressured. For your protection, have all employees agree to the policy in writing.

Under the employee-participation program, employees agree to handle their call backs on their own time. You pay for materials and the employees absorb the cost of their labor. As a variation to this program, you can agree to pay the employee for the first two call backs in a given month, with the employee taking any additional call backs without pay. Before you implement either of these programs, confirm their legality in your area, and have your employees agree to your employment terms in writing.

Bonus incentives

Bonus incentives are another way to curtail call backs. If you can eliminate warranty work by offering bonuses, do it. You won't lose any more money and you won't lose any credibility with your customers.

If you don't like the idea of giving employees bonuses for doing a job the way they should in the first place, hedge your bets. Determine what the maximum annual bonus for any employee will be, and adjust your starting wages to build in a buffer for the bonuses. The employee will feel rewarded with the bonus and you won't be paying extra for services you expect to get out of a fair day's work.

OFFICE EMPLOYEES

Office employees are a little easier to manage than field employees. If you are an office-based owner, your office employees will feel compelled to stay busy. They know you are watching their performance.

Office employees can be intimidated when the boss is close at hand. If this happens, production will drop off or mistakes will multiply. Hire the best help you can find, and then let them do their jobs. If you constantly look over their shoulders, you will do more harm than good.

If you get bored, don't start bending the ear of your office help. When you distract the office workers, your work will not get done. Set an example for your employees. If they see you hanging around the coffee pot swapping stories, they will feel cheated that they don't have the same privileges. If you want to goof off, do it behind closed doors.

Don't neglect the needs and desires of your office employees. If you have a good employee who wants a new chair, buy a new chair. When your workers want a coffee maker, buy a coffee maker. If your employees' requests are reasonable, attend to them. Happy employees are more productive, not to mention nicer to be around.

FIELD EMPLOYEES

Field employees present more management challenges than office help. These employees are mobile and can be difficult to monitor. You might know about every trip your secretary makes to the snack area, but it will be hard pressed to keep up with how many times your field crews take a break.

The best way to keep tabs on your crews is to monitor job production. If the work is getting done on time, what difference does it make if the crew takes three breaks instead of two? If you have good employees that are turning out strong production, leave them alone.

Too much employer presence is not good. You are a boss, not a babysitter. When you hire professionals, expect them to be competent workers. If you make the decision to hire people, you are going to have to trust them to some extent.

If you are concerned about your field crews, talk to your customers. Customers are generally very aware of how crews act. Make some unannounced visits to the job sites. Don't let the crews get too comfortable, but don't crowd them either.

EMPLOYEE MOTIVATION TECHNIQUES

Use employee motivation tactics to increase your business profits. There are books written for the express purpose of showing employers how to motivate their employees. A creative employer can always find ways to influence employees to do better. Let me give you just a few suggestions that might work for your company.

Awards

Awards are welcomed by everyone. You can issue award certificates for everything from perfect attendance to outstanding achievements. These inexpensive pieces of paper can make a world of difference in the way employees act.

An employee that knows she will get a certificate for coming to work every day will think twice before calling in sick when she isn't. While the award might not have a financial value, it becomes a goal. Employees that are working towards a goal will work better.

Money

Money is a great motivator. Since most people work for money, it stands to reason they might work a little harder for extra pay. Any type of bonus program will increase the production rate of your employees.

A day off with pay

Sometimes a day off with pay is worth more to an employee than the value of the wages. This special treat might become a coveted goal. One idea would be to hold a contest where the most productive employee of the month gets a day off with pay. Sure, you'll lose the cost of a day's pay, but how much will you gain from all of your employees during the competition?

Performance ratings

Performance ratings can be compared to awards. If employees know they will be rated on their performance, they might work harder. These ratings should be put in writing and kept in the employees' files.

Titles

Wise business owners know that a lot of people would rather have a fancy title than extra money. In fact, many companies promote people into new titles to avoid giving raises. Even if your company is small, you can hand out impressive titles. For example, instead of calling your field supervisor a foreman, call him a field coordinator. Instead of having a secretary, have an office manager. When you have someone that enters data in a computer all day, change the title from data entry clerk to computer operations manager.

Titles make employees feel better about themselves, and they don't cost you anything. If you are willing to spend a few hours thinking creatively, you can come up with many ways to maximize the performance of your employees.

22

Insurance and retirement options

As a business owner you must consider all aspects of the insurance issue. If your mind is on health insurance, you must acknowledge the fact that you no longer have deductions taken from your paycheck. You must establish your own insurance program, pay all the costs, consider the tax consequences, and determine what impact employees will have on the program you choose.

If you have employees or plan to hire employees, benefit packages are a serious consideration. If you don't offer employees benefits, you might not get or keep the best employees. It has become standard practice for employers to provide their workers with benefits.

Many business owners are not aware of the alternatives and combinations available for insurance, benefits, and retirement plans. If you are your company's only employee, your choices will be easier to make. If you employ others, you will have some studying to do. This chapter is going to prepare you for the kinds of decisions you will have to make.

COMPANY-PROVIDED INSURANCE FOR YOU

Putting an insurance program in place for yourself, when no other employees are involved, is not difficult. However, choosing the right plans will take some research. Health insurance is almost a given. Everyone should try to maintain this type of coverage. Dental insurance is not as critical as health insurance, but it does provide some additional peace of mind. Disability insurance is often ignored, but it can be beneficial if you are injured or suffer a severe illness. Life insurance might not be important if you don't have a family, but if you do, life insurance should be considered a necessity. Key-man insurance isn't needed for a mom-and-pop business, as long as there is enough life insurance in force, but it can become a factor as your business grows. Let's take a closer look at each of these types of coverage and see how they fit into your business plans.

Health insurance

Health insurance is expensive and the plans are complex. Deciding on what type of insurance to get will require research and thought. Let's find out what you should look for in health insurance.

Pre-existing conditions Most insurance companies will not cover expenses related to a pre-existing condition. For example, if you have problems with your back when you obtain new insurance, the insurance company might refuse to cover medical expenses related to your known back problems. If you have had a pregnancy that involved surgery or medical attention beyond the normal child-birth requirements, a reoccurrence of these circumstances might not be covered by your new policy.

It is possible to obtain insurance that covers pre-existing conditions. The premiums for these policies might be higher, but the protection might be worth the additional cost.

Deductible payments The deductible payments for insurance plans vary. Typically, the more you have to pay in deductible expenses, the lower your monthly premiums. A plan with a $200 deductible will cost more on a monthly basis than a plan with a $500 deductible. It is generally considered wise to choose a plan with a higher deductible and lower premium payments.

Limits of standard coverage Before you buy any insurance plan, understand the limits of standard coverage. Not all policies cover all possible circumstances. Read policies closely and ask questions. The insurance company might not have to disclose facts to you unless they are asked direct questions.

Waiting period It is possible that an insurance policy will require a waiting period. These waiting periods stipulate that a specific amount of time must pass before a procedure is covered. For example, most insurance will not cover the costs of a pregnancy until after a waiting period has passed. Since the insured might have been pregnant when the policy was taken out, the waiting period eliminates the risk to the insurance company. Determine if the policy you are considering has a waiting period and if so, what conditions apply to the rules of the waiting period.

Co-payments Average health plans call for the insured to make co-payments. This means that you will be responsible for paying a portion of your medical expenses, even though you are insured. A common co-payment amount is 20 percent. You pay 20 percent and the insurance company pays 80 percent. The split on how much each party pays can vary. You might find that you are responsible for 30 percent of the bills.

Verify how your policy deals with co-payments. Some insurance plans are more generous and pay nearly the entire cost of your medical expenses. For example, you might only pay a few dollars for each office visit to your doctor. These pay-all policies cost more, but they provide excellent coverage and you will not have to come up with large sums of out-of-pocket cash.

Dependent coverage If you have dependents, you will want to know how a policy deals with dependent coverage. Will your dependents receive the same coverage as you? Will the premiums be set at reduced rates for the additional coverage? Are there limits on dependent coverage? Is there an age limit on dependency coverage? All of these are questions you should ask about dependent coverage.

Rate increases Rate increases are a fact of life with insurance though some insurance policies are more prone to rate increases than others. Ask how often the insurance company is allowed to raise its rates. Will you be faced with increases quarterly, semi-annually, or annually? Inquire about caps on the amount of increase at any one interval. For example, if your rates will be subject to an increase on an annual basis, what is the maximum amount the rate can be elevated?

Group advantages As a business owner you might be eligible for group advantages. Some insurance companies take small groups of customers and create a large group. This type of grouping is designed to offer coverage at lower rates. Your company will need at least two employees for this type of coverage. The savings might be worth putting your spouse on the payroll. Check with your insurance representative for the requirements to join a group plan.

Dental insurance

Dental insurance is a blessing for people with bad teeth. If you have paid for crowns or root canals, you know they aren't cheap. Should you buy dental insurance? The decision is yours, but dental insurance can be well worth its cost for the right people. When you shop for dental insurance, ask the same questions you ask about health insurance.

If you decide to buy dental insurance, expect to go through a waiting period for major-expense coverage. While some policies will pick up immediately routine maintenance of your teeth, you will probably have to wait for those needed crowns and caps. The waiting period for major work is usually one year. Many dental plans will pay no more than half of your major expenses. For example, if you are getting a $500 crown, your insurance might only pay $250.

Disability insurance

Disability policies provide you with a percentage of your normal income while you are unable to work. The percentage of your income that is paid will depend on your policy. These policies can also be loaded with pre-existing condition waivers. Let me give you examples of how each type of disability plan might work.

Short-term disability Short-term disability policies will set a limit on the amount of time you can receive benefits. Six months is commonly the maximum period of time you may collect from a short-term policy. There is usually a short waiting period before the disability income (DI) kicks in. In most cases, you will have to be out of work for at least a week before you can collect your DI. The amount you can collect will be a percentage of your normal income. A plan that pays up to 50 percent of your income is not unusual. However, there are generally limits on the maximum amount you can collect in dollar amounts.

For example, your policy may pay 50 percent of your normal weekly pay, but it might stipulate that the maximum you can receive in any given week is $150. Obviously, if you make more than $300 a week, and most plumbing contractors do, you will not be getting half of your income in benefits. Watch out for these little stingers.

Long-term disability Long-term disability is similar to short-term disability. These plans might pay a higher percentage of your income than short-term DI. There will be limits on the minimum and the maximum monthly payments, but the length of time you can collect payments is frequently unlimited.

Life insurance

Life insurance doesn't seem very important until you have dependents. When you are single there is no need to worry about how people will get along without your income when you die. Your mind isn't filled with questions of how your bills will be paid after you are gone or how your child will grow up and be educated. However, when you have people you care for who will be left behind after your death, life insurance becomes important.

How much life insurance is enough?

How much life insurance is enough? The amount of life insurance coverage you need will depend on several factors. The first factor is your number of dependents. A person with only a spouse will need less insurance than a person with a spouse and two children.

Another factor is your income. Many people suggest buying insurance coverage based on a multiple of your annual income. Some people say insurance benefits equal to your annual salary is enough. More people are inclined to believe it is better to have coverage equal to three years worth of income. Your spouse's employment conditions will influence this decision.

If your spouse isn't working, and hasn't worked for some time, your spouse might find it difficult to find a job. If you have been the sole provider, your spouse will have to grieve, adjust to your death, find work, and establish a new life. This is not only stressful, it takes time. Can all of this take place in one year? It could, but it would be a strain. So if you leave behind only one year's worth of benefits, the spouse is under extra pressure. Don't forget, there also will be burial expenses and other related expenses to be paid out of the benefits you bequeath.

Is your spouse capable of being self supportive? If you are leaving behind a spouse and children, the spouse might not have the earning ability to support the remaining family members. If this possibility exists, you should carry enough insurance to allow for investments and long-term support.

If you died today, how many personal and business debts would be left to your spouse? This consideration must be weighed when you decide on an amount of your life insurance.

There are numerous factors to consider before you determine the face amount of your life insurance. Some people look at life insurance as a one-time shot in the arm for the distressed family members. These people assume leaving their spouse $100,000 in cash is more than adequate. In this mind set, the spouse is expected to live off the $100,000 until a new life is built. This isn't a bad plan, but there is another perspective to consider.

In my estate planning, I have structured a way for my wife and daughter to derive most of their annual income needs from the interest of my life insurance dividends. When I die, if the proceeds from my life insurance are invested wisely, the passive income generated will be substantial. This passive income will support my family, without them having to deplete the lump sum of the premium payoff.

My wife and daughter will be well cared for, and the money paid by the insurance company will remain virtually untouched. When my wife passes on, her life insurance dividends can be handled in a similar way. The end result for our daughter will be a comfortable income from her investments and a sizable nest egg in cash.

To generate this type of insurance payoff you have to carry some steep premiums. Not all people are willing to invest their money in life insurance, and I'm not saying you should. I believe you should buy as much life insurance as you feel you need and not a penny more. Now let's look at the various types of insurance.

Term life insurance

Term life insurance is one of the least expensive forms of life insurance you can buy. While it is the cheapest, it might not be the best value. There are many types of term policies. Some of the programs feature premiums that increase annually, others have face amounts that are reduced each year; some might do both.

Term insurance is fine as a supplemental life insurance, but it might not be the best choice for a primary insurance. When you are in your prime earning years and building assets, term policies can protect your family from incurring your debts.

For example, if you are buying a house with a 30-year mortgage and die while there is a substantial loan outstanding, what will your spouse do? If your spouse can't afford the house payments, the house will have to be sold. If you have term life insurance, the proceeds from the policy might be used to satisfy the mortgage on the house. As time passes, the amount you owe on the home is reduced, so the reducing term insurance is not such a bad deal. You are paying only for the insurance you need, while you need it.

If you depend on term life insurance as your only life insurance, you might be underinsured. As you grow older the premiums might go up and the value might go down. If you live a normal life, the policy might not be worth much at the time of your death.

Whole-life policies

Whole-life policies are more expensive than term insurance, but they are more dependable. The face amount of these policies doesn't decrease and the premiums don't go up. As you make your monthly payments you build a cash value in the policy. In effect, you create a savings account of a sort.

Later in life, if you need some quick cash you can borrow against the built-up cash value. Interest rates on these loans are usually low, and you can pay back the money at your discretion. If you reach a point in life where you no longer want to maintain your life insurance, you can cash in a whole-life policy and receive the cash value.

Universal and variable policies

Universal and variable-life policies are variations of whole-life policies. These policies feature investment angles for your premium dollars. As you pay your premiums you build cash value and your account earns interest. The interest you earn is rolled over and is not taxable, unless it is withdrawn. Many business owners choose these policies.

Key-man insurance

Key-man insurance is a form of life insurance that protects a company against the death of a vital employee. Normally, the employee is insured by the employer and the employer pays the insurance premiums. If the employee dies, the proceeds of the insurance goes to the employing company. This gives the company a cash buffer until the key employee can be replaced.

Unless you are in a partnership or a corporation with other stockholders you shouldn't need key-man insurance. Regular life insurance can protect your family and cover your business debts. However, if you have a partner that you depend upon heavily, you might want to set up a key-man plan.

Other options for life insurance

There are many other life insurance options. There are all types of riders that can be added to standard policies, and terms and conditions can be adjusted to meet every conceivable need. Due to the complexity of insurance programs, talk to several insurance professionals before making a buying decision.

CHOOSE AN INSURANCE COMPANY

Not all insurance companies have the same financial strength. The investment abilities of some companies are much better than those of other companies.

Choose your insurance firm carefully. Research the company and attempt to establish its financial power and track record. Talk with state agencies and go to major libraries to find performance ratings on the various companies. Dig deep into a company's background before you depend on them to protect you.

EMPLOYEE BENEFITS

Employee benefits can be even harder to decipher than your own benefits. The strict rules and regulations that govern employee benefits make the chore more challenging. If you fail to execute your duties in the proper manner, you might wind up in serious trouble.

The benefits you offer employees might include any of the insurance coverages we have already discussed. However, when you set up plans for employees, you will have to follow some additional guidelines.

Most companies use an employee policy manual to explain company benefits to their employees. These policy manuals tell employees what benefits they might be eligible for and when their eligibility begins. It is important that you treat all your employees equally. You should not provide benefits for your pet employees and deny the same offering to other employees. If you do this, you are asking for trouble. The policy manual makes it easy for you to set and maintain protocol.

Many employers choose an insurance company that offers multiple benefits in a single plan. The benefits might include medical, dental, life, disability, and accident insurance. This type of employee package can be cost-prohibitive, but it is an attractive feature when you are trying to hire and keep top-notch employees.

Some of these multiplans allow employees to make some of their own coverage choices. The employer gives each employee a set allowance to allocate to various types of coverage. Then the employee is free to customize his or her individual plan. This type of employee package is often referred to as a flexible benefit package or a cafeteria plan.

Other benefits you might offer your employees include paid sick leave, paid personal days, paid vacation, retirement plans, and bonus programs.

Before you make a decision to give benefits to your employees, research the rules and regulations you must follow. Talk to your attorney, your insurance agent, and your state agencies. After talking to these professionals, you should have all the information you need to stay on the right side of the law.

RETIREMENT PLAN OPTIONS

Whether you're looking for a retirement plan for yourself or for your employees, you will have many from which to choose. To prove this point, let's look at some of the most common methods of building retirement capital.

Rental properties

Rental properties can be an ideal source of retirement income for you. Real estate is one of the best ways to keep up with the rising rates of inflation, and inflation is one of your biggest enemies when you plan for retirement. The money earned from some investments will not amount to a hill of beans when you retire. Real estate has the edge in these circumstances because of its typical pattern of appreciation.

Keogh plans

Keogh plans for self-employed people can get a little complicated. If you are self employed, you can contribute up to 25 percent of your earnings to the fund. However, the maximum dollar contribution is capped at $30,000.

The 25 percent you are allowed to contribute is not computed on your gross earnings alone. After you determine how much you are going to put into your Keogh, subtract that amount from your gross earnings. Then you may contribute up to 25 percent of what is left of your earnings. In effect, you can only fund 20 percent of your total earnings. Let's say you had a great year and earned $100,000. You want to contribute $20,000 to your retirement plan. After subtracting the $20,000 from your earnings, you are left with $80,000. Twenty-five percent of $80,000 is $20,000—the maximum you can invest.

A defined-benefit plan can allow larger contributions for older people. However, these plans are expensive to establish and maintain.

If you have employees, these plans become even more confusing. As the employer you not only must deduct the contribution to your personal plan before you arrive at the earnings figure used to factor your maximum contribution, you must also deduct the contributions you make as your part of the employees' contributions.

When you set up a Keogh plan, you must name a trustee. The trustee is usually a financial institution. Before you attempt to establish and use your own Keogh plan, consult with an attorney or investment consultant who is familiar with the rules and regulations.

Pension plans

Pension plans for your employees must be funded in good years and bad years. If you are hiring older employees, they will probably prefer a pension plan over a profit-sharing plan. Pension plans provide a consistent company contribution to the employee's retirement plan.

Pension plans are termed qualified plans. This means they meet the requirements of Section 401 of the Internal Revenue Code and qualify for favorable tax advantages. These tax advantages help you and your employees.

If you decide to use a qualified pension plan, you must cover at least 70 percent of your average employees. The features and benefits of these plans are extensive. For complete details on forming and using such a plan, consult with a qualified professional.

Profit sharing

Profit-sharing plans can also be termed qualified plans. One advantage to you, the employer, is that there is no regulation requiring you to fund the plan in bad economic years.

A formula needs to be established to identify the amount of contributions that will be made to profit-sharing plans. The plan will also detail when contributions will be made. Many new companies prefer profit-sharing plans because there is no mandatory funding in years when a profit is not made.

Social security

Did you know that social security benefits are taxable? If an individual's adjusted gross income, tax-exempt interest, and one-half of the individual's social security benefits exceed $25,000, the social security benefits can be taxed. The maximum tax is one-half of the social security benefits.

Annuities

These investments are safe, pay good interest rates, and the interest you earn is tax deferred until you cash the annuity. If you need access to your money early, you will pay a penalty for early withdrawal. If you plan to let your money work for you in an annuity for 7 to 10 years, annuities are a safe bet.

If you decide to put your money in annuities, shop around. There are a multitude of programs open to you. If you want to investigate annuity plans for employees, talk with professionals in the field. Again, there are many options available for these programs, but there are also rules that must be followed.

Other options

Bonds, art, antiques, diamonds, gold, silver, rare coins, stocks, and mutual funds are all conceivable retirement investments. Any of these forms of investments might return a desirable rate of return, but many require a keen knowledge of the market. For example, if you are not an experienced coin buyer, your rare coin collection might wind up being worth little more than its face value.

For most business owners, sticking to conservative investments is best for retirement. If you have some extra money you can afford to play with, you might diversify your conservative investments with some of the more exciting opportunities available. However, when you are betting on your golden years, play your cards carefully.

LIABILITY INSURANCE

Liability insurance is one type of insurance coverage no business can afford to be without. The extent of coverage needed will vary, but all business ventures should be protected by liability insurance.

General liability insurance protects its holder from claims arising from personal injury or property damage. When a company has a current general liability policy, all representatives of the company are typically covered under the policy, when performing company business.

Without adequate coverage against liability claims, you might lose your business and all your other assets. Contractors are in particular need of this type of insurance. With so many possibilities for accidents on the job site, you can't afford to do business without it.

WORKER'S COMPENSATION INSURANCE

Worker's compensation insurance is insurance that is generally required of companies that have employees who are not close family members. Worker's comp insurance benefits your employees. If employees are injured in the performance of their duties on your payroll, this insurance will help them financially. The employees might receive payment for their medical expenses that are related to the injury. If employees are disabled, they might receive partial disability income from the program. Other events, such as a fatal injury, could result in similar benefits being paid to the employee's heirs.

The cost of worker's compensation insurance will be based on your company's total payroll expenses and the types of work performed by various employees. The rate for a secretary will be much lower than the rate for a plumber. Each employee is put into a job classification and rated for a degree of risk. Once the risk of injury and other factors are assessed, an estimated premium is established.

At the end of the year the insurance carrier will conduct an audit of your company's payroll expenses. The carrier will determine how much was actually paid out in payroll and to what job classifications the wages were paid. At this time, the insurance company will render an accurate accounting of what is owed them or due to your company. Since some preliminary annual estimates are high, it is possible your company will receive a refund. If the original estimate was low, your company must pay the additional premium requirements.

Worker's comp is, at best, a bad experience for companies that have injured personnel. If your company is accident prone, you will pay for it in higher premiums.

Worker's comp for subcontractors

When you engage a subcontractor to work for your company, you might be held responsible for the cost of worker's compensation insurance on that sub. You can avoid this by requiring subcontractors to furnish you with a certificate of insurance before you allow them to do any work.

The certificate of insurance should come directly from the company issuing the insurance. When you receive the certificate of insurance, check it for coverage and expiration. When you are satisfied that the sub has proper insurance, file the certificate for future proof of insurance.

When your insurance company audits you at the end of the year, you might need to produce certificates of insurance on all of your independent contractors. You cannot afford to let your guard down on this one. Paying premiums for insurance for which subcontractors should be responsible will cause you great grief.

Some contractors deduct money from payments due subcontractors when the subs don't carry the necessary insurance. The money is used at the end of the year when the contractors settle up with their insurance companies. While this has been done for years, I don't recommend it. It is best to require the subcontractors to carry and provide proof of their own insurance.

SOME FINAL WORDS

Allow me to give you some final words on insurance and retirement plans. These plans can be quite sophisticated. With the complexity of the circumstances surrounding the plans, you should always consult experts before you make a decision. Make yourself aware of your responsibilities to your employees.

There are many factors that affect how you must treat each employee. Don't assume that part-time employees are not the same as full-time employees under your benefits package. There probably are exceptions to part-time help, but don't make that assumption. Don't assume anything. Employees' rights and the law are too important to guess about. Consult professionals and maintain your integrity as an employer.

The facts I have given you in this chapter are based on my experience and research. I am not an expert on insurance, tax law, general law, or retirement plans. The information I have provided you is more than enough to direct you toward professional advisors, but it is by no means enough to replace professional consultations. Rely only on the advice of expert professionals in all of these areas.

23

Avoid common business traps

How well your business prospers will depend largely on how proficient you become at moving with market trends. Running a business is a time-consuming responsibility. If you don't make time to improve your business as you go along, the business might not last five years.

There are many common business traps that can stop your business dead in its tracks. This chapter is going to show you some of these pitfalls and how you might avoid them.

LOOK TO THE FUTURE

You don't need a crystal ball to look into the future. What you need is determination, time, and skill. Time can be made, and skills can be learned, but you must already possess determination. If you are committed to making your business successful, you can do a fair job of projecting your business future.

How can you judge what your business will encounter three years from now? Our economy runs in cycles. Most contracting businesses are affected in some way by the real estate market. If the construction of new homes is down, most contracting fields suffer. When housing starts are up, contractors seem to thrive. Since the economy is cyclic, you can look back into history to project the future. The clues you find might not be right on the money, but they are likely to render a clear picture of what's in store for your business.

Reading old newspapers at the library is one way to delve into the past. Talking with people who have lived through the tough times is a good way to gain insight into what happened and why it happened. Tracking past political performances can produce clues to the future. The key is spending the time and the effort to look back so that you can look ahead.

If you look deep into the history of the last 20 years, you will find some interesting facts. In the late 70s and early 80s, banks were quick to rise to the problems at hand. Creative financing blossomed and the business world turned itself around.

In the more recent recession of the late 80s and early 90s, the banks did not rally to help. Instead, many of them closed. Business owners in this recession didn't have the high interest rates to combat, but they also didn't have willing lenders to help them with their financial battles.

With interest rates low and efforts being made to get the economy back on track for the mid and late 90s, why aren't people spending money? I believe people are afraid to spend what money they have. Many people are without jobs and the ones that have jobs don't know how long they will have them. Public confidence appears to be at an all-time low. Until confidence is restored, the rebirth of the economy will be painfully slow.

Once you are familiar with the past, you can see trends as they form. You will be able to spot danger signals. These early-warning signs can be enough to save your business from financial ruin. If you like, you can compare your market study with the work of people tracking storms to warn of tornados and hurricanes. Certainly more people have been spared the pain of these vicious storms since scientists have studied and tracked past storms. Unless you have an astute business advisor, you will have to learn to pick up on your own early-warning signals.

LONG-RANGE PLANNING PAYS OFF

Prepare for the worst and you will be able to handle most situations that come your way. Your plans must focus on financial matters, as well as other considerations. As you grow older, how will your business be run? If you do your own field work, how will it get done when you are no longer physically able to do it? How quickly will you allow your business to grow? These are only some of the questions you will want to answer when you plan for the future. Change is inevitable and beyond your control. How you plan for the changes is within your grasp. To have a long-term business, you must have a long-term plan.

BE FLEXIBLE

Businesses don't change themselves; people change them. How will you change your business? You probably don't know yet, but you had better start making plans now for the changes.

Get tired of working in the field

The physical work that has kept you in good shape might become a bit much for you in 10 or 20 years. How will you adjust when you need to get away from the physical work?

Some plumbers plan to stay in the field until the day they retire. Many contractors anticipate hiring employees or subcontractors to pick up the slack in the physical work. Of the two options, I recommend planning on hiring help. You might well get tired of working in the field before you can afford to retire.

If you know that some day you plan to bring employees or subcontractors into your business, start planning for the change now. In your spare time, if you have any, read up on human resources and management skills. The knowledge you gain now will be valuable when you enlist the help of others in your business.

Company growth

Company growth is a pattern that many business owners don't prepare for properly. These owners go about their business and add to it as volume dictates. This is a dangerous way to expand your business. Allowing your company to grow too large too fast can put you out of business. I know it might seem strange that having a bigger business might be worse than maintaining your present size, but it can.

When owners allow their companies to balloon with numerous employees, subcontractors, and jobs, management can become a serious problem. This is especially true for business owners with little management experience. The sudden wealth of quick cash flow and more jobs than you can keep up with is a company killer.

The operating capital that kept your small business floating over rough waters will not be adequate to keep your new, larger business afloat. Overhead expenses will increase along with your business. These expenses might not be recovered with your present pricing structure. All in all, growing too fast can be much worse than not growing at all.

If you want to expand your company, plan for the expansion. Make financial arrangements in advance, and learn the additional skills you will need to guide your business along its growth path.

Continuing education

Many licensed professionals are required by their licensing agencies to participate in continuing education. In New Hampshire, plumbers must attend an annual seminar before they can renew their licenses. Whether your business forces you to pursue continuing education or not, you should. If you don't keep yourself aware of the changes in your industry, you will become outdated and obsolete.

For example, look at how plumbing has changed over the last 20 years. Plastic pipe now is used more often than cast-iron pipe for drains and vents. Copper water pipe is seeing plastic and flexible piping bite into its domain. Faucets are available today that don't have to be touched to be turned on. How would a plumber that hasn't stayed abreast of these changes compete in today's marketplace?

You owe it to yourself and your customers to stay in touch with changes in your field. Read, attend seminars, go to classes, do whatever it takes to stay current on the changes affecting your business.

Bigger jobs

Bigger jobs mean bigger risks. Before you venture into big jobs, make sure you can handle them. Will you have enough money or credit to keep the big jobs and your regular work running smoothly? Do you have enough help to complete your jobs in a timely fashion? If you are required to put up a performance bond, can you? Will you be able to survive financially if the money you're anticipating from the big job is slow to come? Do you have experience running large jobs? This line of questioning could go on for pages, but all the questions are viable ones to ask yourself. You shouldn't tackle big jobs until you are sure you can handle them.

Should you diversify?

At some point you will probably ask yourself this question. To answer it, you will have to spend some time thinking, evaluating, and researching. There is no question that diversifying your company can bring you more income. But it can also cause your successful business to get into trouble. There are many reasons why companies that diversify fail.

When you split your interest into multiple fields, you are less likely to do your best at any one job. For this reason, many companies do better when they don't diversify.

Your geographic location might be a factor in your decision to expand your business operations. The desire to make more money, however, is the most common reason for business alterations. Greed can be a very powerful destroyer. If you want to diversify, do so intelligently. Don't just decide one day you are going to hire a master electrician and expand your plumbing business to include electrical services. What will you do if your master electrician quits?

There are many considerations to think about before you split your time and money into separate business interests. Most people struggle to keep one business healthy. If you get aggressive and open several business ventures, you might find you will lose them all.

Adjusting your company for change is not a task you can complete and be done with. To maintain your business, you must occasionally change your plans. Routine adjustments are normal and should be expected.

RECESSION TECHNIQUES

Hard economic times call for special techniques. If you stay in business long enough, you will need to get creative in order to beat a bad economy. My business has been through two rough recessions. I survived both of them, and my business got stronger because of them. How could a recession make my business stronger? Hard times made me more creative, and my ideas worked, both during and after the hard times. Consequently, I had more business than ever before. Your business can weather the storms of economic slumps, but you will have to work harder and smarter.

When the economy slows down, you must overcome many business obstacles. When interest rates and unemployment are high, people become more conservative in their spending habits. Many people who would normally call plumbers to fix their problems turn to how-to books and try to make home repairs by themselves. This do-it-yourself phase bites into the pockets of all service contractors.

This doesn't mean there is no business to be had. In fact, many of the do-it-yourself homeowners get into the middle of their projects and either make the situation worse or just give up. These frustrated homeowners are going to call someone to correct their problems. It might as well be you.

It is well accepted that recessionary times don't stop all people from spending money. Actually, many people spend money aggressively in slow times. The people who have money know they can get their best deals when the market is down. This group of bargain hunters can provide you with plenty of business. All you have to do is find the customers and win them over. That's not too hard to do, if you put effort into it.

Ideally you should find and secure these spending machines before the economy sinks. You can do this by targeting your marketing and services to the right groups of people. If you are in the right circles when public spending drops, you will not feel the effects of the slowdown as harshly.

I think everyone would agree that word-of-mouth advertising is the best way to get good business. People talk, and if they talk favorably about your business, you will see an increase in sales. By getting in with the right customers, giving extraordinary service, and keeping your name in front of past customers, you can make yourself recession resistant.

When I started my plumbing and remodeling business I wanted to reach several markets. The most coveted market was the up-scale jobs in a specialized community. The people in this community had money and lots of it. They would literally pay $30 an hour to have their light bulbs replaced. When they remodeled a bathroom, they didn't use standard plumbing fixtures. They bought $2,500 gold faucets and expensive fixtures. Most of the homes had tennis courts or swimming pools or both. The area rugs in the foyers often cost thousands of dollars. It would be an understatement to say that it required a special type of contractor to work for these people.

I knew that if I could get into this market I could make strong profits and have stable work. I solicited general contractors that worked in the community. I went directly to the homeowners. It took a little time, but I got in. Once I was in, I did all the work myself. I couldn't afford to have a plumber walk on expensive rugs with muddy boots or make an off-color remark that would ruin my business reputation.

Before long I was spending three days a week, every week, working in this exclusive area. My crews took care of jobs in other areas, while I continued to build up the business in this affluent neighborhood.

When the recession hit, contractors dropped like the proverbial flies. My business suffered and struggled in most areas, but not in my special community. I am convinced that getting into that community saved my business. Even when the rest of the world around me was going downhill, my pet project was as busy as ever. The advance planning and procurement of those wealthy customers kept me going.

You might not have a rich community to tap into, but you do have special opportunities. Large corporations can keep your business afloat in difficult times. If you start doing business with the big companies before money gets tight, you will have an edge during the next economic downturn. Schools and municipal contracts are another source of constant work. If you think about the customer opportunities in your area, I'm sure you can find some that are likely to keep spending, even in bad times.

There is another problem with doing business in recessionary times. The amount of work available shrinks, and the number of people going after the work increases. People laid off from their jobs go into business for themselves. Many of these people don't pay for insurance and other business expenses that the average on-going business does. These over-night businesses operate on the principle that they are only in business until they can find another job. This type of contractor usually works cheap. For contractors carrying normal business overhead, it can be tough to compete against these pop-up contractors.

About all you can do is educate potential customers when you give estimates. Tell the customers that if they get several bids to be wary of extremely low prices. Also, advise the consumer to verify the credentials, insurance, and public standing of contractors before they do business with them. A small percentage of people will deal with people offering the lowest price, but most consumers will look further than price. If you do a good job during your sales pitch, you can win the customer's confidence and get the job, even if your price is higher.

Every business owner wants to know how to stay busy in slow times. Until you have survived recessionary times, you might not have the experience to stay afloat in troubled waters. Since you can't always learn survival skills on a first-hand basis and survive, you must turn to the experience of others for your training.

When times are tough, you might have to alter your business procedures. But how will you do it? Will you lower your prices? Will you eliminate overhead expenses? Any of these options might be the wrong thing to do.

If you lower your prices, you will have a hard time working your prices back up to where they used to be, but sometimes it is the only way to keep food on the table. If you have to lower prices to stay in business, do so with the understanding that getting prices back to normal will take time.

Depending on the nature of your work, discounts might accomplish the same goal as lowered labor rates with less long-term effects. People expect discount offers to end. Run ads offering a discount from your regular labor rates for a limited time only. This tactic will be less difficult to rebound from than a lowering of labor rates.

MOVE AHEAD, DON'T STAGNATE

Many new business owners find something that works and stick with it. This is a good idea, so long as you don't put your business in a rut. For your business to grow and prosper, there will be times when you must step out of your comfort zone.

The struggle to make a new business work can cause an entrepreneur to lose sight of distant goals. When you are responsible for all the business duties, it is easy to ignore your plans for retirement. With the rush of day-to-day needs, you might forget that you wanted to allow yourself a two-week vacation by the end of your second year in business. If you have cranky customers hounding you on the phone, you might forget to pay your supplier bills on time. It is up to you to set the rules, schedules, and goals. If you are lax in your self discipline and management, your business will suffer.

Since the battle for business success can get hectic, it is understandable that some people reach a plateau and rest. I'm not suggesting that you never rest or stop to enjoy your increments of success. However, if you sit around too long, you will be left in the dust by your competitors. Being in business is not a game that allows you to win once and remain the champion. You must win regularly to stay in the game. Until you leave the business, the game is never over. There is always someone trying to cut into your market share.

Appendix

Federal
tax forms

SCHEDULE C-EZ
(Form 1040)

Net Profit From Business
(Sole Proprietorship)
▶ Partnerships, joint ventures, etc., must file Form 1065.
▶ Attach to Form 1040 or Form 1041.

Department of the Treasury
Internal Revenue Service   (0)

OMB No. 1545-0074

1992

Attachment
Sequence No. **09A**

Name of proprietor

Social security number (SSN)

Part I   General Information

**You May Use
This Form
If You:**

- Had gross receipts from your business of $25,000 or less.
- Had business expenses of $2,000 or less.
- Use the cash method of accounting.
- Did not have an inventory at any time during the year.
- Did not have a net loss from your business.
- Had only one business as a sole proprietor.

And You:

- Had no employees during the year.
- Are not required to file **Form 4562**, Depreciation and Amortization for this business. See the instructions for Schedule C, line 13, on page C-3 to find out if you must file.
- Do not deduct expenses for business use of your home.
- Do not have prior year unallowed passive activity losses from this business.

A Principal business or profession, including product or service

B Enter principal business code
(from page 2) ▶

C Business name

D Employer ID number (EIN)

E Business address (including suite or room no.). Address not required if same as on Form 1040, page 1.

City, town or post office, state, and ZIP code

F Was this business in operation at the end of 1992? . . . . ☐ **Yes** ☐ **No**

G How many months was this business in operation during 1992? . . . . ▶

Part II   Figure Your Net Profit

1 **Gross receipts.** If more than $25,000, you **must** use Schedule C. **Caution:** *If this income was reported to you on Form W-2 and the "Statutory employee" box on that form was checked, see* **Statutory Employees** *in the instructions for Schedule C, line 1, on page C-2 and check here* . . . . ▶ ☐ | **1** |

2 **Total expenses.** If more than $2,000, you **must** use Schedule C. See instructions . . . . . | **2** |

3 **Net profit.** Subtract line 2 from line 1. Enter the result here and on Form 1040, line 12, and on Schedule SE, line 2. (Statutory employees **do not** report this amount on Schedule SE, line 2.) If less than zero, you **must** use Schedule C | **3** |

Part III   Information on Your Vehicle. Complete Part III **ONLY** if you are claiming car or truck expenses on line 2.

4 When did you place your vehicle in service for business purposes? (month, day, year) ...... / ...... / ....

5 Of the total number of miles you drove your vehicle during 1992, enter the number of miles you used your vehicle for:

a Business .... **b** Commuting .... **c** Other ....

6 Do you (or your spouse) have another vehicle available for personal use? . . . . ☐ **Yes** ☐ **No**

7 Was your vehicle available for use during off-duty hours? . . . . ☐ **Yes** ☐ **No**

8 **a** Do you have evidence to support your deduction? . . . . ☐ **Yes** ☐ **No**

   b If "Yes," is the evidence written? . . . . ☐ **Yes** ☐ **No**

Instructions

Schedule C-EZ is new for 1992. You may use Schedule C-EZ instead of Schedule C if you operated a business or practiced a profession as a sole proprietorship and you have met all the requirements listed above.

Line A.—Describe the business or professional activity that provided your principal source of income reported on line 1. Give the general field or activity and the type of product or service.

Line B.—Enter on this line the four-digit code that identifies your principal business or professional activity. See page 2 for the list of codes.

Line D.—You need an employer identification number (EIN) only if you had a Keogh plan or were required to file an employment, excise, fiduciary, or alcohol, tobacco, and firearms tax return. If you don't have an EIN, leave line D blank. **Do not** enter your SSN.

Line E.— Enter your business address. Show a street address instead of a box number. Include the suite or room number, if any.

Line 1—Gross Receipts.—Enter gross receipts from your trade or business. Be sure to include any amount you received in your trade or business that was reported on Form(s) 1099-MISC. You must show all items of taxable income actually or constructively received during the year

---

A-1 Net Profit From Business form Department of the Treasury, Internal Revenue Service

SCHEDULES A&B	Schedule A—Itemized Deductions	OMB No. 1545-0074

SCHEDULES A&B
(Form 1040)

Department of the Treasury
Internal Revenue Service (B)

Schedule A—Itemized Deductions

(Schedule B is on back)

▶ **Attach to Form 1040.** ▶ **See Instructions for Schedules A and B (Form 1040).**

OMB No. 1545-0074

1992

Attachment
Sequence No. **07**

Name(s) shown on Form 1040

Your social security number

Medical and Dental Expenses		Caution: *Do not include expenses reimbursed or paid by others.*		
	1	Medical and dental expenses (see page A-1)	1	
	2	Enter amount from Form 1040, line 32 . ⌊ 2 ⌋		
	3	Multiply line 2 above by 7.5% (.075)	3	
	4	Subtract line 3 from line 1. If zero or less, enter -0- . . . . ▶	4	
Taxes You Paid (See page A-1.)	5	State and local income taxes	5	
	6	Real estate taxes (see page A-2)	6	
	7	Other taxes. List—include personal property taxes · ▶ ----------------------------------	7	
	8	Add lines 5 through 7 . . . . ▶	8	
Interest You Paid (See page A-2.) **Note:** Personal interest is not deductible.	9a	Home mortgage interest and points reported to you on Form 1098	9a	
	b	Home mortgage interest not reported to you on Form 1098. If paid to an individual, show that person's name and address. ▶ --------------------------------- ---------------------------------	9b	
	10	Points not reported to you on Form 1098. See page A-3 for special rules	10	
	11	Investment interest. If required, attach Form 4952. (See page A-3.)	11	
	12	Add lines 9a through 11 . . . . ▶	12	
Gifts to Charity (See page A-3.)		Caution: *If you made a charitable contribution and received a benefit in return, see page A-3.*		
	13	Contributions by cash or check	13	
	14	Other than by cash or check. If over $500, you **MUST** attach Form 8283	14	
	15	Carryover from prior year	15	
	16	Add lines 13 through 15 . . . . ▶	16	
Casualty and Theft Losses	17	Casualty or theft loss(es). Attach Form 4684. (See page A-4.) . . . . ▶	17	
Moving Expenses	18	Moving expenses. Attach Form 3903 or 3903F. (See page A-4.). . . . . . ▶	18	
Job Expenses and Most Other Miscellaneous Deductions (See page A-5 for expenses to deduct here.)	19	Unreimbursed employee expenses—job travel, union dues, job education, etc. If required, you **MUST** attach Form 2106. (See page A-4.) ▶	19	
	20	Other expenses—investment, tax preparation, safe deposit box, etc. List type and amount ▶ .... --------------------------------	20	
	21	Add lines 19 and 20	21	
	22	Enter amount from Form 1040, line 32 . ⌊ 22 ⌋		
	23	Multiply line 22 above by 2% (.02)	23	
	24	Subtract line 23 from line 21. If zero or less, enter -0- . . . . ▶	24	
Other Miscellaneous Deductions	25	Other—from list on page A-5. List type and amount ▶ .... -------------------------------- ▶	25	
Total Itemized Deductions	26	Is the amount on Form 1040, line 32, more than $105,250 (more than $52,625 if married filing separately)? • **NO.** Your deduction is not limited. Add lines 4, 8, 12, 16, 17, 18, 24, and 25. ⎫ • **YES.** Your deduction may be limited. See page A-5 for the amount to enter. ⎭ ▶ Caution: *Be sure to enter on Form 1040, line 34, the **LARGER** of the amount on line 26 above or your standard deduction.*	26	

A-2 Schedule A-Itemized Deductions form Department of the Treasury, Internal Revenue Service

Name(s) shown on Form 1040. Do not enter name and social security number if shown on other side.

Your social security number

Schedule B—Interest and Dividend Income

Attachment
Sequence No. **08**

**Part I
Interest
Income**

(See
pages 14
and B-1.)

If you had over $400 in taxable interest income OR are claiming the exclusion of interest from series EE U.S. savings bonds issued after 1989, you must complete this part. List ALL interest you received. If you had over $400 in taxable interest income, you must also complete Part III. If you received, as a nominee, interest that actually belongs to another person, or you received or paid accrued interest on securities transferred between interest payment dates, see page B-1.

Interest Income		Amount	
1 List name of payer—if any interest income is from seller-financed mortgages, see page B-1 and list this interest first ▶			

Note: If you received a Form 1099-INT, Form 1099-OID, or substitute statement from a brokerage firm, list the firm's name as the payer and enter the total interest shown on that form.

		1	
2 Add the amounts on line 1		**2**	
3 Excludable interest on series EE U.S. savings bonds issued after 1989 from Form 8815, line 14. You MUST attach Form 8815 to Form 1040		**3**	
4 Subtract line 3 from line 2. Enter the result here and on Form 1040, line 8a, ▶		**4**	

**Part II
Dividend
Income**

(See
pages 15
and B-1.)

If you had over $400 in gross dividends and/or other distributions on stock, you must complete this part and Part III. If you received, as a nominee, dividends that actually belong to another person, see page B-1.

Dividend Income		Amount	
5 List name of payer—include on this line capital gain distributions, nontaxable distributions, etc. ▶			

Note: If you received a Form 1099-DIV or substitute statement from a brokerage firm, list the firm's name as the payer and enter the total dividends shown on that form.

		5	
6 Add the amounts on line 5		**6**	
7 Capital gain distributions. Enter here and on Schedule D* .	**7**		
8 Nontaxable distributions. (See the inst. for Form 1040, line 9.)	**8**		
9 Add lines 7 and 8		**9**	
10 Subtract line 9 from line 6. Enter the result here and on Form 1040, line 9 ▶		**10**	

*If you received capital gain distributions but do not need Schedule D to report any other gains or losses, see the instructions for Form 1040, lines 13 and 14.

**Part III
Foreign
Accounts
and
Foreign
Trusts**

(See
page B-2.)

If you had over $400 of interest or dividends OR had a foreign account or were a grantor of, or a transferor to, a foreign trust, you must complete this part.

	Yes	No
11a At any time during 1992, did you have an interest in or a signature or other authority over a financial account in a foreign country, such as a bank account, securities account, or other financial account? See page B-2 for exceptions and filing requirements for Form TD F 90-22.1		
b If "Yes," enter the name of the foreign country ▶		
12 Were you the grantor of, or transferor to, a foreign trust that existed during 1992, whether or not you have any beneficial interest in it? If "Yes," you may have to file Form 3520, 3520-A, or 926 .		

For Paperwork Reduction Act Notice, see Form 1040 instructions.

Schedule B (Form 1040) 1992

*U.S. Government Printing Office: 1992 — 315-032

A-2 Continued.

<table>
<tr><td colspan="2">Form 1065
Department of the Treasury
Internal Revenue Service</td><td colspan="2">U.S. Partnership Return of Income
For calendar year 1992, or tax year beginning ...., 1992, and ending ...., 19 .... .
▶ See separate instructions.</td><td>OMB No. 1545-0099
1992</td></tr>
</table>

A Principal business activity	Use the IRS label. Otherwise, please print or type.	Name of partnership	D Employer identification number
B Principal product or service		Number, street, and room or suite no. (If a P.O. box, see page 9 of the instructions.)	E Date business started
C Business code number		City or town, state, and ZIP code	F Total assets (see Specific Instructions) $

G Check applicable boxes: **(1)** ☐ Initial return   **(2)** ☐ Final return   **(3)** ☐ Change in address   **(4)** ☐ Amended return

H Check accounting method: **(1)** ☐ Cash   **(2)** ☐ Accrual   **(3)** ☐ Other (specify) ▶ ....

I   Number of partners in this partnership . . . . ▶ ....

Caution: *Include only trade or business income and expenses on lines 1a through 22 below. See the instructions for more information.*

Income

1a Gross receipts or sales	**1a**		
b Less returns and allowances	**1b**	**1c**	
2 Cost of goods sold (Schedule A, line 8)		**2**	
3 Gross profit. Subtract line 2 from line 1c		**3**	
4 Ordinary income (loss) from other partnerships and fiduciaries *(attach schedule)*		**4**	
5 Net farm profit (loss) *(attach Schedule F (Form 1040))*		**5**	
6 Net gain (loss) from Form 4797, Part II, line 20		**6**	
7 Other income (loss) (see instructions) *(attach schedule)*		**7**	
8 **Total income (loss).** Combine lines 3 through 7		**8**	

Deductions (see instructions for limitations)

9a Salaries and wages (other than to partners)	**9a**		
b Less jobs credit	**9b**	**9c**	
10 Guaranteed payments to partners		**10**	
11 Repairs		**11**	
12 Bad debts		**12**	
13 Rent		**13**	
14 Taxes		**14**	
15 Interest		**15**	
16a Depreciation (see instructions)	**16a**		
b Less depreciation reported on Schedule A and elsewhere on return	**16b**	**16c**	
17 Depletion **(Do not deduct oil and gas depletion.)**		**17**	
18 Retirement plans, etc.		**18**	
19 Employee benefit programs		**19**	
20 Other deductions *(attach schedule)*		**20**	
21 **Total deductions.** Add the amounts shown in the far right column for lines 9c through 20 .		**21**	
22 **Ordinary income (loss)** from trade or business activities. Subtract line 21 from line 8 . .		**22**	

Please Sign Here

Under penalties of perjury, I declare that I have examined this return, including accompanying schedules and statements, and to the best of my knowledge and belief, it is true, correct, and complete. Declaration of preparer (other than general partner) is based on all information of which preparer has any knowledge.

▶ _____   ▶ Date _____
Signature of general partner

Paid Preparer's Use Only	Preparer's signature ▶		Date	Check if self-employed ▶ ☐	Preparer's social security no.
	Firm's name (or yours if self-employed) and address			E.I. No. ▶	
				ZIP code ▶	

A-3   U.S. Partnership Return of Income form   Department of the Treasury, Internal Revenue Service

Schedule A   **Cost of Goods Sold**

1 Inventory at beginning of year	**1**	
2 Purchases less cost of items withdrawn for personal use	**2**	
3 Cost of labor	**3**	
4 Additional section 263A costs (see instructions) *(attach schedule)*	**4**	
5 Other costs *(attach schedule)*.	**5**	
6 **Total.** Add lines 1 through 5	**6**	
7 Inventory at end of year	**7**	
8 **Cost of goods sold.** Subtract line 7 from line 6. Enter here and on page 1, line 2	**8**	

9a Check all methods used for valuing closing inventory:

    (i) ☐ Cost

    (ii) ☐ Lower of cost or market as described in Regulations section 1.471-4

    (iii) ☐ Writedown of "subnormal" goods as described in Regulations section 1.471-2(c)

    (iv) ☐ Other (specify method used and attach explanation) ▶ ....

  b Check this box if the LIFO inventory method was adopted this tax year for any goods *(if checked, attach Form 970)* . ▶ ☐

  c Do the rules of section 263A (for property produced or acquired for resale) apply to the partnership? . . ☐ **Yes** ☐ **No**

  d Was there any change in determining quantities, cost, or valuations between opening and closing inventory? ☐ **Yes** ☐ **No**
    If "Yes," attach explanation.

Schedule B   **Other Information**

	Yes	No
1 Is this partnership a limited partnership?		
2 Are any partners in this partnership also partnerships?		
3 Is this partnership a partner in another partnership?		
4 Is this partnership subject to the consolidated audit procedures of sections 6221 through 6233? If "Yes," see **Designation of Tax Matters Partner** below		
5 Does this partnership meet **ALL THREE** of the following requirements?		
a The partnership's total receipts for the tax year were less than $250,000;		
b The partnership's total assets at the end of the tax year were less than $250,000; **AND**		
c Schedules K-1 are filed with the return and furnished to the partners on or before the due date (including extensions) for the partnership return.		
If "Yes," the partnership is not required to complete Schedules L, M-1, and M-2; Item F on page 1 of Form 1065; or Item J on Schedule K-1		
6 Does this partnership have any foreign partners?		
7 Is this partnership a publicly traded partnership as defined in section 469(k)(2)?		
8 Has this partnership filed, or is it required to file, **Form 8264,** Application for Registration of a Tax Shelter? .		
9 At any time during calendar year 1992, did the partnership have an interest in or a signature or other authority over a financial account in a foreign country (such as a bank account, securities account, or other financial account)? (See the instructions for exceptions and filing requirements for form TD F 90-22.1.) If "Yes," enter the name of the foreign country. ▶		
10 Was the partnership the grantor of, or transferor to, a foreign trust that existed during the current tax year, whether or not the partnership or any partner has any beneficial interest in it? If "Yes," you may have to file Forms 3520, 3520-A, or 926		
11 Was there a distribution of property or a transfer (e.g., by sale or death) of a partnership interest during the tax year? If "Yes," you may elect to adjust the basis of the partnership's assets under section 754 by attaching the statement described under **Elections** on page 5 of the instructions		
12 Was this partnership in operation at the end of 1992?		
13 How many months in 1992 was this partnership actively operated? ▶		

Designation of Tax Matters Partner (See instructions.)

Enter below the general partner designated as the tax matters partner (TMP) for the tax year of this return:

Name of
designated TMP ▶ _____

Identifying
number of TMP ▶ _____

Address of
designated TMP ▶ _____

A-3 Continued

Schedule K　Partners' Shares of Income, Credits, Deductions, Etc.

		(a) Distributive share items		(b) Total amount
Income (Loss)	1	Ordinary income (loss) from trade or business activities (page 1, line 22)	1	
	2	Net income (loss) from rental real estate activities *(attach Form 8825)*	2	
	3a	Gross income from other rental activities **3a**		
	b	Expenses from other rental activities *(attach schedule)* . . **3b**		
	c	Net income (loss) from other rental activities. Subtract line 3b from line 3a	3c	
	4	Portfolio income (loss) (see instructions): **a** Interest income	4a	
	b	Dividend income	4b	
	c	Royalty income	4c	
	d	Net short-term capital gain (loss) *(attach Schedule D (Form 1065))*	4d	
	e	Net long-term capital gain (loss) *(attach Schedule D (Form 1065))*	4e	
	f	Other portfolio income (loss) *(attach schedule)*	4f	
	5	Guaranteed payments to partners	5	
	6	Net gain (loss) under section 1231 (other than due to casualty or theft) *(attach Form 4797)*	6	
	7	Other income (loss) *(attach schedule)*	7	
Deduc-tions	8	Charitable contributions (see instructions) *(attach schedule)*	8	
	9	Section 179 expense deduction *(attach Form 4562)*	9	
	10	Deductions related to portfolio income (see instructions) (itemize)	10	
	11	Other deductions *(attach schedule)*	11	
Invest-ment Interest	12a	Interest expense on investment debts	12a	
	b	**(1)** Investment income included on lines 4a through 4f above	12b(1)	
		(2) Investment expenses included on line 10 above.	12b(2)	
Credits	13a	Credit for income tax withheld	13a	
	b	Low-income housing credit (see instructions):		
		(1) From partnerships to which section 42(j)(5) applies for property placed in service before 1990 . .	13b(1)	
		(2) Other than on line 13b(1) for property placed in service before 1990	13b(2)	
		(3) From partnerships to which section 42(j)(5) applies for property placed in service after 1989	13b(3)	
		(4) Other than on line 13b(3) for property placed in service after 1989	13b(4)	
	c	Qualified rehabilitation expenditures related to rental real estate activities *(attach Form 3468)*	13c	
	d	Credits (other than credits shown on lines 13b and 13c) related to rental real estate activities (see instructions)	13d	
	e	Credits related to other rental activities (see instructions)	13e	
	14	Other credits (see instructions)	14	
Self-Employ-ment	15a	Net earnings (loss) from self-employment	15a	
	b	Gross farming or fishing income	15b	
	c	Gross nonfarm income	15c	
Adjustments and Tax Preference Items	16a	Depreciation adjustment on property placed in service after 1986	16a	
	b	Adjusted gain or loss	16b	
	c	Depletion (other than oil and gas)	16c	
	d	**(1)** Gross income from oil, gas, and geothermal properties	16d(1)	
		(2) Deductions allocable to oil, gas, and geothermal properties	16d(2)	
	e	Other adjustments and tax preference items *(attach schedule)*	16e	
Foreign Taxes	17a	Type of income ▶ .... **b** Foreign country or U.S. possession ▶		
	c	Total gross income from sources outside the United States *(attach schedule)*.	17c	
	d	Total applicable deductions and losses *(attach schedule)*	17d	
	e	Total foreign taxes (check one): ▶ ☐ Paid ☐ Accrued	17e	
	f	Reduction in taxes available for credit *(attach schedule)*	17f	
	g	Other foreign tax information *(attach schedule)*	17g	
Other	18a	Total expenditures to which a section 59(e) election may apply	18a	
	b	Type of expenditures ▶...		
	19	Tax-exempt interest income	19	
	20	Other tax-exempt income	20	
	21	Nondeductible expenses	21	
	22	Other items and amounts required to be reported separately to partners (see instructions) *(attach schedule)*		

		(a) Corporate	(b) Individual		(c) Partnership	(d) Exempt organization	(e) Nominee/Other
Analysis	23a Income (loss). Combine lines 1 through 7 in column (b). From the result, subtract the sum of lines 8 through 12a, 17e, and 18a					**23a**		
				i. Active	ii. Passive			
	b Analysis by type of partner:							
	(1) General partners							
	(2) Limited partners							

A-3　Continued

Caution: *If Question 5 of Schedule B is answered "Yes," the partnership is not required to complete Schedules L, M-1, and M-2.*

Schedule L	Balance Sheets				

		Beginning of tax year		End of tax year	
	Assets	(a)	(b)	(c)	(d)
1	Cash				
2a	Trade notes and accounts receivable . . .				
b	Less allowance for bad debts				
3	Inventories				
4	U.S. government obligations				
5	Tax-exempt securities				
6	Other current assets (attach schedule) . . .				
7	Mortgage and real estate loans				
8	Other investments (attach schedule)				
9a	Buildings and other depreciable assets . . .				
b	Less accumulated depreciation				
10a	Depletable assets				
b	Less accumulated depletion				
11	Land (net of any amortization)				
12a	Intangible assets (amortizable only). . . .				
b	Less accumulated amortization				
13	Other assets (attach schedule)				
14	**Total** assets				
	Liabilities and Capital				
15	Accounts payable				
16	Mortgages, notes, bonds payable in less than 1 year .				
17	Other current liabilities (attach schedule) . . .				
18	All nonrecourse loans				
19	Mortgages, notes, bonds payable in 1 year or more .				
20	Other liabilities (attach schedule)				
21	Partners' capital accounts.				
22	**Total** liabilities and capital.				

Schedule M-1	Reconciliation of Income (Loss) per Books With Income (Loss) per Return (see instructions)

1	Net income (loss) per books		6	Income recorded on books this year not included on Schedule K, lines 1 through 7 (itemize):	
2	Income included on Schedule K, lines 1 through 4, 6, and 7, not recorded on books this year (itemize):		a	Tax-exempt interest $	
3	Guaranteed payments (other than health insurance)		7	Deductions included on Schedule K, lines 1 through 12a, 17e, and 18a, not charged against book income this year (itemize):	
4	Expenses recorded on books this year not included on Schedule K, lines 1 through 12a, 17e, and 18a (itemize):		a	Depreciation $	
a	Depreciation $				
b	Travel and entertainment $		8	Total of lines 6 and 7	
			9	Income (loss) (Schedule K, line 23a). Subtract line 8 from line 5	
5	Total of lines 1 through 4				

Schedule M-2	Analysis of Partners' Capital Accounts

1	Balance at beginning of year		6	Distributions: a Cash	
2	Capital contributed during year			b Property	
3	Net income (loss) per books		7	Other decreases (itemize):	
4	Other increases (itemize):				
			8	Total of lines 6 and 7	
5	Total of lines 1 through 4		9	Balance at end of year. Subtract line 8 from line 5	

A-3 Continued

Form 1120S

U.S. Income Tax Return for an S Corporation

Form 1120S
Department of the Treasury
Internal Revenue Service

For calendar year 1992, or tax year beginning .... , 1992, and ending .... , 19 .....
▶ **See separate instructions.**

OMB No. 1545-0130

1992

A Date of election as an S corporation	**Use IRS label. Otherwise, please print or type.**	**Name**
B Business code no. (see Specific Instructions)		**Number, street, and room or suite no.** (If a P.O. box, see page 8 of the instructions.)
		City or town, state, and ZIP code

C Employer identification number

D Date incorporated

E Total assets (see Specific Instructions)
$

F Check applicable boxes: (1) ☐ Initial return (2) ☐ Final return (3) ☐ Change in address (4) ☐ Amended return
G Check this box if this S corporation is subject to the consolidated audit procedures of sections 6241 through 6245 (see instructions before checking this box) . ▶ ☐
H Enter number of shareholders in the corporation at end of the tax year . . . . ▶

Caution: *Include **only** trade or business income and expenses on lines 1a through 21. See the instructions for more information.*

Income

1a Gross receipts or sales	**b** Less returns and allowances	**c** Bal ▶	**1c**
2 Cost of goods sold (Schedule A, line 8)	**2**
3 Gross profit. Subtract line 2 from line 1c	**3**
4 Net gain (loss) from Form 4797, Part II, line 20 *(attach Form 4797)*	**4**
5 Other income (loss) (see instructions) *(attach schedule)*	**5**
6 **Total income (loss).** Combine lines 3 through 5 . . . . ▶	**6**

Deductions (See instructions for limitations.)

7 Compensation of officers	**7**
8a Salaries and wages	**b** Less jobs credit	**c** Bal ▶	**8c**
9 Repairs	**9**
10 Bad debts	**10**
11 Rents	**11**
12 Taxes	**12**
13 Interest	**13**
14a Depreciation (see instructions)	**14a**	
b Depreciation claimed on Schedule A and elsewhere on return .	**14b**	
c Subtract line 14b from line 14a	**14c**
15 Depletion **(Do not deduct oil and gas depletion.)**	**15**
16 Advertising	**16**
17 Pension, profit-sharing, etc., plans	**17**
18 Employee benefit programs	**18**
19 Other deductions (see instructions) *(attach schedule)*	**19**
20 **Total deductions.** Add lines 7 through 19 . . . . ▶	**20**
21 Ordinary income (loss) from trade or business activities. Subtract line 20 from line 6 . . .	**21**

Tax and Payments

22 **Tax:**	
a Excess net passive income tax *(attach schedule)*	**22a**	
b Tax from Schedule D (Form 1120S)	**22b**	
c Add lines 22a and 22b (see instructions for additional taxes)	**22c**
23 **Payments:**	
a 1992 estimated tax payments	**23a**	
b Tax deposited with Form 7004	**23b**	
c Credit for Federal tax paid on fuels *(attach Form 4136)* . . .	**23c**	
d Add lines 23a through 23c	**23d**
24 Estimated tax penalty (see instructions). Check if Form 2220 is attached. . . . . . ▶ ☐	**24**
25 **Tax due.** If the total of lines 22c and 24 is larger than line 23d, enter amount owed. See instructions for depositary method of payment . . . . ▶	**25**
26 **Overpayment.** If line 23d is larger than the total of lines 22c and 24, enter amount overpaid ▶	**26**
27 Enter amount of line 26 you want: **Credited to 1993 estimated tax** ▶	**Refunded** ▶	**27**

Please Sign Here

Under penalties of perjury, I declare that I have examined this return, including accompanying schedules and statements, and to the best of my knowledge and belief, it is true, correct, and complete. Declaration of preparer (other than taxpayer) is based on all information of which preparer has any knowledge.

▶ _____ _____ ▶ _____
   Signature of officer   Date   Title

Paid Preparer's Use Only

Preparer's signature ▶	Date	Check if self-employed ▶ ☐	Preparer's social security number
Firm's name (or yours if self-employed) and address ▶		E.I. No. ▶
		ZIP code ▶

A-4 U.S. Income Tax Return for an S Corporation form Department of the Treasury, Internal Revenue Service

Schedule A	**Cost of Goods Sold** (See instructions.)		

1	Inventory at beginning of year	**1**	
2	Purchases.	**2**	
3	Cost of labor	**3**	
4	Additional section 263A costs (see instructions) *(attach schedule)*	**4**	
5	Other costs *(attach schedule)*.	**5**	
6	**Total.** Add lines 1 through 5	**6**	
7	Inventory at end of year	**7**	
8	**Cost of goods sold.** Subtract line 7 from line 6. Enter here and on page 1, line 2	**8**	

9a Check all methods used for valuing closing inventory:
 (i) ☐ Cost
 (ii) ☐ Lower of cost or market as described in Regulations section 1.471-4
 (iii) ☐ Writedown of "subnormal" goods as described in Regulations section 1.471-2(c)
 (iv) ☐ Other (specify method used and attach explanation) ▶ ....

 b Check if the LIFO inventory method was adopted this tax year for any goods *(if checked, attach Form 970)*. . . . . . ▶ ☐

 c If the LIFO inventory method was used for this tax year, enter percentage (or amounts) of closing
  inventory computed under LIFO **9c**

 d Do the rules of section 263A (for property produced or acquired for resale) apply to the corporation? . . . . ☐ Yes ☐ No

 e Was there any change in determining quantities, cost, or valuations between opening and closing inventory? . . ☐ Yes ☐ No
  If "Yes," attach explanation.

Schedule B	**Other Information**	

		Yes	No
1	Check method of accounting: **(a)** ☐ Cash **(b)** ☐ Accrual **(c)** ☐ Other (specify) ▶		
2	Refer to the list in the instructions and state the corporation's principal:		
	(a) Business activity ▶ .... **(b)** Product or service ▶		
3	Did the corporation at the end of the tax year own, directly or indirectly, 50% or more of the voting stock of a domestic corporation? (For rules of attribution, see section 267(c).) If "Yes," attach a schedule showing: **(a)** name, address, and employer identification number and **(b)** percentage owned.		
4	Was the corporation a member of a controlled group subject to the provisions of section 1561?		
5	At any time during calendar year 1992, did the corporation have an interest in or a signature or other authority over a financial account in a foreign country (such as a bank account, securities account, or other financial account)? (See instructions for exceptions and filing requirements for form TD F 90-22.1.)		
	If "Yes," enter the name of the foreign country ▶		
6	Was the corporation the grantor of, or transferor to, a foreign trust that existed during the current tax year, whether or not the corporation has any beneficial interest in it? If "Yes," the corporation may have to file Forms 3520, 3520-A, or 926		
7	Check this box if the corporation has filed or is required to file **Form 8264,** Application for Registration of a Tax Shelter . . . . ▶ ☐		
8	Check this box if the corporation issued publicly offered debt instruments with original issue discount . . . ▶ ☐		
	If so, the corporation may have to file **Form 8281,** Information Return for Publicly Offered Original Issue Discount Instruments.		
9	If the corporation: **(a)** filed its election to be an S corporation after 1986, **(b)** was a C corporation before it elected to be an S corporation **or** the corporation acquired an asset with a basis determined by reference to its basis (or the basis of any other property) in the hands of a C corporation, and **(c)** has net unrealized built-in gain (defined in section 1374(d)(1)) in excess of the net recognized built-in gain from prior years, enter the net unrealized built-in gain reduced by net recognized built-in gain from prior years (see instructions) . . . . ▶ $		
10	Check this box if the corporation had subchapter C earnings and profits at the close of the tax year (see instructions) . . . . ▶ ☐		
11	Was this corporation in operation at the end of 1992?.		
12	How many months in 1992 was this corporation in operation?		

Designation of Tax Matters Person (See instructions.)

Enter below the shareholder designated as the tax matters person (TMP) for the tax year of this return:

Name of designated TMP ▶	Identifying number of TMP ▶

Address of designated TMP ▶

A-4 Continued

Schedule K   Shareholders' Shares of Income, Credits, Deductions, etc.

	(a) Pro rata share items		(b) Total amount	
Income (Loss)	1 Ordinary income (loss) from trade or business activities (page 1, line 21)	**1**		
	2 Net income (loss) from rental real estate activities *(attach Form 8825)*	**2**		
	3a Gross income from other rental activities **3a**			
	b Expenses from other rental activities *(attach schedule)*. . **3b**			
	c Net income (loss) from other rental activities. Subtract line 3b from line 3a	**3c**		
	4 Portfolio income (loss):			
	a Interest income	**4a**		
	b Dividend income.	**4b**		
	c Royalty income	**4c**		
	d Net short-term capital gain (loss) *(attach Schedule D (Form 1120S))*	**4d**		
	e Net long-term capital gain (loss) *(attach Schedule D (Form 1120S))*.	**4e**		
	f Other portfolio income (loss) *(attach schedule)*	**4f**		
	5 Net gain (loss) under section 1231 (other than due to casualty or theft) *(attach Form 4797)*	**5**		
	6 Other income (loss) *(attach schedule)*	**6**		
Deductions	7 Charitable contributions (see instructions) *(attach schedule)*	**7**		
	8 Section 179 expense deduction *(attach Form 4562)*.	**8**		
	9 Deductions related to portfolio income (loss) (see instructions) (itemize)	**9**		
	10 Other deductions *(attach schedule)*	**10**		
Investment Interest	11a Interest expense on investment debts	**11a**		
	b (1) Investment income included on lines 4a through 4f above	**11b(1)**		
	(2) Investment expenses included on line 9 above	**11b(2)**		
Credits	12a Credit for alcohol used as a fuel *(attach Form 6478)*	**12a**		
	b Low-income housing credit (see instructions):			
	(1) From partnerships to which section 42(j)(5) applies for property placed in service before 1990	**12b(1)**		
	(2) Other than on line 12b(1) for property placed in service before 1990.	**12b(2)**		
	(3) From partnerships to which section 42(j)(5) applies for property placed in service after 1989	**12b(3)**		
	(4) Other than on line 12b(3) for property placed in service after 1989	**12b(4)**		
	c Qualified rehabilitation expenditures related to rental real estate activities *(attach Form 3468)*	**12c**		
	d Credits (other than credits shown on lines 12b and 12c) related to rental real estate activities (see instructions).	**12d**		
	e Credits related to other rental activities (see instructions)	**12e**		
	13 Other credits (see instructions)	**13**		
Adjustments and Tax Preference Items	14a Depreciation adjustment on property placed in service after 1986	**14a**		
	b Adjusted gain or loss	**14b**		
	c Depletion (other than oil and gas)	**14c**		
	d (1) Gross income from oil, gas, or geothermal properties	**14d(1)**		
	(2) Deductions allocable to oil, gas, or geothermal properties	**14d(2)**		
	e Other adjustments and tax preference items *(attach schedule)*	**14e**		
Foreign Taxes	15a Type of income ▶			
	b Name of foreign country or U.S. possession ▶			
	c Total gross income from sources outside the United States *(attach schedule)*	**15c**		
	d Total applicable deductions and losses *(attach schedule)*	**15d**		
	e Total foreign taxes (check one): ▶ ☐ Paid ☐ Accrued	**15e**		
	f Reduction in taxes available for credit *(attach schedule)*	**15f**		
	g Other foreign tax information *(attach schedule)*	**15g**		
Other	16a Total expenditures to which a section 59(e) election may apply	**16a**		
	b Type of expenditures ▶			
	17 Tax-exempt interest income	**17**		
	18 Other tax-exempt income	**18**		
	19 Nondeductible expenses	**19**		
	20 Total property distributions (including cash) other than dividends reported on line 22 below	**20**		
	21 Other items and amounts required to be reported separately to shareholders (see instructions) *(attach schedule)*			
	22 Total dividend distributions paid from accumulated earnings and profits	**22**		
	23 **Income (loss).** (Required only if Schedule M-1 must be completed.) Combine lines 1 through 6 in column (b). From the result, subtract the sum of lines 7 through 11a, 15e, and 16a.	**23**		

A-4 Continued

Schedule L	Balance Sheets	Beginning of tax year		End of tax year	
	Assets	(a)	(b)	(c)	(d)
1	Cash				
2a	Trade notes and accounts receivable . .				
b	Less allowance for bad debts				
3	Inventories				
4	U.S. Government obligations				
5	Tax-exempt securities				
6	Other current assets (attach schedule) . .				
7	Loans to shareholders				
8	Mortgage and real estate loans				
9	Other investments (attach schedule) . .				
10a	Buildings and other depreciable assets .				
b	Less accumulated depreciation				
11a	Depletable assets				
b	Less accumulated depletion				
12	Land (net of any amortization)				
13a	Intangible assets (amortizable only) . . .				
b	Less accumulated amortization				
14	Other assets (attach schedule)				
15	Total assets				
	Liabilities and Shareholders' Equity				
16	Accounts payable				
17	Mortgages, notes, bonds payable in less than 1 year				
18	Other current liabilities (attach schedule)				
19	Loans from shareholders				
20	Mortgages, notes, bonds payable in 1 year or more				
21	Other liabilities (attach schedule) . . .				
22	Capital stock				
23	Paid-in or capital surplus				
24	Retained earnings				
25	Less cost of treasury stock	(	)	(	)
26	Total liabilities and shareholders' equity . .				

Schedule M-1	Reconciliation of Income (Loss) per Books With Income (Loss) per Return (You are not required to complete this schedule if the total assets on line 15, column (d), of Schedule L are less than $25,000.)		
1	Net income (loss) per books		5 Income recorded on books this year not included on Schedule K, lines 1 through 6 (itemize):
2	Income included on Schedule K, lines 1 through 6, not recorded on books this year (itemize):		a Tax-exempt interest $ ....
3	Expenses recorded on books this year not included on Schedule K, lines 1 through 11a, 15e, and 16a (itemize):		6 Deductions included on Schedule K, lines 1 through 11a, 15e, and 16a, not charged against book income this year (itemize):
a	Depreciation $		a Depreciation $ ....
b	Travel and entertainment $		.... 7 Add lines 5 and 6 . . . .
4	Add lines 1 through 3		8 Income (loss) (Schedule K, line 23). Line 4 less line 7

Schedule M-2	Analysis of Accumulated Adjustments Account, Other Adjustments Account, and Shareholders' Undistributed Taxable Income Previously Taxed (See instructions.)		
		(a) Accumulated adjustments account	(b) Other adjustments account	(c) Shareholders' undistributed taxable income previously taxed
1	Balance at beginning of tax year . . .			
2	Ordinary income from page 1, line 21 . .			
3	Other additions			
4	Loss from page 1, line 21	( )		
5	Other reductions	( )	( )	
6	Combine lines 1 through 5			
7	Distributions other than dividend distributions .			
8	Balance at end of tax year. Subtract line 7 from line 6			

A-4 Continued

Form **1120**	**U.S. Corporation Income Tax Return**	OMB No. 1545-0123
Department of the Treasury Internal Revenue Service	For calendar year 1992 or tax year beginning .... , 1992, ending .... , 19 ... ▶ **Instructions are separate. See page 1 for Paperwork Reduction Act Notice.**	**1992**

A Check if a:
(1) Consolidated return (attach Form 851) ☐
(2) Personal holding co. (attach Sch. PH) ☐
(3) Personal service corp. (as defined in Temporary Regs. sec. 1.441-4T— see instructions) ☐

Use IRS label. Otherwise, please print or type.

Name

Number, street, and room or suite no. (If a P.O. box, see page 6 of instructions.)

City or town, state, and ZIP code

B Employer identification number

C Date incorporated

D Total assets (see Specific Instructions) $

E Check applicable boxes: (1) ☐ Initial return (2) ☐ Final return (3) ☐ Change in address

Income

1a	Gross receipts or sales _____ b Less returns and allowances _____ c Bal ▶	1c
2	Cost of goods sold (Schedule A, line 8)	2
3	Gross profit. Subtract line 2 from line 1c	3
4	Dividends (Schedule C, line 19)	4
5	Interest	5
6	Gross rents	6
7	Gross royalties	7
8	Capital gain net income (attach Schedule D (Form 1120))	8
9	Net gain or (loss) from Form 4797, Part II, line 20 (attach Form 4797) . .	9
10	Other income (see instructions—attach schedule)	10
11	**Total income.** Add lines 3 through 10 . . . . ▶	11

Deductions (See instructions for limitations on deductions.)

12	Compensation of officers (Schedule E, line 4)	12
13a	Salaries and wages _____ b Less jobs credit _____ c Balance ▶	13c
14	Repairs	14
15	Bad debts	15
16	Rents	16
17	Taxes	17
18	Interest	18
19	Charitable contributions (**see instructions for 10% limitation**) . . .	19
20	Depreciation (attach Form 4562) . . . . 20 _____	
21	Less depreciation claimed on Schedule A and elsewhere on return . . . 21a _____	21b
22	Depletion	22
23	Advertising	23
24	Pension, profit-sharing, etc., plans	24
25	Employee benefit programs	25
26	Other deductions (attach schedule)	26
27	**Total deductions.** Add lines 12 through 26 . . . . ▶	27
28	Taxable income before net operating loss deduction and special deductions. Subtract line 27 from line 11	28
29	**Less:** a Net operating loss deduction (see instructions) . . . . . 29a _____	
	b Special deductions (Schedule C, line 20) . . . . 29b _____	29c

Tax and Payments

30	**Taxable income.** Subtract line 29c from line 28	30
31	**Total tax** (Schedule J, line 10)	31
32	**Payments:** a 1991 overpayment credited to 1992	32a _____	
b	1992 estimated tax payments . .	32b _____	
c	Less 1992 refund applied for on Form 4466	32c (_____) d Bal ▶	32d _____
		32e _____
e	Tax deposited with Form 7004	32e
f	Credit from regulated investment companies (attach Form 2439) . . .	32f _____
g	Credit for Federal tax on fuels (attach Form 4136). See instructions . .	32g _____	32h
33	Estimated tax penalty (see instructions). Check if Form 2220 is attached . ▶ ☐	33
34	**Tax due.** If line 32h is smaller than the total of lines 31 and 33, enter amount owed	34
35	**Overpayment.** If line 32h is larger than the total of lines 31 and 33, enter amount overpaid . . .	35
36	Enter amount of line 35 you want: **Credited to 1993 estimated tax ▶** _____ Refunded ▶	36

Please Sign Here

Under penalties of perjury, I declare that I have examined this return, including accompanying schedules and statements, and to the best of my knowledge and belief, it is true, correct, and complete. Declaration of preparer (other than taxpayer) is based on all information of which preparer has any knowledge.

▶ _____
Signature of officer

Date _____

Title _____

Paid Preparer's Use Only

Preparer's signature ▶	Date	Check if self-employed ☐	Preparer's social security number
Firm's name (or yours if self-employed) and address ▶		E.I. No. ▶
		ZIP code ▶

A-5 U.S. Corporation Income Tax Return form Department of the Treasury, Internal Revenue Service

Federal tax forms **247**

Schedule A   **Cost of Goods Sold** (See instructions.)

1	Inventory at beginning of year	**1**
2	Purchases	**2**
3	Cost of labor	**3**
4	Additional section 263A costs (attach schedule)	**4**
5	Other costs (attach schedule)	**5**
6	**Total.** Add lines 1 through 5	**6**
7	Inventory at end of year	**7**
8	**Cost of goods sold.** Subtract line 7 from line 6. Enter here and on page 1, line 2	**8**

9a Check all methods used for valuing closing inventory:

     (i) ☐ Cost   **(ii)** ☐ Lower of cost or market as described in Regulations section 1.471-4

     (iii) ☐ Writedown of "subnormal" goods as described in Regulations section 1.471-2(c)

     (iv) ☐ Other (Specify method used and attach explanation.) ▶ -

   b Check if the LIFO inventory method was adopted this tax year for any goods (if checked, attach Form 970) . . . . . ▶ ☐

   c If the LIFO inventory method was used for this tax year, enter percentage (or amounts) of closing inventory computed under LIFO . . . . | **9c** |

   d Do the rules of section 263A (for property produced or acquired for resale) apply to the corporation? . . . . ☐ Yes   ☐ No

   e Was there any change in determining quantities, cost, or valuations between opening and closing inventory? If "Yes," attach explanation . . . . ☐ Yes   ☐ No

Schedule C   **Dividends and Special Deductions** (See instructions.)

		(a) Dividends received	(b) %	(c) Special deductions: (a) × (b)
1	Dividends from less-than-20%-owned domestic corporations that are subject to the 70% deduction (other than debt-financed stock)		70	
2	Dividends from 20%-or-more-owned domestic corporations that are subject to the 80% deduction (other than debt-financed stock)		80	
3	Dividends on debt-financed stock of domestic and foreign corporations (section 246A)		see instructions	
4	Dividends on certain preferred stock of less-than-20%-owned public utilities . . .		41.176	
5	Dividends on certain preferred stock of 20%-or-more-owned public utilities . . .		47.059	
6	Dividends from less-than-20%-owned foreign corporations and certain FSCs that are subject to the 70% deduction		70	
7	Dividends from 20%-or-more-owned foreign corporations and certain FSCs that are subject to the 80% deduction		80	
8	Dividends from wholly owned foreign subsidiaries subject to the 100% deduction (section 245(b))		100	
9	**Total.** Add lines 1 through 8. See instructions for limitation	/////	/////	
10	Dividends from domestic corporations received by a small business investment company operating under the Small Business Investment Act of 1958		100	
11	Dividends from certain FSCs that are subject to the 100% deduction (section 245(c)(1))		100	
12	Dividends from affiliated group members subject to the 100% deduction (section 243(a)(3))		100	
13	Other dividends from foreign corporations not included on lines 3, 6, 7, 8, or 11 .		/////	
14	Income from controlled foreign corporations under subpart F (attach Form(s) 5471) .		/////	
15	Foreign dividend gross-up (section 78)		/////	
16	IC-DISC and former DISC dividends not included on lines 1, 2, or 3 (section 246(d)) .		/////	
17	Other dividends		/////	
18	Deduction for dividends paid on certain preferred stock of public utilities (see instructions)	/////	/////	
19	**Total dividends.** Add lines 1 through 17. Enter here and on line 4, page 1 . . ▶		/////	
20	Total deductions. Add lines 9, 10, 11, 12, and 18. Enter here and on line 29b, page 1 . . . . ▶			

Schedule E   **Compensation of Officers** (See instructions for line 12, page 1.)

Complete Schedule E only if total receipts (line 1a plus lines 4 through 10 on page 1, Form 1120) are $500,000 or more.

(a) Name of officer	(b) Social security number	(c) Percent of time devoted to business	Percent of corporation stock owned		(f) Amount of compensation
			(d) Common	(e) Preferred	
1		%	%	%	
		%	%	%	
		%	%	%	
		%	%	%	
		%	%	%	

2	Total compensation of officers	
3	Compensation of officers claimed on Schedule A and elsewhere on return	
4	Subtract line 3 from line 2. Enter the result here and on line 12, page 1	

A-5 Continued

Schedule J	**Tax Computation** (See instructions.)		

1 Check if the corporation is a member of a controlled group (see sections 1561 and 1563) . . . . ▶ ☐

2 If the box on line 1 is checked:

a Enter the corporation's share of the $50,000 and $25,000 taxable income bracket amounts (in that order):

   (i) ☐ $ |___|___| **(ii)** ☐ $ |___|___|

b Enter the corporation's share of the additional 5% tax (not to exceed $11,750) ▶ ☐ $ |___|

3 Income tax. Check this box if the corporation is a qualified personal service corporation as defined in section 448(d)(2) (see instructions on page 14). . . . . ▶ ☐ | **3** |

4a Foreign tax credit (attach Form 1118)	**4a**		
b Possessions tax credit (attach Form 5735)	**4b**		
c Orphan drug credit (attach Form 6765)	**4c**		
d Credit for fuel produced from a nonconventional source . .	**4d**		

e General business credit. Enter here and check which forms are attached:

  ☐ Form 3800   ☐ Form 3468   ☐ Form 5884   ☐ Form 6478

  ☐ Form 6765   ☐ Form 8586   ☐ Form 8830   ☐ Form 8826 . . . | **4e** | |

f Credit for prior year minimum tax (attach Form 8827) . . . . | **4f** | |

5 **Total credits.** Add lines 4a through 4f	**5**	
6 Subtract line 5 from line 3	**6**	
7 Personal holding company tax (attach Schedule PH (Form 1120))	**7**	
8 Recapture taxes. Check if from: ☐ Form 4255 ☐ Form 8611	**8**	
9a Alternative minimum tax (attach Form 4626)	**9a**	
b Environmental tax (attach Form 4626)	**9b**	
10 **Total tax.** Add lines 6 through 9b. Enter here and on line 31, page 1	**10**	

Schedule K	**Other Information** (See instructions.)		

		Yes	No

1 Check method of accounting:

a ☐ Cash   **b** ☐ Accrual

c ☐ Other (specify) ▶ ....

2 Refer to the list in the instructions and state the principal:

a Business activity code no. ▶ ....

b Business activity ▶ ....

c Product or service ▶ ....

3 Did the corporation at the end of the tax year own, directly or indirectly, 50% or more of the voting stock of a domestic corporation? (For rules of attribution, see section 267(c).) . . . .

If "Yes," attach a schedule showing: (a) name and identifying number; (b) percentage owned; and (c) taxable income or (loss) before NOL and special deductions of such corporation for the tax year ending with or within your tax year.

4 Did any individual, partnership, corporation, estate, or trust at the end of the tax year own, directly or indirectly, 50% or more of the corporation's voting stock? (For rules of attribution, see section 267(c).) If "Yes," complete a, b, and c below.

a Is the corporation a subsidiary in an affiliated group or a parent-subsidiary controlled group? . . . . . .

b Enter the name and identifying number of the parent corporation or other entity with 50% or more ownership ▶ ....

....

c Enter percentage owned ▶ ....

5 During this tax year, did the corporation pay dividends (other than stock dividends and distributions in exchange for stock) in excess of the corporation's current and accumulated earnings and profits? (See secs. 301 and 316.) . . . . .

If "Yes," file Form 5452. If this is a consolidated return, answer here for the parent corporation and on **Form 851,** Affiliations Schedule, for each subsidiary.

6 Was the corporation a U.S. shareholder of any controlled foreign corporation? (See sections 951 and 957.) . . .

If "Yes," attach Form 5471 for each such corporation. Enter number of Forms 5471 attached ▶ ....

7 At any time during the 1992 calendar year, did the corporation have an interest in or a signature or other authority over a financial account in a foreign country (such as a bank account, securities account, or other financial account)? . . . .

If "Yes," the corporation may have to file Form TD F 90-22.1. If "Yes," enter name of foreign country ▶ ....

8 Was the corporation the grantor of, or transferor to, a foreign trust that existed during the current tax year, whether or not the corporation has any beneficial interest in it? . . .

If "Yes," the corporation may have to file Forms 926, 3520, or 3520-A.

9 Did one foreign person at any time during the tax year own, directly or indirectly, at least 25% of: **(a)** the total voting power of all classes of stock of the corporation entitled to vote, or **(b)** the total value of all classes of stock of the corporation?. . . . .

If "Yes," see page 17 of instructions and

a Enter percentage owned ▶ ....

b Enter owner's country ▶ ....

c The corporation may have to file Form 5472. (See page 18 for penalties that may apply.) Enter number of Forms 5472 attached ▶ ....

10 Check this box if the corporation issued publicly offered debt instruments with original issue discount . ▶ ☐

If so, the corporation may have to file Form 8281.

11 Enter the amount of tax-exempt interest received or accrued during the tax year ▶ $ |_____|

12 If there were 35 or fewer shareholders at the end of the tax year, enter the number ▶ ....

13 If the corporation has an NOL for the tax year and is electing under sec. 172(b)(3) to forego the carryback period, check here . . . . ▶ ☐

A-5 Continued

Schedule L	**Balance Sheets**	Beginning of tax year		End of tax year	
	Assets	(a)	(b)	(c)	(d)
1	Cash				
2a	Trade notes and accounts receivable . . .				
b	Less allowance for bad debts	( )		( )	
3	Inventories				
4	U.S. government obligations				
5	Tax-exempt securities (see instructions) .				
6	Other current assets (attach schedule) . .				
7	Loans to stockholders				
8	Mortgage and real estate loans				
9	Other investments (attach schedule) . . .				
10a	Buildings and other depreciable assets . .				
b	Less accumulated depreciation	( )		( )	
11a	Depletable assets				
b	Less accumulated depletion	( )		( )	
12	Land (net of any amortization)				
13a	Intangible assets (amortizable only) . . .				
b	Less accumulated amortization	( )		( )	
14	Other assets (attach schedule)				
15	Total assets				
	Liabilities and Stockholders' Equity				
16	Accounts payable				
17	Mortgages, notes, bonds payable in less than 1 year				
18	Other current liabilities (attach schedule) . .				
19	Loans from stockholders				
20	Mortgages, notes, bonds payable in 1 year or more				
21	Other liabilities (attach schedule)				
22	Capital stock: **a** Preferred stock . . .				
	b Common stock . . .				
23	Paid-in or capital surplus				
24	Retained earnings—Appropriated (attach schedule)				
25	Retained earnings—Unappropriated . . .				
26	Less cost of treasury stock		( )		( )
27	Total liabilities and stockholders' equity .				

Note: *You are not required to complete Schedules M-1 and M-2 below if the total assets on line 15, column (d) of Schedule L are less than $25,000.*

Schedule M-1	**Reconciliation of Income (Loss) per Books With Income per Return** (See instructions.)

1	Net income (loss) per books		7	Income recorded on books this year not	
2	Federal income tax			included on this return (itemize):	
3	Excess of capital losses over capital gains .			Tax-exempt interest $	
4	Income subject to tax not recorded on books			. . . .	
	this year (itemize):				
	. . . .		8	Deductions on this return not charged	
5	Expenses recorded on books this year not			against book income this year (itemize):	
	deducted on this return (itemize):				
a	Depreciation . . . . $		a	Depreciation . . . . $	
b	Contributions carryover $		b	Contributions carryover $	
c	Travel and entertainment $			. . . .	
	. . . .			. . . .	
	. . . .		9	Add lines 7 and 8	
6	Add lines 1 through 5		10	Income (line 28, page 1)—line 6 less line 9	

Schedule M-2	**Analysis of Unappropriated Retained Earnings per Books (Line 25, Schedule L)**

1	Balance at beginning of year		5	Distributions: **a** Cash	
2	Net income (loss) per books			**b** Stock	
3	Other increases (itemize):			**c** Property	
	. . . .		6	Other decreases (itemize):	
	. . . .			. . . .	
	. . . .		7	Add lines 5 and 6	
4	Add lines 1, 2, and 3		8	Balance at end of year (line 4 less line 7)	

A-5 Continued

SCHEDULE C (Form 1040)	**Profit or Loss From Business** (Sole Proprietorship) ▶ Partnerships, joint ventures, etc., must file Form 1065.	OMB No. 1545-0074 **1992**
Department of the Treasury Internal Revenue Service (0)	▶ **Attach to Form 1040 or Form 1041.** ▶ **See Instructions for Schedule C (Form 1040).**	Attachment Sequence No. **09**

Name of proprietor	Social security number (SSN)

A Principal business or profession, including product or service (see page C-1)

B Enter principal business code (from page 2) ▶

C Business name

D Employer ID number (Not SSN)

E Business address (including suite or room no.) ▶ ....
City, town or post office, state, and ZIP code

F Accounting method: **(1)** ☐ Cash **(2)** ☐ Accrual **(3)** ☐ Other (specify) ▶ ....

G Method(s) used to value closing inventory: **(1)** ☐ Cost **(2)** ☐ Lower of cost or market **(3)** ☐ Other (attach explanation) **(4)** ☐ Does not apply (if checked, skip line H)

	Yes	No
H Was there any change in determining quantities, costs, or valuations between opening and closing inventory? If "Yes," attach explanation		
I Did you "materially participate" in the operation of this business during 1992? If "No," see page C-2 for limitations on losses . .		
J Was this business in operation at the end of 1992?		
K How many months was this business in operation during 1992? . . . . ▶		
L If this is the first Schedule C filed for this business, check here . . . . ▶ ☐		

Part I   Income

1	Gross receipts or sales. **Caution:** *If this income was reported to you on Form W-2 and the "Statutory employee" box on that form was checked, see page C-2 and check here* . . . . ▶ ☐	**1**	
2	Returns and allowances	**2**	
3	Subtract line 2 from line 1	**3**	
4	Cost of goods sold (from line 40 on page 2)	**4**	
5	**Gross profit.** Subtract line 4 from line 3	**5**	
6	Other income, including Federal and state gasoline or fuel tax credit or refund (see page C-2) . .	**6**	
7	**Gross income.** Add lines 5 and 6 . . . . ▶	**7**	

Part II   Expenses (Caution: *Do not enter expenses for business use of your home on lines 8–27. Instead, see line 30.*)

8	Advertising	**8**		**21** Repairs and maintenance . .	**21**	
9	Bad debts from sales or services (see page C-3) . .	**9**		**22** Supplies (not included in Part III) .	**22**	
10	Car and truck expenses (see page C-3—also attach Form 4562) . . .	**10**		**23** Taxes and licenses	**23**	
				24 Travel, meals, and entertainment:		
11	Commissions and fees. . .	**11**		a Travel	**24a**	
12	Depletion.	**12**		b Meals and entertainment .		
13	Depreciation and section 179 expense deduction (not included in Part III) (see page C-3) .	**13**		c Enter 20% of line 24b subject to limitations (see page C-4) . .		
14	Employee benefit programs (other than on line 19) . . .	**14**		d Subtract line 24c from line 24b .	**24d**	
15	Insurance (other than health) .	**15**		**25** Utilities	**25**	
16	Interest:			**26** Wages (less jobs credit) . .	**26**	
a	Mortgage (paid to banks, etc.) .	**16a**		**27a** Other expenses (**list type and amount**):		
b	Other	**16b**		----------------------------------		
17	Legal and professional services .	**17**		----------------------------------		
18	Office expense	**18**		----------------------------------		
19	Pension and profit-sharing plans .	**19**		----------------------------------		
20	Rent or lease (see page C-4):			----------------------------------		
a	Vehicles, machinery, and equipment	**20a**				
b	Other business property .	**20b**		**27b** Total other expenses . . .	**27b**	

28	**Total expenses** before expenses for business use of home. Add lines 8 through 27b in columns . ▶	**28**	
29	Tentative profit (loss). Subtract line 28 from line 7	**29**	
30	Expenses for business use of your home. Attach **Form 8829**	**30**	
31	**Net profit or (loss).** Subtract line 30 from line 29. If a profit, enter here and on Form 1040, line 12. Also, enter the net profit on Schedule SE, line 2 (statutory employees, see page C-5). If a loss, you MUST go on to line 32 (fiduciaries, see page C-5)	**31**	
32	If you have a loss, you MUST check the box that describes your investment in this activity (see page C-5)	**32a** ☐ All investment is at risk. **32b** ☐ Some investment is not at risk.
	If you checked 32a, enter the loss on Form 1040, line 12, and Schedule SE, line 2 (statutory employees, see page C-5). If you checked 32b, you MUST attach **Form 6198.**		

A-6 Profit or Loss From Business form Department of the Treasury, Internal Revenue Service

Part III Cost of Goods Sold (see page C-5)

33	Inventory at beginning of year. If different from last year's closing inventory, attach explanation . .	33
34	Purchases less cost of items withdrawn for personal use	34
35	Cost of labor. Do not include salary paid to yourself	35
36	Materials and supplies	36
37	Other costs	37
38	Add lines 33 through 37	38
39	Inventory at end of year	39
40	**Cost of goods sold.** Subtract line 39 from line 38. Enter the result here and on page 1, line 4 . .	40

Part IV Principal Business or Professional Activity Codes

Locate the major category that best describes your activity. Within the major category, select the activity code that most closely identifies the business or profession that is the principal source of your sales or receipts. **Enter this 4-digit code on page 1, line B.** For example, real estate agent is under the major category of **"Real Estate,"** and the code is "5520." *Note: If your principal source of income is from farming activities, you should file **Schedule F** (Form 1040), Profit or Loss From Farming.*

Agricultural Services, Forestry, Fishing
Code
- 1990 Animal services, other than breeding
- 1933 Crop services
- 2113 Farm labor & management services
- 2246 Fishing, commercial
- 2238 Forestry, except logging
- 2212 Horticulture & landscaping
- 2469 Hunting & trapping
- 1974 Livestock breeding
- 0836 Logging
- 1958 Veterinary services, including pets

Construction
- 0018 Operative builders (for own account)

Building Trade Contractors, Including Repairs
- 0414 Carpentering & flooring
- 0455 Concrete work
- 0273 Electrical work
- 0299 Masonry, dry wall, stone, & tile
- 0257 Painting & paper hanging
- 0232 Plumbing, heating, & air conditioning
- 0430 Roofing, siding & sheet metal
- 0885 Other building trade contractors (excavation, glazing, etc.)

General Contractors
- 0075 Highway & street construction
- 0059 Nonresidential building
- 0034 Residential building
- 3889 Other heavy construction (pipe laying, bridge construction, etc.)

Finance, Insurance, & Related Services
- 6064 Brokers & dealers of securities
- 6080 Commodity contracts brokers & dealers; security & commodity exchanges
- 6148 Credit institutions & mortgage bankers
- 5702 Insurance agents or brokers
- 5744 Insurance services (appraisal, consulting, inspection, etc.)
- 6130 Investment advisors & services
- 5777 Other financial services

Manufacturing, Including Printing & Publishing
- 0679 Apparel & other textile products
- 1115 Electric & electronic equipment
- 1073 Fabricated metal products
- 0638 Food products & beverages
- 0810 Furniture & fixtures
- 0695 Leather footwear, handbags, etc.
- 0836 Lumber & other wood products
- 1099 Machinery & machine shops
- 0877 Paper & allied products
- 1057 Primary metal industries
- 0851 Printing & publishing
- 1032 Stone, clay, & glass products
- 0653 Textile mill products
- 1883 Other manufacturing industries

Mining & Mineral Extraction
- 1537 Coal mining
- 1511 Metal mining

- 1552 Oil & gas
- 1719 Quarrying & nonmetallic mining

Real Estate
- 5538 Operators & lessors of buildings, including residential
- 5553 Operators & lessors of other real property
- 5520 Real estate agents & brokers
- 5579 Real estate property managers
- 5710 Subdividers & developers, except cemeteries
- 6155 Title abstract offices

Services: Personal, Professional, & Business Services

Amusement & Recreational Services
- 9670 Bowling centers
- 9688 Motion picture & tape distribution & allied services
- 9597 Motion picture & video production
- 9639 Motion picture theaters
- 8557 Physical fitness facilities
- 9696 Professional sports & racing, including promoters & managers
- 9811 Theatrical performers, musicians, agents, producers & related services
- 9613 Video tape rental
- 9837 Other amusement & recreational services

Automotive Services
- 8813 Automotive rental or leasing, without driver
- 8953 Automotive repairs, general & specialized
- 8839 Parking, except valet
- 8896 Other automotive services (wash, towing, etc.)

Business & Personal Services
- 7658 Accounting & bookkeeping
- 7716 Advertising, except direct mail
- 7682 Architectural services
- 8318 Barber shop (or barber)
- 8110 Beauty shop (or beautician)
- 8714 Child day care
- 7872 Computer programming, processing, data preparation & related services
- 7922 Computer repair, maintenance, & leasing
- 7286 Consulting services
- 7799 Consumer credit reporting & collection services
- 8755 Counseling (except health practitioners)
- 7732 Employment agencies & personnel supply
- 7518 Engineering services
- 7773 Equipment rental & leasing (except computer or automotive)
- 8532 Funeral services & crematories
- 7633 Income tax preparation
- 7914 Investigative & protective services
- 7617 Legal services (or lawyer)
- 7856 Mailing, reproduction, commercial art, photography, & stenographic services
- 7245 Management services
- 8771 Ministers & chaplains
- 8334 Photographic studios
- 7260 Public relations
- 8733 Research services

- 7708 Surveying services
- 8730 Teaching or tutoring
- 7880 Other business services
- 6882 Other personal services

Hotels & Other Lodging Places
- 7237 Camps & camping parks
- 7096 Hotels, motels, & tourist homes
- 7211 Rooming & boarding houses

Laundry & Cleaning Services
- 7450 Carpet & upholstery cleaning
- 7419 Coin-operated laundries & dry cleaning
- 7435 Full-service laundry, dry cleaning, & garment service
- 7476 Janitorial & related services (building, house, & window cleaning)

Medical & Health Services
- 9274 Chiropractors
- 9233 Dentist's office or clinic
- 9217 Doctor's (M.D.) office or clinic
- 9456 Medical & dental laboratories
- 9472 Nursing & personal care facilities
- 9290 Optometrists
- 9258 Osteopathic physicians & surgeons
- 9241 Podiatrists
- 9415 Registered & practical nurses
- 9431 Offices & clinics of other health practitioners (dieticians, midwives, speech pathologists, etc.)
- 9886 Other health services

Miscellaneous Repair, Except Computers
- 9019 Audio equipment & TV repair
- 9035 Electrical & electronic equipment repair, except audio & TV
- 9050 Furniture repair & reupholstery
- 2881 Other equipment repair

Trade, Retail—Selling Goods to Individuals & Households
- 3038 Catalog or mail order
- 3012 Selling door to door, by telephone or party plan, or from mobile unit
- 3053 Vending machine selling

Selling From Showroom, Store, or Other Fixed Location

Apparel & Accessories
- 3921 Accessory & specialty stores & furriers for women
- 3939 Clothing, family
- 3772 Clothing, men's & boys'
- 3913 Clothing, women's
- 3756 Shoe stores
- 3954 Other apparel & accessory stores

Automotive & Service Stations
- 3558 Gasoline service stations
- 3319 New car dealers (franchised)
- 3533 Tires, accessories, & parts
- 3335 Used car dealers
- 3517 Other automotive dealers (motorcycles, recreational vehicles, etc.)

Building, Hardware, & Garden Supply
- 4416 Building materials dealers
- 4457 Hardware stores
- 4473 Nurseries & garden supply stores
- 4432 Paint, glass, & wallpaper stores

Food & Beverages
- 0612 Bakeries selling at retail
- 3086 Catering services
- 3095 Drinking places (bars, taverns, pubs, saloons, etc.)
- 3079 Eating places, meals & snacks
- 3210 Grocery stores (general line)
- 3251 Liquor stores
- 3236 Specialized food stores (meat, produce, candy, health food, etc.)

Furniture & General Merchandise
- 3988 Computer & software stores
- 3970 Furniture stores
- 4317 Home furnishings stores (china, floor coverings, drapes)
- 4119 Household appliance stores
- 4333 Music & record stores
- 3996 TV, audio & electronic stores
- 3715 Variety stores
- 3731 Other general merchandise stores

Miscellaneous Retail Stores
- 4812 Boat dealers
- 5017 Book stores, excluding newsstands
- 4853 Camera & photo supply stores
- 3277 Drug stores
- 5058 Fabric & needlework stores
- 4655 Florists
- 5090 Fuel dealers (except gasoline)
- 4630 Gift, novelty & souvenir shops
- 4838 Hobby, toy, & game shops
- 4671 Jewelry stores
- 4895 Luggage & leather goods stores
- 5074 Mobile home dealers
- 4879 Optical goods stores
- 4697 Sporting goods & bicycle shops
- 5033 Stationery stores
- 4614 Used merchandise & antique stores (except motor vehicle parts)
- 5884 Other retail stores

Trade, Wholesale—Selling Goods to Other Businesses, etc.

Durable Goods, Including Machinery Equipment, Wood, Metals, etc.
- 2634 Agent or broker for other firms— more than 50% of gross sales on commission
- 2618 Selling for your own account

Nondurable Goods, Including Food, Fiber, Chemicals, etc.
- 2675 Agent or broker for other firms— more than 50% of gross sales on commission
- 2659 Selling for your own account

Transportation, Communications, Public Utilities, & Related Services
- 6619 Air transportation
- 6312 Bus & limousine transportation
- 6676 Communication services
- 6395 Courier or package delivery
- 6361 Highway passenger transportation (except chartered service)
- 6536 Public warehousing
- 6114 Taxicabs
- 6510 Trash collection without own dump
- 6635 Travel agents & tour operators
- 6338 Trucking (except trash collection)
- 6692 Utilities (dumps, snow plowing, road cleaning, etc.)
- 6551 Water transportation
- 6650 Other transportation services
- 8888 Unable to classify

A-6 Continued

Form 4562

Department of the Treasury
Internal Revenue Service (0)

Depreciation and Amortization
(Including Information on Listed Property)

▶ See separate instructions.   ▶ Attach this form to your return.

OMB No. 1545-0172

1992

Attachment
Sequence No. **67**

Name(s) shown on return

Identifying number

Business or activity to which this form relates

Part I   Election To Expense Certain Tangible Property (Section 179) (Note: *If you have any "Listed Property," complete Part V before you complete Part I.*)

		(b) Cost	(c) Elected cost		
1	Maximum dollar limitation (see instructions)			**1**	$10,000
2	Total cost of section 179 property placed in service during the tax year (see instructions) . .			**2**	
3	Threshold cost of section 179 property before reduction in limitation			**3**	$200,000
4	Reduction in limitation. Subtract line 3 from line 2, but do not enter less than -0- . . .			**4**	
5	Dollar limitation for tax year. Subtract line 4 from line 1, but do not enter less than -0- .			**5**	

(a) Description of property	(b) Cost	(c) Elected cost	
6			

7	Listed property. Enter amount from line 26	**7**			
8	Total elected cost of section 179 property. Add amounts in column (c), lines 6 and 7 . . .			**8**	
9	Tentative deduction. Enter the smaller of line 5 or line 8			**9**	
10	Carryover of disallowed deduction from 1991 (see instructions)			**10**	
11	Taxable income limitation. Enter the smaller of taxable income or line 5 (see instructions) . .			**11**	
12	Section 179 expense deduction. Add lines 9 and 10, but do not enter more than line 11 . .			**12**	
13	Carryover of disallowed deduction to 1993. Add lines 9 and 10, less line 12 ▶	**13**			

Note: *Do not use Part II or Part III below for automobiles, certain other vehicles, cellular telephones, computers, or property used for entertainment, recreation, or amusement (listed property). Instead, use Part V for listed property.*

Part II   MACRS Depreciation For Assets Placed in Service ONLY During Your 1992 Tax Year (Do Not Include Listed Property)

(a) Classification of property	(b) Month and year placed in service	(c) Basis for depreciation (business/investment use only—see instructions)	(d) Recovery period	(e) Convention	(f) Method	(g) Depreciation deduction
14 General Depreciation System (GDS) (see instructions):						
a 3-year property						
b 5-year property						
c 7-year property						
d 10-year property						
e 15-year property						
f 20-year property						
g Residential rental property			27.5 yrs.	MM	S/L	
			27.5 yrs.	MM	S/L	
h Nonresidential real property			31.5 yrs.	MM	S/L	
			31.5 yrs.	MM	S/L	
15 Alternative Depreciation System (ADS) (see instructions):						
a Class life					S/L	
b 12-year			12 yrs.		S/L	
c 40-year			40 yrs.	MM	S/L	

Part III   Other Depreciation (Do Not Include Listed Property)

16	GDS and ADS deductions for assets placed in service in tax years beginning before 1992 (see instructions)	**16**	
17	Property subject to section 168(f)(1) election (see instructions)	**17**	
18	ACRS and other depreciation (see instructions)	**18**	

Part IV   Summary

19	Listed property. Enter amount from line 25	**19**	
20	**Total.** Add deductions on line 12, lines 14 and 15 in column (g), and lines 16 through 19. Enter here and on the appropriate lines of your return. (Partnerships and S corporations—see instructions)	**20**	
21	For assets shown above and placed in service during the current year, enter the portion of the basis attributable to section 263A costs (see instructions)	**21**	

A-7 Depreciation and Amortization form Department of the Treasury, Internal Revenue Service

Part V Listed Property—Automobiles, Certain Other Vehicles, Cellular Telephones, Computers, and Property Used for Entertainment, Recreation, or Amusement

For any vehicle for which you are using the standard mileage rate or deducting lease expense, complete only 22a, 22b, columns (a) through (c) of Section A, all of Section B, and Section C if applicable.

Section A—Depreciation (Caution: *See instructions for limitations for automobiles.*)

22a Do you have evidence to support the business/investment use claimed? ☐ **Yes** ☐ **No**   **22b** If "Yes," is the evidence written? ☐ **Yes** ☐ **No**

(a) Type of property (list vehicles first)	(b) Date placed in service	(c) Business/ investment use percentage	(d) Cost or other basis	(e) Basis for depreciation (business/investment use only)	(f) Recovery period	(g) Method/ Convention	(h) Depreciation deduction	(i) Elected section 179 cost
23 Property used more than 50% in a qualified business use (see instructions):								
		%						
		%						
		%						
24 Property used 50% or less in a qualified business use (see instructions):								
		%			S/L –			
		%			S/L –			
		%			S/L –			

25 Add amounts in column (h). Enter the total here and on line 19, page 1 . . . . . **25**

26 Add amounts in column (i). Enter the total here and on line 7, page 1 . . . . **26**

Section B—Information Regarding Use of Vehicles—*If you deduct expenses for vehicles:*
- *Always complete this section for vehicles used by a sole proprietor, partner, or other "more than 5% owner," or related person.*
- *If you provided vehicles to your employees, first answer the questions in Section C to see if you meet an exception to completing this section for those vehicles.*

		(a) Vehicle 1		(b) Vehicle 2		(c) Vehicle 3		(d) Vehicle 4		(e) Vehicle 5		(f) Vehicle 6	
27	Total business/investment miles driven during the year (DO NOT include commuting miles)												
28	Total commuting miles driven during the year												
29	Total other personal (noncommuting) miles driven												
30	Total miles driven during the year. Add lines 27 through 29												
		Yes	No	Yes	No	Yes	No	Yes	No	Yes	No	Yes	No
31	Was the vehicle available for personal use during off-duty hours?												
32	Was the vehicle used primarily by a more than 5% owner or related person?												
33	Is another vehicle available for personal use?												

Section C—Questions for Employers Who Provide Vehicles for Use by Their Employees
Answer these questions to determine if you meet an exception to completing Section B. **Note:** *Section B must always be completed for vehicles used by sole proprietors, partners, or other more than 5% owners or related persons.*

		Yes	No
34	Do you maintain a written policy statement that prohibits all personal use of vehicles, including commuting, by your employees?		
35	Do you maintain a written policy statement that prohibits personal use of vehicles, except commuting, by your employees? (See instructions for vehicles used by corporate officers, directors, or 1% or more owners.)		
36	Do you treat all use of vehicles by employees as personal use?		
37	Do you provide more than five vehicles to your employees and retain the information received from your employees concerning the use of the vehicles?		
38	Do you meet the requirements concerning qualified automobile demonstration use (see instructions)? . .		

Note: *If your answer to 34, 35, 36, 37, or 38 is "Yes," you need not complete Section B for the covered vehicles.*

Part VI Amortization

(a) Description of costs	(b) Date amortization begins	(c) Amortizable amount	(d) Code section	(e) Amortization period or percentage	(f) Amortization for this year
39 Amortization of costs that begins during your 1992 tax year:					
40 Amortization of costs that began before 1992 . . . . **40**					
41 Total. Enter here and on "Other Deductions" or "Other Expenses" line of your return . . . **41**					

A-7 Continued

Depreciation Worksheet

Description of Property	Date Placed in Service	Cost or Other Basis	Business/ Investment Use %	Section 179 Deduction	Depreciation Prior Years	Basis for Depreciation	Method/ Convention	Recovery Period	Rate or Table %	Depreciation Deduction

A-8 Depreciation Worksheet form Department of the Treasury, Internal Revenue Service

Form **8829**	**Expenses for Business Use of Your Home**	OMB No. 1545-1256
	▶ File with Schedule C (Form 1040).	**1991**
Department of the Treasury Internal Revenue Service	▶ See instructions on back.	Attachment Sequence No. **66**

Name of proprietor	Your social security number

Part I   Part of Your Home Used for Business

1	Area used exclusively for business (see instructions). Include area used for inventory storage or as a day-care facility that does not meet exclusive use test	1	
2	Total area of home	2	
3	Divide line 1 by line 2. Enter the result as a percentage	3	%

• For day-care facilities not used exclusively for business, also complete lines 4–6.

• All others, skip lines 4–6 and enter the amount from line 3 on line 7.

4	Total hours facility used for day care during the year. Multiply days used by number of hours used per day	4	hr.
5	Total hours available for use during the year (365 days x 24 hours) (see instructions).	5	8,760 hr.
6	Divide line 4 by line 5. Enter the result as a decimal amount . . .	6	.
7	Business percentage. For day-care facilities not used exclusively for business, multiply line 6 by line 3 (enter the result as a percentage). All others, enter the amount from line 3 . . . . ▶	7	%

Part II   Figure Your Allowable Deduction

			(a) Direct expenses	(b) Indirect expenses	
8	Enter the amount from Schedule C, line 29. (If more than one place of business, see instructions.) . .				8
9	Casualty losses	9			
10	Deductible mortgage interest	10			
11	Real estate taxes	11			
12	Add lines 9, 10, and 11	12			
13	Multiply line 12, column (b) by line 7		13		
14	Add line 12, column (a) and line 13				14
15	Subtract line 14 from line 8. If zero or less, enter -0- .				15
16	Excess mortgage interest (see instructions) . .	16			
17	Insurance	17			
18	Repairs and maintenance	18			
19	Utilities	19			
20	Other expenses	20			
21	Add lines 16 through 20	21			
22	Multiply line 21, column (b) by line 7		22		
23	Carryover of operating expenses from 1990 . .		23		
24	Add line 21 in column (a), line 22, and line 23				24
25	Allowable operating expenses. Enter the **smaller** of line 15 or line 24				25
26	Limit on excess casualty losses and depreciation. Subtract line 25 from line 15				26
27	Excess casualty losses (see instructions)		27		
28	Depreciation of your home from Part III below		28		
29	Carryover of excess casualty losses and depreciation from 1990 . .		29		
30	Add lines 27 through 29				30
31	Allowable excess casualty losses and depreciation. Enter the **smaller** of line 26 or line 30 . .				31
32	Add lines 14, 25, and 31				32
33	Casualty losses included on lines 14 and 31. (Carry this amount to **Form 4684**, Section B.). .				33
34	Allowable expenses for business use of your home. Subtract line 33 from line 32. Enter here and on Schedule C, line 30 . . . . ▶				34

Part III   Depreciation of Your Home

35	Enter the **smaller** of your home's adjusted basis or its fair market value (see instructions) . .	35	
36	Value of land included on line 35	36	
37	Basis of building. Subtract line 36 from line 35	37	
38	Business basis of building. Multiply line 37 by line 7	38	
39	Depreciation percentage (see instructions)	39	%
40	Depreciation allowable. Multiply line 38 by the percentage on line 39. Enter here and on line 28 above .	40	

Part IV   Carryover of Unallowed Expenses to 1992

41	Operating expenses. Subtract line 25 from line 24. If less than zero, enter -0-	41	
42	Excess casualty losses and depreciation. Subtract line 31 from line 30. If less than zero, enter -0- .	42	

A-9 Expenses for Business Use of Your Home form Department of the Treasury, Internal Revenue Service

General Instructions

Paperwork Reduction Act Notice.—We ask for the information on this form to carry out the Internal Revenue laws of the United States. You are required to give us the information. We need it to ensure that you are complying with these laws and to allow us to figure and collect the right amount of tax.

The time needed to complete and file this form will vary depending on individual circumstances. The estimated average time is: **Recordkeeping, 52 min.; Learning about the law or the form,** 7 min.; **Preparing the form,** 1 hr., 13 min.; and **Copying, assembling, and sending the form to the IRS,** 20 min.

If you have comments concerning the accuracy of these time estimates or suggestions for making this form more simple, we would be happy to hear from you. You can write to both the IRS and the Office of Management and Budget at the addresses listed in the instructions for Form 1040.

Purpose of Form

Use Form 8829 to figure the allowable expenses for business use of your home on **Schedule C** (Form 1040) and any carryover to 1992 of amounts not deductible in 1991.

You must meet specific requirements to deduct expenses for the business use of your home. Even if you meet these requirements, your deductible expenses are limited. For details, get **Pub. 587,** Business Use of Your Home.

Who May Deduct Expenses for Business Use of a Home

General rule.—You may deduct business expenses that apply to a part of your home **only** if that part is exclusively used on a regular basis:

● As your principal place of business for any of your trades or businesses; or

● As a place of business used by your patients, clients, or customers to meet or deal with you in the normal course of your trade or business; or

● In connection with your trade or business if it is a separate structure that is not attached to your home.

Exception for storage of inventory.—You may also deduct expenses that apply to space within your home if it is the **only** fixed location of your trade or business. The space must be used on a regular basis to store inventory from your trade or business of selling products at retail or wholesale.

Exception for day-care facilities.—If you use space in your home on a regular basis in your trade or business of providing day care, you may be able to deduct the business expenses even though you use the same space for nonbusiness purposes.

Specific Instructions

Part I

Lines 1 and 2.—You may use square feet to determine the area on lines 1 and 2. If the rooms in your home are about the same size, you may figure area using the number of rooms instead of square feet. You may use any other reasonable method if it accurately figures your business percentage on line 7.

Line 4.—Enter the total number of hours the facility was used for day care during the year.

Example. Your home is used Monday through Friday for 12 hours per day for 250 days during the year. It is also used on 50 Saturdays for 8 hours per day. Enter 3,400 hours on line 4 (3,000 hours for weekdays plus 400 hours for Saturdays).

Line 5.—If you started or stopped using your home for day care in 1991, you must prorate the number of hours based on the number of days the home was available for day care. Cross out the preprinted entry on line 5. Multiply 24 hours by the number of days available and enter the result.

Part II

Enter as direct or indirect expenses only expenses for the business use of your home (i.e., expenses allowable only because your home is used for business). Other expenses, such as salaries, supplies, and business telephone expenses, which are deductible elsewhere on Schedule C, should not be entered on Form 8829.

Direct expenses benefit only the business part of your home. They include painting or repairs made to the specific area or room used for business. Enter 100% of your direct expenses on the appropriate expense line in column (a).

Indirect expenses are for keeping up and running your entire home. They benefit both the business and personal parts of your home. Generally, enter 100% of your indirect expenses on the appropriate expense line in column (b). **Exception:** If the business percentage of an indirect expense is different from the percentage on line 7, enter only the business part of the expense on the appropriate line in column (a), and leave that line in column (b) blank. For example, your electric bill is $800 for lighting, cooking, laundry, and television. If you reasonably estimate $300 of your electric bill is for lighting and you use 10% of your home for business, enter $30 on line 19 in column (a) and leave line 19 in column (b) blank.

Line 8.—If all of the gross income from your trade or business is from the business use of your home, enter on line 8 the amount from Schedule C, line 29.

If part of the income is from a place of business other than your home, you must first determine the part of your gross income (Schedule C, line 7) from the business use of your home. In making this determination, consider the amount of time you spend at each location as well as other facts. After determining the part of your gross income from the business use of your home, subtract from that amount the total from Schedule C, line 28. Enter the result on line 8 of Form 8829.

Lines 9, 10, and 11.—Enter only the amounts that would be deductible whether or not you used your home for business (i.e., amounts allowable as itemized deductions on **Schedule A** (Form 1040)).

Treat **casualty losses** as personal expenses for this step. Figure the amount to enter on line 9 by completing Form 4684, Section A. When figuring line 17 of Section A, enter 10% of your adjusted gross income excluding the gross income from business use of your home and the deductions attributable to that income. Include on line 9 of Form 8829 the amount from Form 4684, Section A, line 18. See line 27 to deduct part of the casualty losses not allowed because of the limits on Form 4684, Section A.

Do not file or use that Form 4684 to figure the amount of casualty losses to deduct on Schedule A. Instead, complete a separate Form 4684 to deduct the personal portion of your casualty losses.

On line 10, include only **mortgage interest** that would be deductible on Schedule A and that qualifies as a direct or indirect expense. Do not include interest on a mortgage loan that did not benefit your home (e.g., a home equity loan used to pay off credit card bills, to buy a car, or to pay tuition costs).

Line 16.—If the amount of home mortgage interest you deduct on Schedule A is limited, enter the part of the excess mortgage interest that qualifies as a direct or indirect expense. Do not include mortgage interest on a loan that did not benefit your home (explained above).

Line 20.—If you rent rather than own your home, include the rent you paid on line 20, column (b).

Line 23.—If you were unable to deduct all of your 1990 operating expenses due to the limit on the deductible amount, enter on line 23 the amount of operating expenses you are carrying forward to 1991.

Line 27.—Multiply your casualty losses in excess of the amount on line 9 by the business percentage of those losses and enter the result.

Line 29.—If you were unable to deduct all of your 1990 excess casualty losses and depreciation due to the limit on the deductible amount, enter the amount of excess depreciation and casualty losses you are carrying forward to 1991.

Part III

Lines 35 through 37.—Enter on line 35 the cost or other basis of your home, or if less, the fair market value of your home on the date you first used the home for business. **Do not** adjust this amount for depreciation claimed or changes in fair market value after the year you first used your home for business. Allocate this amount between land and building values on lines 36 and 37.

Show on an attached schedule the cost or other basis of additions and improvements placed in service after you began to use your home for business. Do not include any amounts on lines 35 through 38 for these expenditures. Instead, see the instructions for line 40.

Line 39.—If you first used your home for business in 1991, enter the percentage for the month you first used it for business.

Jan.	3.042%	July	1.455%
Feb.	2.778%	Aug.	1.190%
March	2.513%	Sept.	0.926%
April	2.249%	Oct.	0.661%
May	1.984%	Nov.	0.397%
June	1.720%	Dec.	0.132%

If you first used your home for business before 1991 and after 1986, enter 3.175%. If the business use began before 1987 or you stopped using your home for business before the end of the year, see **Pub. 534,** Depreciation, for the percentage to enter.

Line 40.—Include on line 40 depreciation on additions and improvements placed in service after you began using your home for business. See Pub. 534 to figure the amount of depreciation allowed on these expenditures. Attach a schedule showing how you figured depreciation on any additions or improvements. Write "See attached" below the entry space.

Complete and attach **Form 4562,** Depreciation and Amortization, if you first used your home for business in 1991 or you are depreciating additions or improvements placed in service in 1991. If you first used your home for business in 1991, enter on Form 4562, in column (c) of line 14h, the amount from line 38 of Form 8829. Then enter on Form 4562, in column (g) of line 14h, the amount from line 40 of Form 8829.

A-9 Continued

SCHEDULE E
(Form 1040)

Department of the Treasury
Internal Revenue Service   (0)

Supplemental Income and Loss

(From rental real estate, royalties, partnerships, estates, trusts, REMICs, etc.)
▶ Attach to Form 1040 or Form 1041.
▶ See Instructions for Schedule E (Form 1040).

OMB No. 1545-0074

1992

Attachment
Sequence No. **13**

Name(s) shown on return

Your social security number

Part I   Income or Loss From Rental Real Estate and Royalties   Note: *Report income and expenses from the rental of personal property on **Schedule C** or **C-EZ**. Report farm rental income or loss from **Form 4835** on page 2, line 39.*

1	Show the kind and location of each **rental real estate property:**	2	For each rental real estate property listed on line 1, did you or your family use it for personal purposes for more than the greater of 14 days or 10% of the total days rented at fair rental value during the tax year? (See page E-1.)	Yes	No
A	....		A		
B	....		B		
C	....		C		

Income:			Properties			Totals (Add columns A, B, and C.)	
			A	B	C		
3	Rents received	3				3	
4	Royalties received	4				4	
Expenses:							
5	Advertising	5					
6	Auto and travel (see page E-2) .	6					
7	Cleaning and maintenance . . .	7					
8	Commissions	8					
9	Insurance	9					
10	Legal and other professional fees	10					
11	Management fees	11					
12	Mortgage interest paid to banks, etc. (see page E-2)	12				12	
13	Other interest	13					
14	Repairs	14					
15	Supplies	15					
16	Taxes	16					
17	Utilities	17					
18	Other (list) ▶	18					
19	Add lines 5 through 18	19				19	
20	Depreciation expense or depletion (see page E-2)	20				20	
21	Total expenses. Add lines 19 and 20	21					
22	Income or (loss) from rental real estate or royalty properties. Subtract line 21 from line 3 (rents) or line 4 (royalties). If the result is a (loss), see page E-2 to find out if you must file **Form 6198** . . .	22					
23	Deductible rental real estate loss. **Caution:** *Your rental real estate loss on line 22 may be limited. See page E-3 to find out if you must file **Form 8582** . . . .*	23	( )	( )	( )		
24	**Income.** Add positive amounts shown on line 22. **Do not** include any losses					24	
25	**Losses.** Add royalty losses from line 22 and rental real estate losses from line 23. Enter the total losses here					25	( )
26	Total rental real estate and royalty income or (loss). Combine lines 24 and 25. Enter the result here. If Parts II, III, IV, and line 39 on page 2 do not apply to you, also enter this amount on Form 1040, line 18. Otherwise, include this amount in the total on line 40 on page 2					26	

A-10   Supplemental Income and Loss form Department of the Treasury, Internal Revenue Service

Name(s) shown on return. Do not enter name and social security number if shown on other side. | Your social security number

Note: *If you report amounts from farming or fishing on Schedule E, you must enter your gross income from those activities on line 41 below.*

Part II   **Income or Loss From Partnerships and S Corporations**

IT you report a loss from an at-risk activity, you MUST check either column **(e)** or **(f)** of line 27 to describe your investment in the activity. See page E-3. If you check column **(f)**, you must attach **Form 6198**.

27	(a) Name	(b) Enter **P** for partnership; **S** for S corporation	(c) Check if foreign partnership	(d) Employer identification number	Investment At Risk? (e) All is	(f) Some is not at risk
A						
B						
C						
D						
E						

	Passive Income and Loss		Nonpassive Income and Loss		
	(g) Passive loss allowed (attach **Form 8582** if required)	**(h)** Passive income from **Schedule K–1**	**(i)** Nonpassive loss from **Schedule K–1**	**(j)** Section 179 expense deduction from **Form 4562**	**(k)** Nonpassive income from **Schedule K–1**
A					
B					
C					
D					
E					
28a Totals					
b Totals					

29	Add columns (h) and (k) of line 28a	29
30	Add columns (g), (i), and (j) of line 28b	30 ( )
31	Total partnership and S corporation income or (loss). Combine lines 29 and 30. Enter the result here and include in the total on line 40 below	31

Part III   **Income or Loss From Estates and Trusts**

32	(a) Name	(b) Employer identification number
A		
B		
C		

	Passive Income and Loss		Nonpassive Income and Loss	
	(c) Passive deduction or loss allowed (attach **Form 8582** if required)	**(d)** Passive income from **Schedule K–1**	**(e)** Deduction or loss from **Schedule K–1**	**(f)** Other income from **Schedule K–1**
A				
B				
C				
33a Totals				
b Totals				

34	Add columns (d) and (f) of line 33a	34
35	Add columns (c) and (e) of line 33b	35 ( )
36	Total estate and trust income or (loss). Combine lines 34 and 35. Enter the result here and include in the total on line 40 below	36

Part IV   **Income or Loss From Real Estate Mortgage Investment Conduits (REMICs)—Residual Holder**

37	(a) Name	(b) Employer identification number	(c) Excess inclusion from Schedules Q, line 2c (see page E-4)	(d) Taxable income (net loss) from Schedules Q, line 1b	(e) Income from Schedules Q, line 3b

38	Combine columns (d) and (e) only. Enter the result here and include in the total on line 40 below	38

Part V   **Summary**

39	Net farm rental income or (loss) from **Form 4835**. Also, complete line 41 below	39
40	TOTAL income or (loss). Combine lines 26, 31, 36, 38, and 39. Enter the result here and on Form 1040, line 18 . . . . ▶	40
41	**Reconciliation of Farming and Fishing Income:** Enter your **gross** farming and fishing income reported in Parts II and III and on line 39 (see page E-4)	41

A-10   Continued

Form **1040**

Department of the Treasury—Internal Revenue Service

U.S. Individual Income Tax Return **1992** (L)   IRS Use Only—Do not write or staple in this space.

For the year Jan. 1–Dec. 31, 1992, or other tax year beginning   , 1992, ending   , 19   OMB No. 1545-0074

Label

(See instructions on page 10.)

Use the IRS label. Otherwise, please print or type.

L A B E L   H E R E

Your first name and initial   Last name   **Your social security number**

If a joint return, spouse's first name and initial   Last name   **Spouse's social security number**

Home address (number and street). If you have a P.O. box, see page 10.   Apt. no.

City, town or post office, state, and ZIP code. If you have a foreign address, see page 10.

For Privacy Act and Paperwork Reduction Act Notice, see page 4.

Presidential Election Campaign

(See page 10.)

Do you want $1 to go to this fund?   Yes   No

If a joint return, does your spouse want $1 to go to this fund?   Yes   No

Note: Checking "Yes" will not change your tax or reduce your refund.

Filing Status

(See page 10.)

Check only one box.

1   Single

2   Married filing joint return (even if only one had income)

3   Married filing separate return. Enter spouse's social security no. above and full name here. ▶

4   Head of household (with qualifying person). (See page 11.) If the qualifying person is a child but not your dependent, enter this child's name here. ▶

5   Qualifying widow(er) with dependent child (year spouse died ▶ 19). (See page 11.)

Exemptions

(See page 11.)

If more than six dependents, see page 12.

6a   Yourself. If your parent (or someone else) can claim you as a dependent on his or her tax return, **do not** check box 6a. But be sure to check the box on line 33b on page 2

b   Spouse

c   Dependents:

(1) Name (first, initial, and last name)	(2) Check if under age 1	(3) If age 1 or older, dependent's social security number	(4) Dependent's relationship to you	(5) No. of months lived in your home in 1992

d   If your child didn't live with you but is claimed as your dependent under a pre-1985 agreement, check here ▶

e   Total number of exemptions claimed

No. of boxes checked on 6a and 6b

No. of your children on 6c who:
• lived with you
• didn't live with you due to divorce or separation (see page 13)

No. of other dependents on 6c

Add numbers entered on lines above ▶

Income

Attach Copy B of your Forms W-2, W-2G, and 1099-R here.

If you did not get a W-2, see page 9.

Attach check or money order on top of any Forms W-2, W-2G, or 1099-R.

7   Wages, salaries, tips, etc. Attach Form(s) W-2   **7**

8a   **Taxable** interest income. Attach Schedule B if over $400   **8a**

b   **Tax-exempt** interest income (see page 15). DON'T include on line 8a **8b**

9   Dividend income. Attach Schedule B if over $400   **9**

10   Taxable refunds, credits, or offsets of state and local income taxes from worksheet on page 16   **10**

11   Alimony received   **11**

12   Business income or (loss). Attach Schedule C or C-EZ   **12**

13   Capital gain or (loss). Attach Schedule D   **13**

14   Capital gain distributions not reported on line 13 (see page 15)   **14**

15   Other gains or (losses). Attach Form 4797   **15**

16a   Total IRA distributions **16a**   b Taxable amount (see page 16)   **16b**

17a   Total pensions and annuities **17a**   b Taxable amount (see page 16)   **17b**

18   Rents, royalties, partnerships, estates, trusts, etc. Attach Schedule E   **18**

19   Farm income or (loss). Attach Schedule F   **19**

20   Unemployment compensation (see page 17)   **20**

21a   Social security benefits **21a**   b Taxable amount (see page 17)   **21b**

22   Other income. List type and amount—see page 18   **22**

23   Add the amounts in the far right column for lines 7 through 22. This is your **total income** ▶ **23**

Adjustments to Income

(See page 18.)

24a   Your IRA deduction from applicable worksheet on page 19 or 20 **24a**

b   Spouse's IRA deduction from applicable worksheet on page 19 or 20 **24b**

25   One-half of self-employment tax (see page 20) **25**

26   Self-employed health insurance deduction (see page 20) **26**

27   Keogh retirement plan and self-employed SEP deduction **27**

28   Penalty on early withdrawal of savings **28**

29   Alimony paid. Recipient's SSN ▶ **29**

30   Add lines 24a through 29. These are your **total adjustments** ▶ **30**

Adjusted Gross Income

31   Subtract line 30 from line 23. This is your **adjusted gross income.** If this amount is less than $22,370 and a child lived with you, see page EIC-1 to find out if you can claim the "Earned Income Credit" on line 56 ▶ **31**

A-11   U.S. Individual Income Tax Return form   Department of the Treasury, Internal Revenue Service

			32	
Tax Compu-tation	32	Amount from line 31 (adjusted gross income)	32	
	33a	Check if: ☐ **You** were 65 or older, ☐ Blind; ☐ **Spouse** was 65 or older, ☐ Blind.		
		Add the number of boxes checked above and enter the total here . ► 33a ☐		
(See page 22.)	b	If your parent (or someone else) can claim you as a dependent, check here ► 33b ☐		
	c	If you are married filing separately and your spouse itemizes deductions or you are a dual-status alien, see page 22 and check here . . . . ► 33c ☐		
	34	Enter the larger of your: { **Itemized deductions** from Schedule A, line 26, **OR** **Standard deduction** shown below for your filing status. **But if you checked any box on line 33a or b,** go to page 22 to find your standard deduction. **If you checked box 33c,** your standard deduction is zero. • Single—$3,600 • Head of household—$5,250 • Married filing jointly or Qualifying widow(er)—$6,000 • Married filing separately—$3,000 }	34	
	35	Subtract line 34 from line 32	35	
	36	If line 32 is $78,950 or less, multiply $2,300 by the total number of exemptions claimed on line 6e. If line 32 is over $78,950, see the worksheet on page 23 for the amount to enter	36	
	37	**Taxable income.** Subtract line 36 from line 35. If line 36 is more than line 35, enter -0-	37	
If you want the IRS to figure your tax, see page 23.	38	Enter tax. Check if from **a** ☐ Tax Table, **b** ☐ Tax Rate Schedules, **c** ☐ Schedule D, or **d** ☐ Form 8615 (see page 23). Amount, if any, from Form(s) 8814 ► **e** _____	38	
	39	Additional taxes (see page 23). Check if from **a** ☐ Form 4970 **b** ☐ Form 4972 . .	39	
	40	Add lines 38 and 39 . . . . ►	40	

Credits	41	Credit for child and dependent care expenses. Attach Form 2441	41		
	42	Credit for the elderly or the disabled. Attach Schedule R .	42		
(See page 23.)	43	Foreign tax credit. Attach Form 1116	43		
	44	Other credits (see page 24). Check if from **a** ☐ Form 3800 **b** ☐ Form 8396 **c** ☐ Form 8801 **d** ☐ Form (specify)_____	44		
	45	Add lines 41 through 44		45	
	46	Subtract line 45 from line 40. If line 45 is more than line 40, enter -0- . . . ►		46	

Other Taxes	47	Self-employment tax. Attach Schedule SE. Also, see line 25	47	
	48	Alternative minimum tax. Attach Form 6251	48	
	49	Recapture taxes (see page 25). Check if from **a** ☐ Form 4255 **b** ☐ Form 8611 **c** ☐ Form 8828 .	49	
	50	Social security and Medicare tax on tip income not reported to employer. Attach Form 4137	50	
	51	Tax on qualified retirement plans, including IRAs. Attach Form 5329	51	
	52	Advance earned income credit payments from Form W-2	52	
	53	Add lines 46 through 52. This is your **total tax** . . . . ►	53	

Payments	54	Federal income tax withheld. If any is from Form(s) 1099, check ► ☐	54		
	55	1992 estimated tax payments and amount applied from 1991 return .	55		
Attach Forms W-2, W-2G, and 1099-R on the front.	56	**Earned income credit.** Attach Schedule EIC	56		
	57	Amount paid with Form 4868 (extension request)	57		
	58	Excess social security, Medicare, and RRTA tax withheld (see page 26) .	58		
	59	Other payments (see page 26). Check if from **a** ☐ Form 2439 **b** ☐ Form 4136	59		
	60	Add lines 54 through 59. These are your **total payments** . . . . . ►		60	

Refund or Amount You Owe	61	If line 60 is more than line 53, subtract line 53 from line 60. This is the amount you **OVERPAID** ►	61	
	62	Amount of line 61 you want **REFUNDED TO YOU**. . . . . ►	62	
	63	Amount of line 61 you want **APPLIED TO YOUR 1993 ESTIMATED TAX** ►	63	
Attach check or money order on top of Form(s) W-2, etc., on the front.	64	If line 53 is more than line 60, subtract line 60 from line 53. This is the **AMOUNT YOU OWE.** Attach check or money order for full amount payable to "Internal Revenue Service." Write your name, address, social security number, daytime phone number, and "1992 Form 1040" on it	64	
	65	Estimated tax penalty (see page 27). Also include on line 64	65	

Sign Here Keep a copy of this return for your records.	Under penalties of perjury, I declare that I have examined this return and accompanying schedules and statements, and to the best of my knowledge and belief, they are true, correct, and complete. Declaration of preparer (other than taxpayer) is based on all information of which preparer has any knowledge.			
	Your signature	Date	Your occupation	
	Spouse's signature. If a joint return, BOTH must sign.	Date	Spouse's occupation	

Paid Preparer's Use Only	Preparer's signature ►	Date	Check if self-employed ☐	Preparer's social security no.
	Firm's name (or yours if self-employed) and address ►		E.I. No.	
			ZIP code	

*U.S. Government Printing Office: 1992 — 315-033

A-11 Continued

Department of the Treasury
Internal Revenue Service (0)

Employee Business Expenses

▶ See separate instructions.

▶ Attach to Form 1040.

OMB No. 1545-0139

1991

Attachment
Sequence No. **54**

Your name	Social security number	Occupation in which expenses were incurred

Part I   **Employee Business Expenses and Reimbursements**

STEP 1   Enter Your Expenses

			Column A Other Than Meals and Entertainment		Column B Meals and Entertainment	
1	Vehicle expense from line 22 or line 29	1				
2	Parking fees, tolls, and local transportation, including train, bus, etc.	2				
3	Travel expense while away from home overnight, including lodging, airplane, car rental, etc. **Do not** include meals and entertainment	3				
4	Business expenses not included on lines 1 through 3. **Do not** include meals and entertainment	4				
5	Meals and entertainment expenses. (See instructions.)	5				
6	**Total expenses.** In Column A, add lines 1 through 4 and enter the result. In Column B, enter the amount from line 5.	6				

Note: *If you were not reimbursed for any expenses in Step 1, skip line 7 and enter the amount from line 6 on line 8.*

STEP 2   Enter Amounts Your Employer Gave You for Expenses Listed in STEP 1

7	Enter amounts your employer gave you that were **not** reported to you in Box 10 of Form W-2. Include any amount reported under code "L" in Box 17 of your Form W-2. (See instructions.)	7				

STEP 3   Figure Expenses To Deduct on Schedule A (Form 1040)

8	Subtract line 7 from line 6	8				
	Note: *If **both columns** of line 8 are zero, **stop here.** If Column A is less than zero, report the amount as income and enter -0- on line 10, Column A. See the instructions for how to report.*					
9	Enter 20% (.20) of line 8, Column B	9				
10	Subtract line 9 from line 8	10				
11	Add the amounts on line 10 of both columns and enter the total here. **Also enter the total on Schedule A (Form 1040), line 19.** (Qualified performing artists and individuals with disabilities, see the instructions for special rules on where to enter the total.) ▶	11				

A-12   Employee Business Expenses form   Department of the Treasury, Internal Revenue Service

| **Part II** | Vehicle Expenses (See instructions to find out which sections to complete.) |

Section A.—General Information

			(a) Vehicle 1	**(b)** Vehicle 2
12	Enter the date vehicle was placed in service	12	/ /	/ /
13	Total mileage vehicle was used during 1991	13	miles	miles
14	Miles included on line 13 that vehicle was used for business	14	miles	miles
15	Percent of business use (divide line 14 by line 13)	15	%	%
16	Average daily round trip commuting distance	16	miles	miles
17	Miles included on line 13 that vehicle was used for commuting	17	miles	miles
18	Other personal mileage (add lines 14 and 17 and subtract the total from line 13)	18	miles	miles

19 Do you (or your spouse) have another vehicle available for personal purposes? . . ☐ Yes ☐ No

20 If your employer provided you with a vehicle, is personal use during off duty hours permitted? ☐ Yes ☐ No ☐ Not applicable

21a Do you have evidence to support your deduction? ☐ Yes ☐ No   21b If "Yes," is the evidence written? ☐ Yes ☐ No

Section B.—Standard Mileage Rate (Use this section only if you own the vehicle.)

| 22 | Multiply line 14 by 27.5¢ (.275). Enter the result here and on line 1. (Rural mail carriers, see instructions.) . . . . | 22 | | |

Section C.—Actual Expenses

			(a) Vehicle 1			**(b)** Vehicle 2		
23	Gasoline, oil, repairs, vehicle insurance, etc.	23						
24a	Vehicle rentals	24a						
b	Inclusion amount	24b						
c	Subtract line 24b from line 24a	24c						
25	Value of employer-provided vehicle (applies only if 100% of annual lease value was included on Form W-2. See instructions.)	25						
26	Add lines 23, 24c, and 25 . .	26						
27	Multiply line 26 by the percentage on line 15 . . .	27						
28	Enter amount from line 38 below	28						
29	Add lines 27 and 28. Enter total here and on line 1.	29						

Section D.—Depreciation of Vehicles (Use this section only if you own the vehicle.)

			(a) Vehicle 1			**(b)** Vehicle 2		
30	Enter cost or other basis. (See instructions.)	30						
31	Enter amount of section 179 deduction. (See instructions.) .	31						
32	Multiply line 30 by line 15. (See instructions if you elected the section 179 deduction.) . . .	32						
33	Enter depreciation method and percentage. (See instructions.)	33						
34	Multiply line 32 by the percentage on line 33. (See instructions.) .	34						
35	Add lines 31 and 34	35						
36	Enter the limitation amount from the table in the line 36 instructions	36						
37	Multiply line 36 by the percentage on line 15 . . .	37						
38	Enter the **smaller** of line 35 or line 37. Also enter the amount on line 28 above	38						

A-12 Continued

SCHEDULE D	**Capital Gains and Losses**	OMB No. 1545-0074
(Form 1040)	(And Reconciliation of Forms 1099-B for Bartering Transactions)	19**92**
(0)	▶ Attach to Form 1040. ▶ See Instructions for Schedule D (Form 1040).	
Department of the Treasury Internal Revenue Service	▶ For more space to list transactions for lines 1a and 9a, get Schedule D-1 (Form 1040).	Attachment Sequence No. **12A**

Name(s) shown on Form 1040	Your social security number

Caution: *Add the following amounts reported to you for 1992 on Forms 1099-B and 1099-S (or on substitute statements): (a) proceeds from transactions involving stocks, bonds, and other securities, and (b) gross proceeds from real estate transactions not reported on another form or schedule. If this total does not equal the total of lines 1c and 9c, column (d), attach a statement explaining the difference.*

Part I — Short-Term Capital Gains and Losses—Assets Held One Year or Less

(a) Description of property (Example, 100 shares 7% preferred of "XYZ" Co.)	(b) Date acquired (Mo., day, yr.)	(c) Date sold (Mo., day, yr.)	(d) Sales price (see page D-2)	(e) Cost or other basis (see page D-3)	(f) LOSS If (e) is more than (d), subtract (d) from (e)	(g) GAIN If (d) is more than (e), subtract (e) from (d)
1a Stocks, Bonds, Other Securities, and Real Estate. Include Form 1099-B and 1099-S Transactions. See page D-3.						
1b Amounts from Schedule D-1, line 1b. Attach Schedule D-1						
1c Total of All Sales Price Amounts. Add column (d) of lines 1a and 1b ▶ **1c**						
1d Other Transactions.						

2	Short-term gain from sale or exchange of your home from Form 2119, line 17 or 23 .	**2**	
3	Short-term gain from installment sales from Form 6252, line 26 or 37	**3**	
4	Short-term gain or (loss) from like-kind exchanges from Form 8824	**4**	
5	Net short-term gain or (loss) from partnerships, S corporations, and fiduciaries .	**5**	
6	Short-term capital loss carryover from 1991 Schedule D, line 36	**6**	
7	Add lines 1a, 1b, 1d, and 2 through 6, in columns (f) and (g).	**7** ( )	
8	**Net short-term capital gain or (loss).** Combine columns (f) and (g) of line 7	**8**	

Part II — Long-Term Capital Gains and Losses—Assets Held More Than One Year

9a Stocks, Bonds, Other Securities, and Real Estate. Include Form 1099-B and 1099-S Transactions. See page D-3.						
9b Amounts from Schedule D-1, line 9b. Attach Schedule D-1						
9c Total of All Sales Price Amounts. Add column (d) of lines 9a and 9b ▶ **9c**						
9d Other Transactions.						

10	Long-term gain from sale or exchange of your home from Form 2119, line 17 or 23 .	**10**	
11	Long-term gain from installment sales from Form 6252, line 26 or 37 . . .	**11**	
12	Long-term gain or (loss) from like-kind exchanges from Form 8824. . . .	**12**	
13	Net long-term gain or (loss) from partnerships, S corporations, and fiduciaries .	**13**	
14	Capital gain distributions	**14**	
15	Gain from Form 4797, line 8 or 10	**15**	
16	Long-term capital loss carryover from 1991 Schedule D, line 43	**16**	
17	Add lines 9a, 9b, 9d, and 10 through 16, in columns (f) and (g) . . .	**17** ( )	
18	**Net long-term capital gain or (loss).** Combine columns (f) and (g) of line 17	**18**	

A-13 Capital Gains and Losses form Department of the Treasury, Internal Revenue Service

Name(s) shown on Form 1040. Do not enter name and social security number if shown on other side. | Your social security number

Part III   Summary of Parts I and II

19	Combine lines 8 and 18 and enter the net gain or (loss). If a gain, also enter the gain on Form 1040, line 13	19	

Note: *If both lines 18 and 19 are gains, see Part IV below.*

20   If line 19 is a (loss), enter here and as a (loss) on Form 1040, line 13, the **smaller** of:

a   The (loss) on line 19; **or**

b   ($3,000) or, if married filing a separate return, ($1,500) . . . .   **20** (   )

Note: *When figuring whether line 20a or 20b is smaller, treat both numbers as positive.*
Complete Part V if the loss on line 19 is more than the loss on line 20 OR if Form 1040, line 37, is zero.

Part IV   Tax Computation Using Maximum Capital Gains Rate

USE THIS PART TO FIGURE YOUR TAX ONLY IF BOTH LINES 18 AND 19 ARE GAINS, AND:

You checked filing status box:	AND	Form 1040, line 37, is over:	You checked filing status box:	AND	Form 1040, line 37, is over:
1		$51,900	3		$43,250
2 or 5		$86,500	4		$74,150

21	Enter the amount from Form 1040, line 37	21
22	Enter the **smaller** of line 18 or line 19	22
23	Subtract line 22 from line 21	23
24	Enter: $21,450 if you checked filing status box 1; $35,800 if you checked filing status box 2 or 5; $17,900 if you checked filing status box 3; or $28,750 if you checked filing status box 4	24
25	Enter the **greater** of line 23 or line 24	25
26	Subtract line 25 from line 21	26
27	Figure the tax on the amount on line 25. Use the Tax Table or Tax Rate Schedules, whichever applies	27
28	Multiply line 26 by 28% (.28)	28
29	Add lines 27 and 28. Enter here and on Form 1040, line 38, and check the box for Schedule D . .	29

Part V   Capital Loss Carryovers from 1992 to 1993

30	Enter the amount from Form 1040, line 35. If a loss, enclose the amount in parentheses	30
31	Enter the loss from line 20 as a positive amount	31
32	Combine lines 30 and 31. If zero or less, enter -0-	32
33	Enter the **smaller** of line 31 or line 32	33

Note: *If both lines 8 and 20 are losses, go to line 34; otherwise, skip lines 34-38.*

34	Enter the loss from line 8 as a positive amount		34
35	Enter the gain, if any, from line 18	35	
36	Enter the amount from line 33	36	
37	Add lines 35 and 36		37
38	**Short-term capital loss carryover to 1993.** Subtract line 37 from line 34. If zero or less, enter -0- .		38

Note: *If both lines 18 and 20 are losses, go to line 39; otherwise, skip lines 39-45.*

39	Enter the loss from line 18 as a positive amount		39
40	Enter the gain, if any, from line 8	40	
41	Enter the amount from line 33	41	
42	Enter the amount, if any, from line 34 . .	42	
43	Subtract line 42 from line 41. If zero or less, enter -0-	43	
44	Add lines 40 and 43		44
45	**Long-term capital loss carryover to 1993.** Subtract line 44 from line 39. If zero or less, enter -0- .		45

Part VI   Election Not To Use the Installment Method. Complete this part **only** if you elect out of the installment method and report a note or other obligation at less than full face value.

46	Check here if you elect out of the installment method . . . . ▶ ☐
47	Enter the face amount of the note or other obligation . . . . ▶ ....
48	Enter the percentage of valuation of the note or other obligation . . . ▶ .... %

Part VII   Reconciliation of Forms 1099-B for Bartering Transactions.
Complete this part **only** if you received one or more Forms 1099-B or substitute statements reporting **bartering income.**

		Amount of bartering income from Form 1099-B or substitute statement reported on form or schedule
49	Form 1040, line 22	49
50	Schedule C, C-EZ, D, E, or F (specify) ▶	50
51	Other form or schedule (identify). If nontaxable, indicate reason—attach additional sheets if necessary:	51
52	**Total.** Add lines 49 through 51. This amount should be the same as the total bartering income on all Forms 1099-B and substitute statements received for bartering transactions	52

A-13   Continued

Schedule 1

(Form 1040A)

Interest and Dividend Income for Form 1040A Filers (L)

1992

OMB No. 1545-0085

Name(s) shown on Form 1040A	Your social security number
	: :

Part I **Interest income** (See pages 24 and 54.)	Complete this part and attach Schedule 1 to Form 1040A if: • You had over $400 in taxable interest, or • You are claiming the exclusion of interest from series EE U.S. savings bonds issued after 1989. If you received, as a nominee, interest that actually belongs to another person, see page 54. **Note:** *If you received a Form 1099–INT, Form 1099–OID, or substitute statement, from a brokerage firm, enter the firm's name and the total interest shown on that form.*

1	List name of payer—if any interest is from seller-financed mortgages, see page 54		Amount	
		1		
2	Add the amounts on line 1.	2		
3	Excludable interest on series EE U.S. savings bonds issued after 1989 from Form 8815, line 14. You MUST attach Form 8815 to Form 1040A.	3		
4	Subtract line 3 from line 2. Enter the result here and on Form 1040A, line 8a.	4		

Part II **Dividend income** (See pages 24 and 55.)	Complete this part and attach Schedule 1 to Form 1040A if you had over $400 in dividends. If you received, as a nominee, dividends that actually belong to another person, see page 55. **Note:** *If you received a Form 1099–DIV, or substitute statement, from a brokerage firm, enter the firm's name and the total dividends shown on that form.*

5	List name of payer		Amount	
		5		
6	Add the amounts on line 5. Enter the total here and on Form 1040A, line 9.	6		

A-14 Interest and Dividend Income form Department of the Treasury, Internal Revenue Service

Form **8822**	**Change of Address**	OMB No. 1545-1163

Form **8822**
(Rev. May 1992)
Department of the Treasury
Internal Revenue Service

Change of Address

▶ **Please type or print.**

▶ **See instructions on back.**   ▶ **Do not attach this form to your return.**

OMB No. 1545-1163
Expires 5-31-95

Part I   **Complete This Part To Change Your Home Mailing Address**

Check **ALL** boxes this change affects:

1 ☐ Individual income tax returns (Forms 1040, 1040A, 1040EZ, 1040NR, etc.)

▶ If your last return was a joint return and you are now establishing a residence separate from the spouse with whom you filed that return, check here . . . . ▶ ☐

2 ☐ Employment tax returns for household employers (Forms 942, 940, and 940-EZ)

▶ Enter your employer identification number here . . . . ▶ _____

3 ☐ Gift, estate, or generation-skipping transfer tax returns (Forms 706, 709, etc.)

▶ For Forms 706 and 706NA, enter the decedent's name and social security number below.

▶ Name   ▶ Social security number

4a Your name (first name, initial, and last name)	**4b** Your social security number
5a Spouse's name (first name, initial, and last name)	**5b** Spouse's social security number

6 Prior name(s). See instructions

7a Your old address (no., street, city or town, state, and ZIP code). If a P.O. box or foreign address, see instructions	Apt. no.
7b Spouse's old address, if different from line 7a (no., street, city or town, state, and ZIP code). If a P.O. box or foreign address, see instructions	Apt. no.
8 New address (no., street, city or town, state, and ZIP code). If a P.O. box or foreign address, see instructions	Apt. no.

Part II   **Complete This Part To Change Your Business Mailing Address or Business Location**

Check **ALL** boxes this change affects:

9 ☐ Employment, excise, and other business returns (Forms 720, 941, 990, 1041, 1065, 1120, etc.)
10 ☐ Employee plan returns (Forms 5500, 5500 C/R, and 5500EZ)
11 ☐ Business location

12a Business name	**12b** Employer identification number

13 Old address (no., street, city or town, state, and ZIP code). If a P.O. box or foreign address, see instructions	Room or suite no.
14 New address (no., street, city or town, state, and ZIP code). If a P.O. box or foreign address, see instructions	Room or suite no.
15 New business location (no., street, city or town, state, and ZIP code). If a foreign address, see instructions	Room or suite no.

Part III   **Signature**

Daytime telephone no. of person to contact (optional) ▶ ( )

Please Sign Here

▶ _____   _____   ▶ _____   _____
Your signature   Date   Spouse's signature. If joint return, both should sign   Date

▶ _____   _____   _____
If Part II completed, signature of owner, officer, or representative   Date   Title

---

A-15 Change of Address form Department of the Treasury, Internal Revenue Service

Privacy Act and Paperwork Reduction Act Notice

We ask for this information to carry out the Internal Revenue laws of the United States. We may give the information to the Department of Justice and to other Federal agencies, as provided by law. We may also give it to cities, states, the District of Columbia, and U.S. commonwealths or possessions to carry out their tax laws. And we may give it to foreign governments because of tax treaties they have with the United States.

If you fail to provide the Internal Revenue Service with your current mailing address, you may not receive a notice of deficiency or a notice and demand for tax. Despite the failure to receive such notices, penalties and interest will continue to accrue on the tax deficiencies.

The time needed to complete and file this form will vary depending on individual circumstances. The estimated average time is 16 minutes.

If you have comments concerning the accuracy of this time estimate or suggestions for making this form more simple, we would be happy to hear from you. You can write to both the **Internal Revenue Service**, Washington, DC 20224, Attention: IRS Reports Clearance Officer, T:FP; and the **Office of Management and Budget**, Paperwork Reduction Project (1545-1163), Washington, DC 20503. **DO NOT** send this form to either of these offices. Instead, see **Where To File** on this page.

Purpose of Form

You may use Form 8822 to notify the Internal Revenue Service if you changed your home or business mailing address or your business location. If this change also affects the mailing address for your children who filed income tax returns, complete and file a separate Form 8822 for each child.

Note: *If you moved after you filed your return and you are expecting a refund, also notify the post office serving your old address. This will help forward your check to your new address.*

Prior Name(s)

If you or your spouse changed your name due to marriage, divorce, etc., complete line 6. Also, be sure to notify the **Social Security Administration** of your new name so that it has the same name in its records that you have on your tax return. This prevents delays in processing your return and safeguards your future social security benefits.

P.O. Box

If your post office does not deliver mail to your street address and you have a P.O. box, show your P.O. box number instead of your street address.

Foreign Address

If your address is outside of the United States or its possessions or territories, enter the information in the following order: number, street, city, province or state, postal code, and country. **Do not** abbreviate the country name. Be sure to include any apartment, room, or suite number in the space provided.

Employee Plan Returns

A change in the mailing address for employee plan returns must be shown on a separate Form 8822 unless the **Exception** below applies.

Exception. If the employee plan returns were filed with the same service center as your other returns (individual, business, employment, gift, estate, etc.), you do not have to use a separate Form 8822. See **Where To File** below.

Where To File

Send this form to the **Internal Revenue Service Center** shown below for your old address. But if you checked the box on line 10 (employee plan returns), send it to the address shown in the far right column.

If your old address was in:	Use this address:
Florida, Georgia, South Carolina	Atlanta, GA 39901
New Jersey, New York (New York City and counties of Nassau, Rockland, Suffolk, and Westchester)	Holtsville, NY 00501
New York (all other counties), Connecticut, Maine, Massachusetts, New Hampshire, Rhode Island, Vermont	Andover, MA 05501
Alaska, Arizona, California (counties of Alpine, Amador, Butte, Calaveras, Colusa, Contra Costa, Del Norte, El Dorado, Glenn, Humboldt, Lake, Lassen, Marin, Mendocino, Modoc, Napa, Nevada, Placer, Plumas, Sacramento, San Joaquin, Shasta, Sierra, Siskiyou, Solano, Sonoma, Sutter, Tehama, Trinity, Yolo, and Yuba), Colorado, Idaho, Montana, Nebraska, Nevada, North Dakota, Oregon, South Dakota, Utah, Washington, Wyoming	Ogden, UT 84201
California (all other counties), Hawaii	Fresno, CA 93888

Indiana, Kentucky, Michigan, Ohio, West Virginia	Cincinnati, OH 45999
Kansas, New Mexico, Oklahoma, Texas	Austin, TX 73301
Delaware, District of Columbia, Maryland, Pennsylvania, Virginia	Philadelphia, PA 19255
Alabama, Arkansas, Louisiana, Mississippi, North Carolina, Tennessee	Memphis, TN 37501
Illinois, Iowa, Minnesota, Missouri, Wisconsin	Kansas City, MO 64999
American Samoa	Philadelphia, PA 19255
Guam	Commissioner of Revenue and Taxation 855 West Marine Dr. Agana, GU 96910
Puerto Rico (or if excluding income under section 933) Virgin Islands: Nonpermanent residents	Philadelphia, PA 19255
Virgin Islands: Permanent residents	V. I. Bureau of Internal Revenue Lockharts Garden No. 1A Charlotte Amalie, St. Thomas, VI 00802
Foreign country: U.S. citizens and those filing Form 2555 or Form 4563	Philadelphia, PA 19255
All A.P.O. and F.P.O. addresses	Philadelphia, PA 19255

Employee Plan Returns ONLY (Form 5500 series)

If the principal office of the plan sponsor or the plan administrator was in:	Use this address:
Connecticut, Delaware, District of Columbia, Foreign Address, Maine, Maryland, Massachusetts, New Hampshire, New Jersey, New York, Pennsylvania, Puerto Rico, Rhode Island, Vermont, Virginia	Holtsville, NY 00501
Alabama, Alaska, Arkansas, California, Florida, Georgia, Hawaii, Idaho, Louisiana, Mississippi, Nevada, North Carolina, Oregon, South Carolina, Tennessee, Washington	Atlanta, GA 39901
Arizona, Colorado, Illinois, Indiana, Iowa, Kansas, Kentucky, Michigan, Minnesota, Missouri, Montana, Nebraska, New Mexico, North Dakota, Ohio, Oklahoma, South Dakota, Texas, Utah, West Virginia, Wisconsin, Wyoming	Memphis, TN 37501
All Form 5500EZ filers	Andover, MA 05501

A-15 Continued

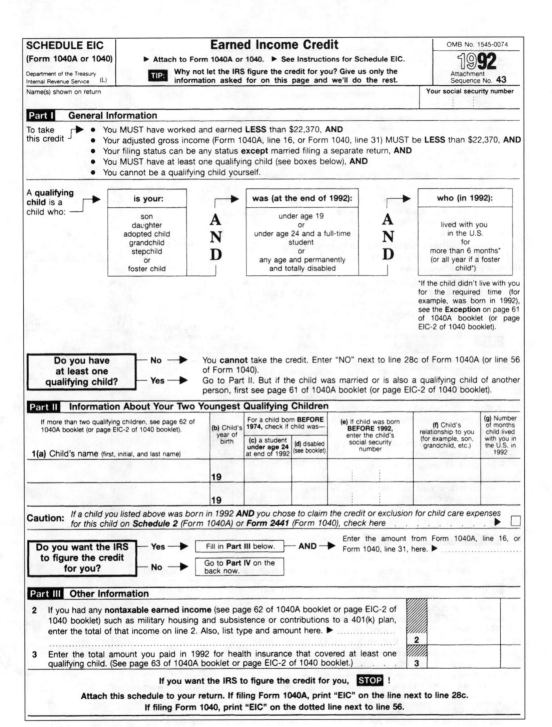

SCHEDULE EIC
(Form 1040A or 1040)

Department of the Treasury
Internal Revenue Service (L)

Earned Income Credit

▶ Attach to Form 1040A or 1040. ▶ See Instructions for Schedule EIC.

TIP: Why not let the IRS figure the credit for you? Give us only the information asked for on this page and we'll do the rest.

OMB No. 1545-0074

1992

Attachment Sequence No. **43**

Name(s) shown on return

Your social security number

| **Part I** | **General Information** |

To take this credit ▶
- You MUST have worked and earned **LESS** than $22,370, **AND**
- Your adjusted gross income (Form 1040A, line 16, or Form 1040, line 31) MUST be **LESS** than $22,370, **AND**
- Your filing status can be any status **except** married filing a separate return, **AND**
- You MUST have at least one qualifying child (see boxes below), **AND**
- You cannot be a qualifying child yourself.

A **qualifying child** is a child who: ▶

is your:
son
daughter
adopted child
grandchild
stepchild
or
foster child

A N D

was (at the end of 1992):
under age 19
or
under age 24 and a full-time student
or
any age and permanently and totally disabled

A N D

who (in 1992):
lived with you in the U.S. for more than 6 months* (or all year if a foster child*)

*If the child didn't live with you for the required time (for example, was born in 1992), see the **Exception** on page 61 of 1040A booklet (or page EIC-2 of 1040 booklet).

Do you have at least one qualifying child?

— No ▶ You **cannot** take the credit. Enter "NO" next to line 28c of Form 1040A (or line 56 of Form 1040).

— Yes ▶ Go to Part II. But if the child was married or is also a qualifying child of another person, first see page 61 of 1040A booklet (or page EIC-2 of 1040 booklet).

| **Part II** | **Information About Your Two Youngest Qualifying Children** |

If more than two qualifying children, see page 62 of 1040A booklet (or page EIC-2 of 1040 booklet).

1(a) Child's name (first, initial, and last name)

	(b) Child's year of birth	For a child born **BEFORE** 1974, check if child was—		**(e)** If child was born **BEFORE 1992**, enter the child's social security number	**(f)** Child's relationship to you (for example, son, grandchild, etc.)	**(g)** Number of months child lived with you in the U.S. in 1992
		(c) a student **under age 24** at end of 1992	**(d)** disabled (see booklet)			
	19					
	19					

Caution: If a child you listed above was born in 1992 **AND** you chose to claim the credit or exclusion for child care expenses for this child on **Schedule 2** (Form 1040A) or **Form 2441** (Form 1040), check here ▶ ☐

Do you want the IRS to figure the credit for you?

— Yes ▶ Fill in **Part III** below. — **AND** ▶ Enter the amount from Form 1040A, line 16, or Form 1040, line 31, here. ▶

— No ▶ Go to **Part IV** on the back now.

| **Part III** | **Other Information** |

2 If you had any **nontaxable earned income** (see page 62 of 1040A booklet or page EIC-2 of 1040 booklet) such as military housing and subsistence or contributions to a 401(k) plan, enter the total of that income on line 2. Also, list type and amount here. ▶ ....

2

3 Enter the total amount you paid in 1992 for health insurance that covered at least one qualifying child. (See page 63 of 1040A booklet or page EIC-2 of 1040 booklet.) . . . .

3

If you want the IRS to figure the credit for you, STOP !

Attach this schedule to your return. If filing Form 1040A, print "EIC" on the line next to line 28c.

If filing Form 1040, print "EIC" on the dotted line next to line 56.

A-16 Earned Income Credit form Department of the Treasury, Internal Revenue Service

Part IV **Figure Your Earned Income Credit**—You can take **ALL THREE** parts of the credit if you qualify

BASIC CREDIT

4 Enter the amount from line 7 of Form 1040A or Form 1040 (wages, salaries, tips, etc.). If you received a taxable scholarship or fellowship grant, see page 64 of 1040A booklet (or page EIC-3 of 1040 booklet) for the amount to enter | 4 |

5 If you had any **nontaxable earned income** (see page 62 of 1040A booklet or page EIC-2 of 1040 booklet) such as military housing and subsistence or contributions to a 401(k) plan, enter the total of that income on line 5. Also, list type and amount here. ▶ .... | 5 |

6 **Form 1040 Filers Only:** If you were self-employed **or** reported income and expenses on Sch. C or C-EZ as a statutory employee, enter the amount from the worksheet on page EIC-3 of 1040 booklet | 6 |

7 Add lines 4, 5, and 6. This is your **earned income.** If $22,370 or more, you **cannot** take the earned income credit. Enter "NO" next to line 28c of Form 1040A (or line 56 of Form 1040) ▶ | 7 |

8 Use the amount on **line 7** above to look up your credit in **TABLE A** on pages **65 and 66** of 1040A booklet (or pages **EIC-4 and 5** of 1040 booklet). Then, enter the credit here | 8 | |

9 Enter your **adjusted gross income** (from Form 1040A, line 16, or Form 1040, line 31). If $22,370 or more, you **cannot** take the credit ▶ | 9 |

10 **Is line 9 $11,850 or more?**

   • **YES.** Use the amount on **line 9** to look up your credit in **TABLE A** on pages **65 and 66** of 1040A booklet (or pages **EIC-4 and 5** of 1040 booklet). Then, enter the credit here | 10 | |

   • **NO.** Enter the amount from line 8 on line 11.

11 If you answered "YES" to line 10, enter the **smaller** of line 8 or line 10 here. This is your **basic credit** | 11 |

   NEXT: *To take the health insurance credit, fill in lines 12–16. To take the extra credit for a child born in 1992, fill in lines 17–19. Otherwise, go to line 20 now.*

HEALTH INSURANCE CREDIT —Take this credit **ONLY** if you paid for health insurance that covered at least one qualifying child.

12 Look at the amount on **line 7** above. Use that amount to look up your credit in **TABLE B** on page **67** of 1040A booklet (or page **EIC-6** of 1040 booklet). Then, enter the credit here | 12 | |

13 Look at the amount on **line 9** above. **Is line 9 $11,850 or more?**

   • **YES.** Use the amount on **line 9** to look up your credit in **TABLE B** on page **67** of 1040A booklet (or page **EIC-6** of 1040 booklet). Then, enter the credit here | 13 | |

   • **NO.** Enter the amount from line 12 on line 14.

14 If you answered "YES" to line 13, enter the **smaller** of line 12 or line 13 here. | 14 | |

15 Enter the total amount you paid in 1992 for health insurance that covered at least one qualifying child. (See page 64 of 1040A booklet or page EIC-3 of 1040 booklet.) | 15 | |

16 Enter the **smaller** of line 14 or line 15 here. This is your **health insurance credit** | 16 |

EXTRA CREDIT FOR CHILD BORN IN 1992 —Take this credit **ONLY** if:

   • You listed in Part II a child born in 1992, **AND** ◀

   • You did not take the credit or exclusion for child care expenses on **Schedule 2** or **Form 2441** for the same child.

   TIP: You can take **both** the **basic credit** and the **extra credit** for your child born in 1992.

17 Look at the amount on **line 7** above. Use that amount to look up your credit in **TABLE C** on page **68** of 1040A booklet (or page **EIC-7** of 1040 booklet). Then, enter the credit here | 17 | |

18 Look at the amount on **line 9** above. **Is line 9 $11,850 or more?**

   • **YES.** Use the amount on **line 9** to look up your credit in **TABLE C** on page 68 of 1040A booklet (or page **EIC-7** of 1040 booklet). Then, enter the credit here | 18 | |

   • **NO.** Enter the amount from line 17 on line 19.

19 If you answered "YES" to line 18, enter the **smaller** of line 17 or line 18 here. This is your **extra credit for a child born in 1992** | 19 |

TOTAL EARNED INCOME CREDIT

20 Add lines 11, 16, and 19. Enter the total here and on Form 1040A, line 28c (or on Form 1040, line 56). This is your **total earned income credit** ▶ | 20 |

A-16 Continued

Glossary

abatement The termination or reduction of an expenditure.

accelerated depreciation The depreciation of an item at a higher rate in the early years of its useful life than in the later years.

accord An agreement between two parties describing the method for discharging an obligation.

accounts payable Liabilities to creditors, such as an open account with a trade supplier.

accounts receivable Claims against debtors, such as customers owing money for services rendered.

accrued expense Expenses that have been incurred, but that remain unpaid.

accrued income Income that has been earned, but that has not been received.

accrued interest Interest that has accumulated since a loan was originated and since the last interest payment was made.

acquisition cost The cost incurred to acquire an item.

active income Income derived in the form of wages or salary.

ad hoc committee A temporary group created to deal with a specific problem or situation.

adjusted gross income Total of money received after all allowable deductions and exclusions have been claimed.

ad valorem tax A tax based on appreciated value or cost, such as a personal property tax.

aging schedule A list of outstanding accounts receivables that shows the accounts grouped by the length of time any accounts have been past due—also known as an aging report.

allonge An individual form that is attached to a negotiable form, such as a contract, to allow space for multiple signatures.

amortization A fee schedule set to pay an interest and principal amount of a loan over a routine period of time that will settle the debt or loan at a given maturity date.

annual percentage rate An annual rate of interest that reflects all interest to be paid in a given year. The annual percentage rate (APR) for a loan is arrived at by dividing the total annual interest paid by the balance due on the loan.

applied cost A cost applied to a specific project or job, such as a permit for the Smith job.

applied overhead Overhead expenses applied to specific projects, such as the cost of supervision for the Smith job.

appreciation An increase in value.

articles of incorporation Documents detailing the terms and conditions of a corporation in compliance with state laws.

balance sheet A statement showing a company's financial strength on a given date. Balance sheets disclose all liabilities and assets.

bilateral contract A contract affecting two parties.

bylaws Rules and regulations generated by a corporation to specify and govern methods for doing business.

capital assets Items of value owned by a company or individual.

capital gains Income derived from the sale of capital assets.

certificate of incorporation A document issued by a state authority giving authorization for an organization to act as a corporation.

closed corporation A corporation that is held closely by a few individuals and one where stock is seldom issued.

closed-end credit Credit with a maximum limit set for borrowing and where no additional funding is allowed without approval.

collateral An asset pledged as security for a loan.

common stock Stock issued by a corporation where no guarantee of dividends is offered.

credit A credit, pertaining to bookkeeping, is an amount on a balance sheet that indicates a decrease in assets.

debit A debit, pertaining to bookkeeping, is an amount on a balance sheet that indicates an increase in assets.

discretionary income Income remaining after all essential expenses have been paid.

earned income Money received within a given period of time for the production or marketing of goods and services.

fiscal year A period of time, not exceeding 12 months, from one balancing period of accounts to the next.

fixed overhead Expenses that do not fluctuate with a rise or fall in production, such as rent.

gross profit An amount of money from net sales after the cost of goods and services have been deducted.

hypothecation An act of pledging an asset as security for a loan without transferring title or possession of the asset.

income statement A detailed financial report of a company's income, expenses, and losses that shows the resulting net income for a set period of time.

internal audit An audit performed on a company by the company being audited.

net capital gains The amount arrived at when capital losses are subtracted from capital gains.

net income An amount of income that remains after all expenses and taxes have been paid.

net operating income (NOI) An amount of income that remains after all expenses have been paid, but before taxes are paid.

net worth A value, such as for a company, that is established by the company's capital assets after all liabilities and expenses are deducted.

open-end credit Credit that can be used at any time until such time the credit limit is reached.

par value Pertaining to corporate stock, par value is the face value of a share of stock.

passive income Money derived from an activity where the receiver is not actively engaged in earning of the income, such as income from professionally managed rental properties.

per diem A term meaning a basis of one day. For example, a per diem penalty of $50 would result in a penalty of $50 for each day the penalty was assessed.

preferred stock Stock from a corporation where a dividend is guaranteed to be paid before any dividends are paid on common stock.

pro forma financial statement A statement projecting a company's financial position based on a hypothetical situation.

spreadsheet A report containing multiple columns that allows quick evaluation of various entries.

umbrella policy A type of insurance policy that covers more than a general liability policy does.

write-off A reduction in an account due to unfavorable circumstances, such as with uncollectable accounts receivables.

Index